Center for Basque Studies
Occasional Papers Series, No. 17

EVA MENDIETA

In Search of Catalina de Erauso:
The National and Sexual Identity of
the Lieutenant Nun

Translated by

Angeles Prado

Center for Basque Studies
University of Nevada, Reno
Reno, Nevada

This book was published with generous financial support from the Basque Government.

Center for Basque Studies
Occasional Papers Series, No. 17
Series Editor: Joseba Zulaika

Center for Basque Studies
University of Nevada, Reno
Reno, Nevada 89557
http://basque.unr.edu

Cover and Series design © 2009 Jose Luis Agote.
Cover photograph: Amaia Mendieta, 2009.

Library of Congress Cataloging-in-Publication Data

Mendieta, Eva.
    In search of Catalina de Erauso : the national and sexual identity of the lieutenant nun / Eva Mendieta ; translated by Angeles Prado.
        p. cm. -- (Occasional papers series / Center for Basque Studies ; no. 16)
    Summary: "An investigation of the life and historical milieu of Catalina de Erauso (1592-1650), the lieutenant nun, with emphasis on her national and gender identities"--Provided by publisher.
    Includes bibliographical references and index.
    ISBN 978-1-877802-87-4 (hardcover)
    1. Erauso, Catalina de, b. ca. 1592. 2. Spain--Biography. 3. Latin America--Biography. 4. Soldiers--Latin America--Biography. 5. Women soldiers--Latin America--Biography. 6. Basques--Latin America--Biography. 7. New Spain--History--17th century. 8. National characteristics--Case studies. 9. Gender identity--Case studies. 10. Nuns--Spain--País Vasco--Biography. I. Title.
    CT1358.E7M46 2009
    946.08092--dc22
    [B]
                                    2009035405

To my daughter Silvia and to the memory of
my grandmother Josefina Baigorri.

TABLE OF CONTENTS

Acknowledgments

My adventure with Catalina de Erauso began when my friend from SUNY Albany, Donald Keenan, sent me a message in which he said I absolutely had to read the fascinating story of "a Basque transvestite nun." Hard to resist such an introduction. The curiosity about the figure started shaping into a research project thanks in part to the never-ending conversations with Amaia Mendieta, Marisa García-Verdugo, and Isabel Molina in Indiana and Bilbao. Later they were given the dubious honor of reading multiple versions of the manuscript. I would like to thank them for their patience and unwavering support. I owe my deepest gratitude to William A. Douglass of the Center for Basque Studies at the University of Nevada, Reno. Our communications have greatly contributed to the intellectual axis in which my vision of Catalina de Erauso developed. In a review of the most recent English edition of Catalina de Erauso's *Autobiografía*, Douglass remarked that one area that lacked further research was the relevance of Basque networks of support in the territories and at the time in which Erauso lived. I decided to organize my interest around this subject and Professor Douglass' insights and commentary are behind whatever value this book might have in this respect. I also thank Professor Douglass for urging me to confront the subject of Erauso's sexuality in all its complexity. I had the great fortune of counting on Angeles Prado as translator of the manuscript into English. Her wide knowledge, her meticulous attention to detail, and her commitment to the work have produced a rendition that in many cases supersedes that of the original. I thank Indiana University Northwest for several research scholarships that allowed me to dedicate my time fully to the writing of the manuscript. And finally, thank you to my wonderful family. Their devotion knows no limits, and it has carried me through the entire gestation of this project.

Introduction

Buckle up your seat belt, Dear Reader, since you are in for a wild ride! Catalina de Erauso, the subject of this incisive biography, was one of the more controversial (and certainly bizarre) figures of the early seventeenth century. A celebrated and controversial individual, and as such the object of an excessive amount of scrutiny, her person and story are nevertheless fascinatingly blurred at the edges. Above all, she is a quintessential liminal character caught up within not a single identity crisis but several. For, like many of her compatriots, she was a European imperialist interloper in the Spanish-American colonial world. Although a loyal subject and handmaiden of her monarch, she was a member of Spain's most unique ethnic collectivity—the Basques. As such, she was both part of a sub-group whose members were prone to (and eminently capable of) providing critical mutual support to one another and, for that very privilege and posture, the object of the resentment and animosity of many Native Americans, Creoles, and Old-World-born, non-Basque Spaniards alike.

Most strikingly, Catalina, who was christened a girl and educated in a convent (before fleeing it) in her native town of Donostia-San Sebastián in the Basque province of Gipuzkoa, lived her entire adult life as Antonio Erauso—soldier, adventurer, and ne'er-do-well! In this latter guise, Catalina/Antonio cut a wide swath through Peruvian and Chilean society, accounting for several deaths in sword fights that led to harried escapes, including one from the gallows as the noose was being placed around her neck. At the same time, she was an admired hero of the military campaigns against the Indians of Peru and Chile, many of whom she dispatched on the field of battle. When her gender issues became public, Catalina/Antonio, or the so-called Lieutenant Nun, became both the celebratory object of contemporary curiosity and the protagonist of enduring literary fame. This was all facilitated by a text, the *Autobiografía*, possibly written by Catalina herself (but maybe not). That narrative ends with its protagonist in Naples, having just received from the pope unexpected (given the mores of the age) permission to continue life as a man. She/he returned to the New World to spend his/her remaining days as an obscure muleteer.

So why recount this oft-told tale? One could simply answer that it is precisely the well-worn subject that lends itself to periodic synthesis—witness the hundreds if not thousands of books about figures like George Washington or Napoleon Bonaparte that in

Eva Mendieta

effect update and tell the story about the story. It is always fascinating to review who said what and when about controversial historical figures. The present book is simply the most recent and excellent synthesis of its subject matter. However, there are two ways in which it goes well beyond any other treatise of Catalina de Erauso's life (including her own), which makes the present text unique with respect to the others.

The first difference regards Mendieta's detailed analysis of the *Autobiografía* in terms of what it can tell us about the existence of a Basque ethnic web within both Spanish society and Spain's New World colonial enterprise. It is not that we were unaware of such a complex. It has certainly been acknowledged by several contemporaries in general terms and described in action during such specific events as the civil war between Basques and all others in the mining camp of Potosí (in which Catalina took part). However, I am unaware of any account that surpasses the present one in demonstrating the individuation of Basque identity for strategic (often self-defensive) purposes in the everyday life of the Hispanic world. In this regard, Catalina's story is an illuminating window on a largely undocumented process.

The second unique contribution of the present work is its discussion of Catalina/Antonio's ambiguity regarding gender identity. The issues of transvestitism and homosexuality have received the obvious attention in many of the previous treatments of this life story. The present text, in fact, makes a significant contribution along these lines by providing a thorough review of the attitudes within seventeenth-century Spain and Spanish America toward cross-dressing and lesbianism in order to contextualize Catalina's behavior. However, Mendieta then takes the significant step of reviewing the evidence in light of the most recent medical research on the etiology of transsexualism or gender dysphoria in order to make what I find to be the convincing case that Catalina/Antonio was a man trapped in a female body rather than a woman disguised in a male persona. Nevertheless, like most of everything else about this larger-than-life individual, there are ways in which this remains but plausible speculation that will likely remain beyond our capacity to ever prove definitively.

Enjoy.

William A. Douglass

CHAPTER ONE

Catalina de Erauso's Other Stories

Who was Catalina de Erauso, the Lieutenant Nun? In this book I intend to answer that question by concentrating on aspects of Erauso's life that have not been examined in depth, yet are crucial for an understanding of her as a person and as a literary character. How can one fail to be fascinated by her? A woman, yet a man; a soldier, yet a nun; Spanish, yet Basque. Catalina de Erauso embodied some very real contradictions and conflicts of her historical period, and she transcended them in her own way. She became a stage on which we see how tensions between different identities played out in sixteenth- and seventeenth-century Spain, particularly the tensions between two sexual identities, male and female, and between the different national identities within Spain. The purpose of this book is, then, to explore the different facets of Erauso's persona: her sexual identity and the factors which determined her choice of gender roles; and her ethnic origin and its impact on her life and her self-image. I believe that for a full understanding of her historical figure, in all its complexity, these aspects of her life must be given full consideration.

In the first place, it is impossible to comprehend Erauso without considering her national origin: that is, her Basque identity. It has been pointed out that the central role played by the Basque community in American colonial society has yet to be studied. Although a few interesting references to it can be found, we lack an overall vision of just what the Basque collective entity in the Americas represented during the Early Modern Period.[1] In the following pages, I will try to show that the text of Erauso's autobiography provides important insights that illuminate the narrative of the Basques as a collective group. It is a matter of what, paraphrasing William A. Douglass, one could describe as the importance of "the Basque element" in her biography, and the significance of this text in understanding the dynamic of the Basque presence in Spain and the New World at the end of the sixteenth and at the beginning of the seventeenth centuries.[2]

The life of Catalina de Erauso ranks as a privileged portrait of the colonial society of her time, and of the role played in it by the Basques, but because hers is such an extraordinary and atypical biography, those who have studied it have overlooked, in large part, the relevancy of aspects which were not foregrounded in the creation of her legendary figure—aspects such as her ethnic origin and its importance in the trajectory of her life.[3] As we will see, in the *Autobiografía* Erauso depicted herself as a member of a well-defined Basque community that continually accompanied her during her travels and in her adventures, both in Spain and in Latin America. Her Basque identity placed her firmly within a framework defined by strong and deep social networks of solidarity shared by Basques: networks that, for example, assured her a passage on a sailing ship destined for colonial America, provided employment upon reaching the continent, and, on more than one occasion, also saved her life. A recurrent motif throughout her life story is that Erauso sought and found help, employment, lodging, and protection with relatives or friends of relatives who, although they did not recognize her, protected her simply because of her origin. In the unstable and violent world of that historical period, the sense of belonging to a community that would provide the protection and support she needed could not fail to be a fundamental structure in her life. I do not pretend that "the Basque element" is a central theme in the *Autobiografía*. It is not; however, given the turbulent and dynamic nature of the seventeenth-century Baroque world—where, as in her own case, nothing is what it appears to be—it is clearly evident that the feeling of belonging to a community is decidedly an advantage for a character who through her own transgressive actions seems to have placed herself on the outer edges of society, beyond the margins of conventionally accepted behavior.

The purpose of this study is, therefore, to contribute to the understanding of Erauso's character by providing a detailed view of the relevancy of her Basque identity in the narrative of her life. Having introduced that general topic, I will next specifically identify the events and the people who shape her biography in this particular way in order to obtain a clearer idea of the significance of her ethnic origin in the trajectory of her life, explaining also how this influence is effected. With this in mind I searched for the historical Erauso in the text of her memoirs, and having examined the vicissitudes of her life—a singularly extraordinary one, I might add—I have been able to corroborate the degree to which relationships with persons of her own ethnic origin, and participation in the trades and professions that form part of the Basque tradition, were both decisive factors in her life. When I discuss these factors I will also deal with the conflicts that emerged as a result of the economic and political rivalries among the national groups that comprised modern Spain. During the historical period that concerns us, Spain had only recently begun to exist as a modern state, and was constructing a national identity which had no relationship to the respective identities of the various regions that comprised it. As we follow Erauso's steps, our journey will lead us through the social reality of Spain and that of her colonies in the Americas. We will observe how people traveled, worked, amused themselves, and made friends; how they loved, as well as how they fought. We will try to draw some conclusions about that social reality, whether viewed from within the limited scope of an individual life, or within the larger one of the different nationalities that made up the Spanish Crown. In crucial situations, the historical Erauso availed herself of the protection that her Basque identity provided, and this advantage assured her survival in a life that was full of adventure and recurrent insecurity. In the end, she prevailed as an individual, and her heterodox persona prevailed. To explain her astounding success, it is necessary to address many other factors. Unlike the focus of other recent studies on Catalina de Erauso, my own interest is not so much in the literary character herself as in the person who remained hidden beneath the character; this is particularly so in the first part of the book which is devoted to the topic of national identity.

When, upon leaving the convent, Erauso exchanged her woman's clothing for that of a man, the transformation that took place was tantamount to a ritualistic gender change. Erauso, except in very specific circumstances, would not appear again as a woman. When she discarded her nun's habit, Erauso also symbolically discarded the restrictions of her sex and began a personal adventure in which she tried to discover her true self.[4] This second part of my study focuses on Erauso's sexual identity. In order to understand it, we will need to refer to the sexual ideology of her epoch, to transvestism, to homosexuality, and to transgenderism: in short, the whole complex of factors that shaped sex and gender reality during the historical period in which our protagonist was born. Recent research has paid special attention to Erauso's homosexuality. With respect to this, my own approach, although it does not overlook her sexual preferences, goes beyond them, and seeks to analyze all those elements which have a bearing on her choice of gender (Is Erauso a man or a woman?), and on her own female sexuality (and homosexuality) as they were understood in that period. In addition, I believe we need to comprehend what it meant socially and economically to be a woman in her world, first in the Basque territories themselves, and later in the larger territories through which she moved in Spain and in colonial America. Erauso's life stood in direct opposition to the kind of existence that would normally correspond to a Spanish woman in the seventeenth century; it represented a virtual rejection of her female identity and the consequent need to construct a gender identity more in keeping with her own experience. In this sense, I will devote attention to the significance of her life as it contributes to a deeper understanding of what life was like for a woman of her time—the nature of the conflicts she faced, and the possible alternatives available to her. Again, my approach is more historical than literary; instead of trying to link her to literary archetypes with which she clearly can be identified, I intend to place the real Erauso in the social, legal, religious, and political world of her times. To that end, we must address the legal codes that were then in force, and examine the import of her life within the context of both the national and the local laws which regulated collective life in the sixteenth and seventeenth centuries.

Below I will introduce the principal themes that will be discussed in the study of Erauso's national and sexual identity, so that we can later see what these identities represented in her life and in her time on both sides of the Atlantic. These are the "other stories" which have yet to be told about Catalina de Erauso's life.

Ruins of the church of San Sebastián the Ancient. Lithography by Alejandro Fernández
(Revista Vascongada).

Convent of San Sebastián the Ancient in the eighteenth and nineteenth centuries. Lithography by Alejandro Fernández (Revista Vascongada).

National Identity: Erauso "the Basque"

By virtue of the education she received, the kinds of work she did, the language she spoke, and the social relationships she cultivated, Erauso was a representative Basque person of her time. If we were to listen to Erauso's voice for a moment, we would hear her speaking in the Basque language (or Euskara, her mother tongue) within a close circle of persons who are of Basque origin, or "*vizcaínos,*" as they were called in that period. She was bound to them by of a sense of solidarity that became very important in the difficult and perilous world in which she moved about.

I will explore contemporaneous historical documents that allude to the solidarity among persons of Basque origin, and how that solidarity is perceived by other ethnic groups (Chapter 3). As we look at colonial society, it is essential to consider the concept of *paisanaje,* or loyalty to one's regional origin, and the proclivity to unite and support one another through a network of associations and economic relationships. In their declarations, various colonial authorities provided an image of the Basque as an individual who was integrated in a community,

> in the "Basque nation" which distinguished itself from other groups because it was char-
> acterized by a high degree of cohesion and solidarity. By availing ourselves of documents
> from the colonial period we can profile the stereotypical Basque by enumerating the char-
> acteristics that define that person: a strong consciousness of group unity, of "us against
> them"; a devotion to the land of one's birth; a spirit of solidarity which reveals itself
> through mutual assistance and aid; an innate sense of justice; a fierce defense of liberty;
> a kind of crudeness and at times violence; intense ambition, as revealed in the desire to
> monopolize or take control; entrepreneurial initiative; a willingness to work hard and be
> responsible; and loyalty to others in the group. In short, the Basque's individualism is not
> at odds with a deep-rooted tradition of alliance.[5]

In my analysis of this particular strand of the narrative, we will see how Basque cama-
raderie had an effect on different aspects of Erauso's life: for example, in facilitating her travel (Chapter 4); in providing her with shelter and with work (Chapter 5); in saving her life when she was in trouble with the law (Chapter 6); or in simply lending her a helping hand and offering her friendship and companionship. For an expatriate who lived a hand-to-mouth existence, who was unable to settle down in one place and create a circle of friends who made life easier and more pleasant, it was only in the existence of a collective group that had representatives far and wide, that such an individual would find a true sense of belonging. Wherever several members of the group were found, they embodied that community with all its concomitant rights and obligations.

Beyond the strictly biographical details we will see that many of the episodes of Erauso's life must be viewed within the historical context of the group to which she belonged. For example, I will begin by placing her within the general framework of traditional Basque emigration, specifically as a member of the Basque contingent that emigrated during the Conquest of the New World. We will also come across references to clashes between competing factions representing various regions of Spain, factions that placed the Basques in direct conflict with the other groups (Chapter 7). Still other episodes of Erauso's life reflect the force and significance of the prevailing *fueros,* or privileges granted by the Spanish Crown, as they applied to the development of economic sectors traditionally dominated by the Basques: for example, mining and the public secretarial services then performed by clerks. All these topics are mentioned in the text of her narrative; and by examining them more closely I hope to contribute to a better understanding of the historical and cultural framework within which the widely celebrated episodes of her life took place.

Her Sexual Identity

Erauso's extraordinary life began when she fashioned a man's clothing from the nun's habit she was wearing after escaping from the convent. From that moment on, she always considered herself to be a man, and led a life accessible only to men. She was able to travel and to work, enjoying a freedom of movement denied to the majority of women in Renaissance Spain; whereas had her true sexual identity been known, she would have been taken as a prostitute or a sexually immoral woman, since any woman who chose to transgress the restrictions of that time would have been labeled as such.

It is precisely the concealment of her sexual identity that makes her life so fascinating and sensational. Without this detail, the story of Lieutenant Antonio de Erauso, the name she chose to go by during most of her life, would resemble something between a picaresque novel and a soldier's chronicle, an interesting and entertaining work, but all things considered, a tale that would not have achieved the enormous popularity of the *Autobiografía.* The duality with respect to her sexual gender is replicated in the difficulty which is posed when we try to identify the literary genre to which the work belongs. The *Autobiografía* can be associated with three narrative forms which have an autobiographical nature: with the picaresque novel and the soldier's journal, both of which contain masculine and feminine characters, but are usually written by men; and with religious autobiography, which was a distinctively feminine type of writing.[6] Erauso's image as a juvenile delinquent who robs, murders, and deceives, as she traveled incessantly from one place to another, evokes the principal characteristics of the picaresque novel.[7] The text also qualifies as a travel and adventure saga, and thus bears a close relationship to the historical chronicles of the New World, to the novels of chivalry, and to the Byzantine novel. Thus we see that both the character's gender and the literary genre of the work itself possess the same hybrid quality.

Erauso changed her gender because she had, in fact, transformed herself into another person; the change went far beyond a disguise which merely concealed her identity, but did not reconstruct it. For Erauso, the alteration in her attire was not a just a costume; it was a permanent second skin. In the part of my book that deals with her sexual identity (Chapter 11), I will explore Erauso's gender transformation into Antonio, and link it to the convention of transvestism in sixteenth- and seventeenth-century Europe. I will also address Erauso's homosexuality. Was Catalina de Erauso homosexual? Which episodes of her *Autobiografía* could persuade us to affirm that she was? Here we sometimes tread on less solid ground, but I believe that her sexual preference is a facet of her personality that cannot be overlooked, and in the final instance represents an undeniable component of her sexual identity.

In the analysis of her sexual identity I will also address the social dimension involved in choosing a man's role. Her flight from the convent represents Erauso's refusal to accept the social proscriptions imposed on women. When Erauso chose to become a man, she was implicitly rejecting her female identity. We are forced, then, to ask ourselves what it was like to be a woman in Spain during the sixteenth and seventeenth centuries (Chapter 10). Was it similar in all the territories of the Spanish Crown or were there differences that applied in the Basque territories (Chapter 9)? In order to answer these questions it is necessary to consider the possible life choices which Erauso rejected, and to that end we will outline those philosophical and socioeconomic factors which defined the social roles assigned to women during that period in the aforementioned territories. In a like manner, in order to define Erauso's own view of women in her time, we will examine the way she portrayed the other female figures that appear in the story.

Catalina de Erauso: The Story Told in Her Own Words

We will first examine the basic facts of her biography, facts already familiar to many. Catalina de Erauso, the daughter of a distinguished family of noble ancestry, was born in Donostia-San Sebastián in 1592.* At the age of four she entered the convent of San Sebastián El Antiguo and lived there until, following an argument with a nun who beat her, she went into the chamber of her aunt, the Mother Superior, robbed the keys of the convent, and escaped forever. Erauso was fifteen years old. Just outside the convent, she hid in a nearby forest, cut her hair, and, as explained earlier, she created a man's garb from the nun's habit she was wearing. She would live and dress as a man for the rest of her days. Working for several masters, she traveled throughout Spain, and ended up in Seville where she sailed for the New World. There she spent her adult life; and there— without her true sexual identity ever being discovered—she starred in the picaresque and military adventures which brought her fame. When she was near death, Erauso confessed her secret to a bishop, and overnight became a real celebrity: "The Lieutenant Nun." Under this new identity she returned to Spain briefly, and then traveled back to the Americas, which remained, for the rest of her life, her adopted homeland.

Research regarding the *Autobiografía* of Catalina de Erauso has been hampered because the original copy of the text, given to Bernardino de Guzmán in 1625, has not

---

* For the most part, the present work will use Basque-language orthography for toponyms (place-names of villages, towns, provinces and so on in the Basque Country). Where applicable, the Spanish or French equivalents will appear, on first mention, in parentheses. However, we use the bilingual variant of Erauso's birthplace, Donostia (Basque)-San Sebastián (Castilian).

been found. The oldest known copy of the text bears the title *Vida i sucesos de la Monja Alférez, o Alférez Catarina D[oña] Catarina de Araujo [sic] doncella, natural de S[an]Sebastián, Prov[inci]a de Guipúzcoa. Escrita por ella misma en 18 de Sept[iembr]e 1646 [sic].* Juan Bautista Muñoz made this copy in 1784, from a manuscript which belonged to the poet Cándido María Trigueros, and donated it to the Biblioteca de la Real Academia de la Historia. This same manuscript is the one reproduced by Joaquín María Ferrer in the first (1829), and second (1838) editions, under the title *Historia de la Monja Alférez, Catalina de Erauso, escrita por ella misma.*[8] Ferrer's edition was later to be the basis of numerous translations and reworkings. To these documents it is necessary to add two manuscripts discovered in 1995 by Pedro Rubio Merino in the Archivo Capitular of Seville. These manuscripts are copies which date either from the end of the seventeenth or the beginning of the eighteenth century, and in some respects they contain significant variations of Ferrer's text, variations which I will point out at the appropriate moment.

In spite of what the title affirms (Written by Herself) the question of authorial authenticity has been disputed, and, for the time being, the fact remains that we cannot know who wrote the text. Could it really have been Erauso? In Chapter 2, I propose to answer that question by paying careful attention to the narrative voice; I will examine the language of the text to see if it coincides with what might be assumed regarding Erauso's own linguistic identity, in particular with respect to her mastery of both Spanish and Euskara. We will also consider the art with which the narrator tells the tale, and draw conclusions regarding the skill it demonstrates.

The Veracity of the Story

Ever since the appearance of Ferrer's first edition, the publication of this work has usually been accompanied by other historical documents that attest to the historical truthfulness not only of Catalina de Erauso's life story, but also to the veracity of the adventures that are narrated in her biography.[9] The historicity of most of the characters to whom we will refer has been confirmed in documents and in records of various kinds. Among the most important are the two *Peticiones* made by Erauso to the Crown in which she asks for payment for the military service rendered, and a third in which she asks to be compensated for having been robbed while she was in France. Accompanying Erauso's *Peticiones* are numerous affidavits made by witnesses, two *Relaciones* (news pamphlets, or broadsides), published in 1625, and three *Relaciones* published in Mexico. The first two Mexican *Relaciones* are practically identical to those published in Madrid, but the *Tercera Relación* (1653) continues the story of her life until her death. These accounts, written by different anonymous authors and sold to the public, serialized Erauso's life, narrating it in installments. To grasp the extent of Catalina de Erauso's popularity in her time on both sides of the Atlantic, one has only to know that in these *Relaciones* her name is not even mentioned because it is assumed that everyone knew who she was.[10] In some cases, the events narrated are corroborated by historical fact; in others, they appear only in the *Autobiografía.*

In any case, regardless of their factual historicity, their inclusion in the text reflects certain cultural referents which the author associates with our protagonist and her times.

The Reception of the *Autobiografía*

The interest awakened by this radically unconventional and original woman has varied, mirroring the cultural and philosophical world associated with a given particular historical period. Following her extraordinary popularity during her own lifetime, we find no mention of her after her death, and during the Enlightenment her figure was consigned to almost total oblivion. In the eighteenth century, she stirred the curiosity of only a few learned scholars who pored over documents and historical accounts.[11] In 1829, however, all of this changed when Jose María Ferrer published his Paris edition of the *Historia de la monja alférez Doña Catalina de Erauso escrita por ella misma e ilustrada con notas y documentos*. Ferrer became Erauso's adoptive father, and almost two centuries after her death, he launched her again into the orbit of historical celebrity. A year after its publication (1830), it appeared in both French and German translations. The original work spawned innumerable reworkings, translations, plays, and poetry, all based on the protagonist.[12] In the twentieth century the number of reprints increased, although in general nothing was added to Ferrer's original research. As I searched American and Spanish libraries for materials related to Erauso, countless versions of her story kept surfacing, some of them extremely fictionalized and bearing only a slight resemblance to the original. At the close of the century three critical editions worthy of note appear: Rima R. Vallbona's (1992), Marjorie Garber's (1996), and Angel Esteban's (2002),[13] and there was renewed interest in Erauso's figure, especially as it was viewed from the perspective of gender studies. If we consider the fact that during Catalina de Erauso's lifetime only one-fourth of the population could read, we must conclude that the enormous popularity of her biography was owed in large part to Juan Pérez de Montalban's well-known play (1629), through which it became widely known. While those who were literate belonged to upper-class society, "at the end of the sixteenth century it was the theatre, both in Spain and in England, that reached the masses."[14] The reawakened interest in the Lieutenant Nun which emerged at the close of the twentieth century and continued into the beginning of the present one is reflected in new studies devoted to the *Autobiografía* as well as to Montalban's play: "Catalina's figure appears in movies, in plays, in stories, and even in comics and comic strips."[15] Many historical novels and works of fiction recreate her life,[16] and her complete *Autobiografía*, or fragments of it, can be found in contemporary anthologies and even in textbooks.[17]

The Plot of the *Autobiografía*

But let us return to her story. Immediately after escaping from the convent, her first steps took her to Vitoria-Gasteiz where she worked for three months for Doctor Francisco de Cerralta: "Seeing that I read Latin well, he took a fancy to me, and got the idea in his head that I should continue my training as his student. When I let him know that I wasn't interested, he pleaded and insisted and finally went so far as to lay a hand on me. With this, I decided to leave him, and that is exactly what I did."[18] From there she traveled to Valladolid where she served as a page for seven months until, faced with the imminent danger of being discovered by her own father, she departed for Bilbao. Here her wandering life really began, initiated, very much in the picaresque mode, with a street fight in Bilbao, for which she ended up spending a month in jail.

> I managed to attract the attention of some of the town's youths who encircled me, edging up closer and closer, until finally I had had enough and picked up some stones and let one of them have it—where I cannot say, because I didn't see. I was arrested and thrown in jail, and there I remained one long month, until the boy I had hit got better and I was set free, my pockets several *cuartos* lighter for the cost of my stay.[19]

From Bilbao she moved on to Lizarra (Estella) in Navarre, and later to Seville and to Cádiz. From there she made her big leap to the New World, where she lived for practically the rest of her life.

In Latin America, we witness Erauso's tumultuous life, punctuated by numerous masters, battles, travels, gambling fights, slayings, and, frequently, problems with the law. Although the periods of relative calm are few, her success as a soldier and as a merchant (her two most important endeavors) is noteworthy. Erauso performs very well as the manager of Juan de Urquiza's shops in Panama and in Peru, so much so that Urquiza left her in charge of the business. These were the golden days of peace and prosperity. But they did not last long. As she herself declared, "Who would have guessed those tranquil days were numbered or that trouble lay just around the corner!"[20] Shortly thereafter, we witness the first in a series of the violent clashes she participated in, which seemed to be very common in those times. The cause of the dispute was trivial, as was repeatedly the case in the numerous fights that start at gambling tables and end in bloody conflicts and deaths. In this instance Erauso was at the theater and she complained because the person seated in front of her cut off her view. "I asked him if he wouldn't mind moving a bit to the side, he responded in a nasty tone . . . Then he told me I'd best disappear, or he'd be forced to cut my face open."[21] The next morning Erauso went out looking for him and the unavoidable confrontation took place.

> I approached him from behind and said, "Ah, Señor Reyes!"
> He turned and asked, "What do you want?"
> I said, "This is the face you were thinking of cutting up," and gave him a slash worth ten stitches.
> He clutched at the wound with both hands, his friend drew his sword and came at me, and I went at him with my own. We met, I thrust the blade through his left side, and down he went.
> I ran straight into the church, followed just as quickly by the sheriff don Mendo de Quiñones, a knight of the order of Alcántara, who dragged me out, and carted me to jail—the first I was ever in— and clapped me in irons, and threw me in a cell.[22]

Although she affirms here that this is the first time she was ever in jail, previously she had stated that after her fight in Bilbao, she "was arrested and thrown in jail." However, now she could be making reference to her first time in jail in the New World. This episode typifies all the events that repeatedly occur throughout her life, events which arose from different circumstances but had similar consequences.

After the relatively stable period represented by her employment with Urquiza, her luck ran out, and she was discharged from her job as a merchant. She decided to be a soldier, and so began her military career. Its highest point was her participation in the battle of Valdivia for which she was rewarded with promotion to the rank of second lieutenant. The narrative continues with more gambling problems and another sword fight. The description is at times nimble and entertaining; for example, while she was in Charcas (today, Sucre in Bolivia), Erauso played a card game with a merchant. She tells us that the game was going on smoothly until,

> on one particular hand, the merchant who was already smarting from his losses said, "I raise you."
>
> I said, "How much do you raise?" and he said again, "I raise you."
>
> Again I asked, "How much?"
>
> He slammed down a doubloon and said "I raise you a cuckhold's horn!"
>
> "Fine," I said, "I'll see you that horn and raise you the one that is still on your head!"
>
> He swept the cards from the table and drew his dagger. I drew my own, the others at the table grabbed us and pulled us apart, and then we went on playing, with everyone side-stepping the issue, well into the night. I left to go home, but I hadn't gone far when I turned the corner and who should I meet up with but this same merchant, who draws his sword and comes at me. I pulled out my own blade and we fell to fighting—we parried, but before long I ran him through, and down he went.
>
> The fracas raised a crowd of people, including the police, and they tried to arrest me. I fought them back, taking two wounds in the process, and retreated to the safety of the cathedral. Here I held up for few days on my master's advice, until one evening, when the hour seemed ripe, the byways clear, I slipped off to Piscobamba.[23]

Through many vicissitudes and hardships, Erauso endured. Time after time, conflict, struggle, and flight appear as motifs in her narrative. She was sentenced to death twice, and more than three times she found herself just on the edge of an armed encounter. She killed seven people—among them her own brother—got herself into gambling scrapes and into more than one unsavory relationship with women.

For many years no one suspected that she was a female until, badly wounded and at death's door, she revealed herself in a confession to the Bishop of Guamanga. The confession itself is worth quoting:

> Your Grace, all of this that I have told you . . . in truth, it is not so. The truth is this: that I am a woman, that I was born in such and such a place, the daughter of this man and this woman, that at a certain age I was placed in a convent with a certain aunt; that I was raised there and took the veil and became a novice, and that when I was about to profess

my final vows, I left the convent for such and such a reason, went to such and such place, undressed myself, dressed myself up again, cut my hair, traveled here and there, embarked, disembarked, hustled, killed, maimed, wreaked havoc, and roamed about until coming to a stop in this very instant, at the feet of Your Eminence.[24]

While in the manuscript published by Ferrer, Erauso, near death, spontaneously confessed, in Rubio Merino's manuscript the confession was induced by the Bishop, who suspected the truth: "He took my hand, came close, and asked me, in a low voice, if I was a woman. I answered yes."[25] In Merino's manuscript, the revelation of her true sex is not part of an account which summarizes her life, as in the passage just quoted, but is rather a much simpler affirmation: "He asked me who I was, where I was from, and whose daughter I was. I answered him. He took me aside and asked me if I was a nun, and why and how I left the convent. I explained it to him."[26] Sherry Velasco notes that although different versions of her life report similar events, "in the small variations between the copies, we can see that her story has been open to interpretation from the very beginning. Since most of the critics agree about the historicity of certain episodes and activities in Catalina's life, the personal motivations behind these actions are what intrigue and frustrate those who try to discover the truth behind the legend of the Lieutenant Nun."[27]

Though this moment marks the end of her public deception, Catalina de Erauso did not alter the way she lived, dressed, and felt, consistent with her self-definition as a man. Given the impact of the Bishop's judgment of her, this represents a pivotal moment in her life, as it would be in the lives of other unorthodox nuns. If the bishop gave his approval, their lives, through the publication of biographies and autobiographies, become part of established tradition and are accepted as exemplary. But if, on the contrary, she was censured, the latitude allowed for a woman's activity would be seriously limited. And so, Erauso's fate hung on the decision of the Bishop of Guamanga. We know that he was astounded when he heard her story, and that he offered her his official protection. She in turn characterizes him in her *Autobiografía* as a saintly, kind man and she repeatedly professes to feel real affection for him.[28] The confession regarding her sexual identity transformed her into an instant celebrity. When the Bishop accompanied her as she entered the convent where she would reside for some time, they could hardly enter the church because of the crowds that had come out to see her. They awaited her in the convent with all candles burning.[29]

Nun and soldier, enveloped in the myth of the New World, a leading player in duels, in real and legendary battles, Catalina de Erauso's life story has all the ingredients to make it widely popular in both Spain and Latin America, and even reach other European countries. When she returned to Spain, she was received as a celebrity. She traveled to Cádiz, Seville, and Madrid, where she hid from crowds who had come to see her dressed as a man. Back again in the Old World, she had two objectives: first, that the king recognize her service and grant her a pension, in which she succeeded: "They received me and ruled in my favor, granting me at the king's suggestion, a pension of eight hundred crowns a year, which is a little less than the sum I had asked for."[30] Next, Erauso traveled to Rome to ask the Pope's permission to continue dressing as a man: "I left Genoa for Rome. I kissed the feet of the Blessed Pope, Urban the Eighth; and told him in brief and as well as I could the story of my life and travels, the fact that I was a woman, and that I had kept my virginity. His Holiness seemed amazed to hear such things, and graciously gave me leave to pursue my life in men's clothing."[31] Thus she accomplished her second objective.

Erauso's narrative, recounted in her own words, stops here. Her autobiography leaves her in the streets of Naples, but we know, through other documents, that shortly thereafter she returned to Latin America, from whence she would never return.

CHAPTER TWO

Who Wrote the *Autobiografía* of Catalina de Erauso? Authorship and Language in the *Autobiografía*

Who actually wrote the autobiography of Catalina de Erauso? Given the state of the current scholarship on this question, we do not know with certainty. All the known editions of her autobiography are based on copies of an original that was never found, and we have no edition that predates the eighteenth century. We do not know whether it was Erauso herself who wrote it or dictated it; whether she told her story to another person who composed it; or whether a third person looked into the facts of the well-known story and gave it written form. This makes any discussion of authorship difficult, or at least inconclusive, since we do not know the original tone of the narrator's voice nor can we definitively establish the text. I will then restate the original question in a way that might allow me to suggest a partial answer. Could Catalina de Erauso have been the author of her own autobiography? In order to come to a conclusion, I will focus on the only evidence we have available to us: the narrative voice and the text itself. However, it is uncertain to what degree these aspects coincide with those of the original text.

The narrative voice and the text pose two principal problems. With respect to the voice, what, we ask, can we deduce from the author's language and its distinctiveness? Can this voice be related to what we can assume to be Erauso's linguistic reality, particularly as it refers to her mastery of Euskara and Castilian? What are the characteristics of her literary voice, and what conclusions can we draw about her narrative skill? And with respect to the text, what is its intention? How could the author have been privy to so many historically accurate details? Are we to assume that certain episodes, particularly the most picaresque ones, are later additions? I intend to answer these questions, with the understanding that although the final result of my inquiry may not give us definitive answers, it will allow us to assign a greater likelihood of truth to some possibilities than to others. I will leave aside, temporarily, the thread of Erauso's story in order to address the linguistic history of the Basque Territory in the centuries that concern us, specifically the sixteenth and seventeenth centuries. We should not forget that Erauso must be seen as a woman who lived in a particular historical period that extends from the end of the sixteenth century into the first third of the following century.

Language Use in the Basque Country (Sixteenth and Seventeenth Centuries)

Thanks to the active support of the Crown, Castilian was consolidated as the official national language of Spain at the close of the sixteenth century. In such important domains as government administration, education, and jurisprudence, Castilian was the dominant language. Two decrees of Philip II ordained that Castilian be used in the instruction of all the sciences, and all the teachers of Castilian were required to pass a test that demonstrated their proficiency in the language.[1] In the Basque provinces, as in the rest of the kingdom, Castilian became the language of culture. At this time, Euskara was still exclusively an oral language and was far from becoming a linguistic code in which children and adults could learn to read and write, or study mathematics, Latin, spelling— in short, all those learning activities that then constituted elementary education.

To illustrate the importance of Castilian in the political life of the Basque Country, Koldo Zuazo reminds us that in 1613, the most important political body of the province, the General Assembly of Bizkaia (Vizcaya), required that all candidates who ran for office demonstrate a mastery of Castilian.[2] According to a document of 1682, the same requirement existed for the political representatives of Araba (Álava).[3] The ascendancy of Castilian in the sixteenth century, along with substantial contact with people from other regions of the Crown, both played an important role in the Basques' growing awareness of their linguistic differentiation.

Thanks to a series of political changes that occurred in the Basque Country during the sixteenth century, the Basque population became aware of the ethnolinguistic ties that united them. With the pacification of the western zone of the Basque Country and the conquest of Navarre (1512), a linguistically coherent territory was configured. At the same time, when the three Basque provinces came under the rule of the king of Castile, the entire Basque Country integrated into a single political universe, and the Basques of all provinces, both in Spain and in the Americas, found themselves involved in shared enterprises; there they noticed (and were reminded of) their striking linguistic differences with the other territories that comprised the realm. On the one hand, this convergence of Basques from all the regions would, linguistically, give rise to a feeling of shared identity, a consciousness that was not felt previously with such clarity. Andrés de Poza, after affirming that the Basques "did not get along nor do get along within their homeland," observed that "outside it, it is noteworthy that they respect each other, love each other and help each other; and this is explained by a single fact, that they are compatriots of the Basque language."[4] On the other hand, the awareness of this linguistic unity would soon be accompanied by the recognition of its difference from that of the other nationalities of the kingdom. As the contact between the different linguistic groups that comprised the Crown became more intense, their respective differences became more evident to all;

and not just because the common language that bound the Basque population had no similarity to Castilian, but also because of the characteristic manner in which they spoke Castilian, in contrast to the way it was spoken by other groups.

Spanish Golden Age writers such as Lope de Vega, Tirso de Molina, Quevedo, and Cervantes provide evidence of this linguistic peculiarity; in their works we find numerous satirical portrayals of Basques who express themselves in fractured Castilian. Their authorial intention is to convey that Basques find it difficult to express themselves in a language they have not mastered. The characterizations are, nevertheless, sometimes contradictory; for example, in Cervantes the *vizcaínos* (literally, Bizkaians but also meaning Basques in general) are at times depicted as the laughing stock of the Castilians; while at other times, they are portrayed as models of correct speech. While Sancho is acting as the governor of the island of Barataria, a courier arrives with a letter addressed to him or to his secretary. Sancho asks "Which of you is my secretary?" "I am, señor," said one of those present, "for I can read and write, and am a Biscayan." "With that addition," said Sancho, "you might be secretary to the Emperor himself. Open this paper and see what it says."[5] In contrast with these testimonies, in other places in *Don Quixote* or in the short comedy, *El vizcaíno fingido* (The Bizkaian Imposter), Cervantes pokes good-humored fun at the almost unintelligible Castilian spoken by the Basques. In Chapter 9 (Part I), Don Quixote meets a group of ladies being escorted by a Basque squire. Believing that they are captive princesses, the knight tries to prevent the coach from going on.

> The Biscayan went up to Don Quixote and seized his lance, addressing him in bad Castilian and worse Biscayan. "Go away; good riddance, gentleman. By God that made me, if you no leave coach I kill you or I not Basque."
>
> Don Quixote understood the gentleman quite well and answered him quietly, "If thou wert a gentleman, as thou art none, I should have already chastised thy folly and rashness, miserable creature."
>
> "I no gentleman!" exclaimed the Biscayan. "I swear to God like Christian you lying. If you throw lance and draw sword, soon see who better man. Basque on land on sea gentleman, by devil, and you lying if you say different."[6]

In a similar fashion, in the short comedy *El vizcaíno fingido* the Castilian spoken by the imposter Quiñones is nonsensical. His speech, "Me Biscayan, kissem hands, you me serve," has to be translated by his friend. "The Biscayan gentlemen says that he kisses the hand of your lady, and that he is at your service." To this, the lady whom he addresses answers: "Oh! What a pretty language. I don't understand it but it seems very pretty." Here we find a pointed reference to a kind of fractured Basque-Spanish speech that by this time had become a cliché, used in the derisive characterization of a "Bizkaian." In the rest of the play Quiñones continues to make utterances that are incomprehensible and must be "translated" by his friend; when they are not translated, the ladies cannot understand the meaning. Here are a few examples. Quiñones says "*Dama que quedaste, tan buena como entraste*" ("Lady that stays good as entered"). The perplexed lady then inquires, "What did he say, señor Solórzano?" "That the lady who is standing here—who is you—is just as good as the one who entered." "My gracious, how prettily the man talks, even though I don't understand him." And in still another similar comical exchange, the Bizkaian says, "*Vamos que vino que subes y bajas, lengua es grillos y corma es pies; tarde vuelvo, señora; Dios que te guárdate*" ("Wine up and wine down, tongue in irons and feet in chains. Later come back, lady. God you keep"). She again is forced to ask, "What did he say, señor Solórzano?" to which the translator replies, "That the wine handcuffs his tongue and ties his feet, but he'll be back this afternoon and may God keep you ladies."[7] Here is a fictional character who, for all intents and purposes, speaks another language, and whose speech must be translated by a "bilingual" speaker.

Of course Cervantes is being satirical and ironic when he exaggerates and distorts the syntax of Basque speech in this way. Such characterizations do not reproduce the usual syntactical interferences caused by certain Basque grammatical structures, since they seem to affect all types of structures, and distort them in unpredictable ways. But these portrayals in literary works remain as an undeniable record of the assumption that every Basque speaks the Basque language, thus providing another indirect testimony of the vitality of Euskara during that historical period. It is taken for granted that every Basque is bilingual, and that Euskara is his dominant language; however, we know that this simplification distorts the facts, because for the most part those Basques who demonstrated their social mobility within the Spanish Empire were men with considerable education, who occupied administrative posts in which correct oral and written Spanish were indispensable. It is evident, then, that the linguistic reality is a complex one, but the stereotype of the Basque ridiculed in this way is comical and amusing; understandably, it takes on a life of its own, quite apart from the reality itself.

An unusually large number of Basques occupied positions as public or government notaries or clerks; this bureaucratic influence of the Basques in Spain and in the Americas was often thought to be excessive. Mateo Alemán voices his complaint, giving reasons that reflect the opinions held during that period with respect to language:

> What can be deduced from this absurdity is that it was introduced by some Biscayan minister; for, all things considered, that tells you the whole story, like the letter he wrote to his parents in the following manner. 'Father sir, I fine you are, letter I write, mother you read, iron you don't sell, nobody you wants it. God you keep.' And since some warrants or royal documents were written like this by those who were in charge of the writing, even more followed.[8]

It defies logic to believe that those who succeeded in asserting their power as clerks and royal secretaries in the field of public administration would express themselves so poorly in Castilian. Perhaps—and precisely to counteract that power—there was an attempt to foster an image of the Basque who was laughable because of his absurd language constructs.

Because it has a bearing on the topic of language itself, we must also consider the remarkable development of elementary education in the Basque territory. From the sixteenth century on, families for whom Euskara was the first language made sure that their children, who knew Euskara very well, also studied Castilian "in an academic way, better even than the way it is learned in Castile."[9] With these words, Julio Caro Baroja casts doubt on the validity of that stereotype of the Basque who speaks Castilian badly, at least as it applies to members of the middle class from the sixteenth through the nineteenth centuries. This is borne out by the fact that the most important authors of treatises as well as the teachers of calligraphy were disproportionately Basque. Nevertheless, Caro Baroja's opinion is at odds with the literary stereotypes previously referred to. This "Bizkaian syntax," widely mirrored by Golden Age writers, is ascribed to fictional characters that were well educated by necessity, as would have been the case with those who worked in public or ecclesiastical administration. A case in point would be the Bishop of Cuzco, Sebastián de Lartaum, "with a doctorate from Alcalá de Henares, a native of Gipuzkoa [Guipúzcoa], a very erudite man," who, nevertheless "spoke with a marked accent, as if he had not studied or been educated, although this was not the case when it came to theological matters or Latin."[10] It appears that here a distinction is being drawn between the speech he used when referring to scholarly subjects, in which case he was very erudite; or his normal everyday speech, in which case he spoke with a very evident accent. It is difficult to evaluate these subjective opinions. As it applied to the lower social class, the stereotype of the Basque who spoke Spanish imperfectly probably came close to reflecting the reality, and apparently it was noticed by other Spanish émigrés in the New World. The less-than-perfect mastery of Castilian must have posed a problem for labor relations, as suggested in the following statement made by Esteban de Garibay with reference to his fellow countrymen: "What they lack in the Castilian language, they make up for in weaponry and military and naval matters."[11] Nevertheless, with respect to the more privileged social classes, we have to assume that a mastery of Castilian would have been the norm.

Another linguistic aspect that has hardly been examined is the distinction between different dialects of the Basque language, dialects that during the colonial period came into contact in a much more generalized way than before. According to Ibon Sarasola, at the end of the sixteenth century Basque speakers were grouped by their provincial dialect as follows: speakers of Bizkaian, 105,000; of Navarrese, 90,000; of Low Navarrese (Nafarroa Beherea or Basse Navarre in the Northern Basque Country (Iparralde)), 60,000; and of Gipuzkoan, 50,000.[12] Although these dialects are mutually intelligible, the differences between them do not fail to be perceived by speakers of the respective dialects when they interact with each other. Pedro de Axular, one of the first authors in the Basque language, expresses this opinion in the prologue to his work *Gero* (Later), published in Bordeaux:

> I know as well that I cannot include all the varieties of spoken Euskara, because Euskara is spoken in many and varied ways in the Basque Territory: in Navarre, in Low Navarre, in Zuberoa [Soule], in Lapurdi [Labourd], in Bizkaia, in Gipuzkoa, in Araba, and in many other places. One says *behatzea*, and another *so egitea* [to express "observe"]. One says *haserretzea*, and the other *samurtzea* [anger or angry] . . . In short, each in his own way and man-

ner. All Basques do not have the same laws and customs, nor do they have the same way of speaking Euskara, because politically they constitute different states.[13]

Another difference that does not fail to go unnoticed is the change in the speech of fellow countrymen who spent a great deal of time away from the villages where they were born, who when they returned sometimes spoke with an accent that had been modified as a result of being in continual contact with speakers of other languages. What we witness then, among the Basques of the time, is the development of a dual linguistic consciousness of their own; this is produced on the one hand by what we might describe as the intralinguistic contact between the distinct varieties of Euskara, and on the other hand by the interlinguistic contact between Euskara and Castilian.

Without a doubt, the use of the Basque language during the sixteenth and seventeenth centuries was a very important factor, if not *the* essential factor in defining the Basque ethnic identity. In contrast with what would occur later in the eighteenth and nineteenth centuries, practically all the inhabitants of the Basque territory were Basque speakers who possessed, in varying degrees, Castilian proficiency, extending from basic knowledge to perfect mastery of the language. The definition of a *vizcaíno* (Bizkaian) (which as we know was the equivalent of *vasco* or *vascongado*, that is, Basque) had an extremely important linguistic component. Ferrer defines the term in his edition of the *Autobiografía*.

> As is the case in some provinces of Spain, in America the name of *vizcaínos* is given to all those who are natives of the three provinces and of Navarre, *because all of them speak vascuence* [Euskara], which is their common language, just as it is for the inhabitants of Lapurdi and the French Navarrese [inhabitants of Low Navarre], and for this reason, in Spain and in the Americas, they easily pass for nationals.[14]

We know with certainty that many of the Basques who emigrated to the Americas spoke Euskara; the testimonies that record the vitality of the language among *vizcaínos* in American territories are numerous. Fernández de Oviedo points out that in the expedition led by Simón de Alcazaba to the Strait of Magellan in 1534, some of the mutineers were judged by the Basque Juan de Charchoaga and "other *vizcaínos,*" and that "the trial was conducted in *vascuence.*"[15] Still another document is a letter (part of which is written in Basque) penned in 1537 by the friar Juan de Zumárraga, in connection with a trial involving some properties in Durango (Bizkaia) that the Bishop had given to his nephew.[16] In 1632, the historian Bernal Díaz del Castillo notes that the Basques who were coming to the New World used the Basque language to communicate with each other.[17] An additional example of the imprint of the Basque language in colonial culture can be found in the works of the celebrated Mexican writer, Sor Juana Inés de la Cruz, to whom we will devote more attention in Chapter 10. One of her *villancicos* (Christmas songs) contains some Basque phrases, recited by a Bizkaian: "*Ay que se va. Galdu naiz, Nere vici gucico galdu naiz.*" ("Well, there it goes. I've lost it, I've lost it forever").[18] She thus offers a clue that points to her paternal ancestry.[19] Sor Juana's verses in Basque are preceded by a series of verses in which once again, the poetic "*I* is expressed through the stereotyped speech of the Bizkaians."[20] The first stanza of the verses sung by the Bizkaian reads: "Señora Andre María / Why do you go to heaven / And not want to remain / in your home Aracaçu?" With such a transposition of elements in the sentence, Sor Juana reveals the existence of the famous "Basque syntax" in the Castilian spoken by Basques in Latin America. Koldobika J. Bijuesca traces these verses in Euskara by Sor Juana to two sources: the *"poesía galante vizcaína"* (literally, "Bizkaian courteous poetry," a type of verse that falls between the learned and the popular), and a type of poetry that circulated in Mexico during the second half of the seventeenth century: "We theorize that Sor Juana was acquainted with that poetry, understood it very well and included it in her *villancicos* for the [Feast of the] Assumption of 1685."[21] We have, therefore, a number of indirect testimonies of the presence and vitality of Euskara in the Americas during the Early Modern Age.

According to Zubiaur, in the period extending from the thirteenth through the eighteenth centuries, the Basque-speaking territory remains stable. He situates the geographic border between the two languages in Portugalete and Urduña (Orduña) in central/western Bizkaia, southern Araba, and in Navarre from Lizarra (Estella), up to Erronkari (Roncal) and the Northern Basque Country or Iparralde. In the interior, Euskara was the general and sole language for the common people, especially in Gipuzkoa, the birthplace of Erauso. With respect to Navarre, a manuscript of 1587 offers a list of the villages of the province and identifies 451 as Basque-speaking, while 58 are Castilian-speaking.[22] The fact that the linguistic border remained stable during so many centuries does not mean, however, that nothing had changed. The annexation of Araba, Bizkaia, and Gipuzkoa to the Spanish Empire brought with it the arrival of a small minority of royal bureaucrats, clerks, and merchants who spoke only Castilian and functioned as agents reinforcing the use of Castilian in daily life. Their presence gave rise to the emergence of a social bilingualism that applied to the noble and urban classes, attracted as they were by the prestige associated with, as well as the practical necessity for, proficiency in the official language of the kingdom. Thus began a slow but progressive erosion of the Basque-speaking territory, causing the growth of a kind of vertical bilingualism "in which a large part of the population would be monolingual Basque-speaking or Euskaldun, and a relatively small part of the population—the upper classes, the nobles, and the clergy, etc.—would be bilingual Basque-Castilian."[23] We should not, however, forget the very small proportion of Castilian monolinguals previously mentioned.

The sixteenth century was also the century that gave us the first texts in Basque. The first text written in the Basque language was published in Bordeaux in 1545: the *Primitiae linguae vasconum* (First Basque Language) is a small collection of poems composed by Mosén Benarte Dechepare, a parish priest of Eiheralarre (Saint Michel le Vieu), in Low Navarre. The volume contains religious poems that end with an invocation to the Virgin Mary, "Lesson to Those in Love," linking the first part of the volume to the second part, which in turn is devoted to worldly love. Two compositions at the end of the book pay homage to the Basque language; in one of them we find the well-known verses *"Heuskara ialgi adi plazara!"* ("Basque, go forth into the street!"). Perhaps this suggests the author's concern that in the public sphere, Euskara was disappearing. In this same century, the Basque apologists (for example, Garibay and Poza) published their treatises, which can be considered as a defense of a language that was losing ground as well as social prestige, given its exclusively oral, rather than written, character, and being marginalized by the ascendancy of new national languages like French and Castilian.[24]

To a certain degree, the usage of one or the other language depended on the speakers' social class. The less well-off and less educated population, who had less need to associate with people outside their social circle (farmers, cattle raisers, blacksmiths) above all spoke Euskara, although some may have used Castilian in their dealings with the upper class. In this regard, Adela Colera points out that in the village of Azpeitia, in Gipuzkoa, those ordinances that applied to the poor had to be translated into the Basque language and proclaimed orally throughout the village in order to insure that they would be understood by all. Andrés de Loyola (a nephew of St. Ignatius of Loyola) acted as translator of such documents, a fact that demonstrates that the more learned classes (nobles, gentlemen, priests) were bilingual.[25] Ordinances dating from the middle of the eighteenth century (found in the Municipal Archive of Eibar, Gipuzkoa) regarding the elections announced by the *corregidor* (the king's direct representative in the provinces) also had to be translated into Euskara.[26] Pedro de Axular, who dedicates his work *Gero* (1643) to the reader, underscores the importance of writing in Euskara "particularly for those who know only this language."[27] If it is certainly true that the more privileged social classes must have used Castilian in their dealings with the Crown, it would be no less true that they must have used the Basque language in their frequent dealings with the townspeople. The bilingualism of the middle and upper classes is, thus, more than probable. That the lower classes were characterized by a less-than-perfect bilingualism, with Euskara as the dominant language, seems to be corroborated by what we can presume was their contribution to the predominance of *seseo* (the pronunciation of "c" before "i" and "e," and the pronunciation of "z" as "s") in the New World. The Basque émigrés would have contributed to the predominance of *seseo* because their own pronunciation of the romance language was influenced by the phonetics of their maternal Euskara.[28] The preservation of the lateral articulation /l/ in Paraguay, as well as the articulation of the asibilants r, rr, and tr, in various Latin American zones, have also been attributed to the Basque influence.[29]

Several lawsuits of the sixteenth and seventeenth centuries refer to the need for interpreters because the interested parties possessed a limited knowledge of Castilian. For example, there was the case of a seventeen-year-old girl, María de Fuica, who was the victim of a violent sexual assault, and for whom the *corregidor* of Bilbao felt obliged to name a translator because "she does not know how to speak Castilian with clarity."[30] We find similar situations in trials during which the lawyers for the defense sometimes complained that the witnesses' depositions were recorded without the use of translators, rendering the depositions unreliable; still another case points out that a Basque magistrate did not know Castilian either.[31]

To draw conclusions regarding the historical usage of the Basque language we have to rely largely, as we have seen, on indirect testimonies. Additional indirect proof of the use of the language in the territory can be found in the abundance of translations of books used for religious education during the sixteenth and seventeenth centuries. In keeping with the spirit of the Council of Trent (1545–63), the ecclesiastical authorities found it necessary to promote translations so that all Christians could come to know the Christian doctrine, or at least its principal articles, "in their own tongue." In 1561, Sancho de Elso's *Doctrina christiana* (Christian Doctrine) was published; it is the first known catechism in the Basque language.[32] Besides these books there are also a few collections of proverbs and a conversational guide in Euskara, written by Rafael Mikoleta from the city of Bilbao. This guide offers more indirect proof of the vitality that Euskara enjoyed in the city of Bilbao during that period, inasmuch as the conversational knowledge of the language was considered necessary for the activities of daily life in the urban area.[33] To add still greater complexity to the linguistic situation, we have also to consider the presence of the Gascon language in Gipuzkoa. According to Ramón Menéndez Pidal, Gascon was the customary language of documents written during the Middle Ages in Donostia-San Sebastián and Pasaia (Pasajes), and it continued to be used until the nineteenth century. There are numerous records regarding the Gascon colony in Donostia-San Sebastián and its environs; for example, in a 1611 trial of several women accused of practicing witchcraft in Hondarribia (Fuenterrabía), the witnesses of this town and those of Oiartzun (Oyarzun) were questioned in Euskara, but those who came from Donostia-San Sebastián and Pasaia were questioned in Gascon.[34]

Catalina de Erauso's Language Use

Now, let us summarize some of the general observations we have provided to see how they apply to the life and times of Catalina de Erauso. She was born at the end of the sixteenth century in Donostia-San Sebastián to a noble and wealthy family, although in comparison to the fortune once possessed by her paternal grandfather, the family had come down in the world. In sixteenth-century Donostia-San Sebastián, the social class to which the Erausos belonged was bilingual. We can assume with certainty that the entire native population possessed a mastery of Euskara. A cursory look at the individuals who lived in the convent of San Sebastián el Antiguo, where Erauso was raised and educated, would clearly reveal that the great majority of the nuns who lived there (with whom she shared her daily existence until she was fifteen years old) were Basque. José Ignacio Tellechea Idígoras mentions some of their surnames: Aliri, Argarte, Yarza, Elduayen, Escilla, Zapiain, Altuna, Sagarraga, Arriola, Zuloaga, Arancibia, Iturrieta, Echebelz, Bezcanga, Aldama, Echeverría, Echeverri, Asua, Arotz, Garagarz, Amas, and the three Erauso sisters.[35] Without a doubt, Erauso also knew Castilian: we know that she learned to read and write there, and this she could only have done in Castilian. To her mastery of Euskara and Castilian we should also add her knowledge of Latin.

It is clear that the years she spent in the convent provided her with an education she could hardly have received elsewhere. Electra Arenal and Stacy Schlau, who have examined the ambiance of the convents in the seventeenth century, point out that the nuns got a significantly better education than did the rest of the female population.[36] If by reason of her social class and her education we must suppose that Erauso was bilingual, we still do not know if it was a bilingualism in which she was equally proficient in both languages; or if, on the contrary, one of the two was dominant. I think we can assume that Euskara was the language of communication within the convent. After all, we are referring to a community of Basque women who lived at the end of the sixteenth and the beginning of the seventeenth century and in that community the need to communicate in Castilian with that group who only spoke Castilian would have been minimal. If it existed at all, it would affect only the nuns who had positions of authority and responsibility in the Order—for example, those nuns who had to deal directly with non-Basque benefactors and administrators from the nobility and the merchant class.

With respect to language proficiency in the upper classes, Vallbona comes to a different conclusion: "In evaluating the present manuscript we must keep in mind that, coming as she did from an upper-class family of that period, Catalina de Erauso's native language was Basque, *and for that very reason she was monolingual*; when she is four years old she goes to live in a convent protected as well as directed by Basques."[37] As I pointed out previously, it would appear that it was precisely the privileged classes who were not monolingual. Given what we know about their commercial enterprises and their constant contact with the multifaceted government administration, they were the ones who found it necessary to have greater mastery of Castilian. We know that the Erauso family belonged to this group not just because of its social class, but also because Erauso's father was the mayor of Donostia-San Sebastián, a position he could not have held in 1589 unless he knew how to speak, read, and write Castilian. It is obvious that such an appointment would presuppose frequent and continual contact with the business and industrial sectors connected to the Crown.

The linguistic reality of the convent aside, we know that Catalina de Erauso spoke Euskara because she herself tells us that. On two or three occasions, when she finds herself in serious predicaments that would in all likelihood lead to her imprisonment or death, the voice of a Bizkaian is suddenly heard, speaking to her in Basque, telling her where to go or what to do to get out of the tight spot she is in. This, of course, is done in the assurance that only she (or other Basques whose comradeship is taken for granted) will understand. Secret codes have a double advantage: they draw us closer to comrades and keep others, whom we fear, at bay.

In the text it is clear that Basque is equivalent to Basque-speaking. An individual's identity may be unknown, but if that person is known to be of Basque origin, the use of a common language is unquestioned. While this fact allows us to draw a conclusion, it simultaneously poses a question. The use of Euskara between the Basques in the text of the *Autobiografía* leads us to conclude that the knowledge of Euskara was generalized throughout the population of an entire territory that, in terms of its geographic borders, was stable. When someone is identified as a Basque, no one asks if that individual is from this or that province; for all, a mastery of common language is taken for granted.

This leads us to pose the following question: Would Euskara be the preferred language of communication among Basques outside their native territory, when they met or had dealings with each other? Or, to put it another way, would Erauso normally speak Euskara to all the Basques with whom she developed close and continuous relationships throughout her life? For a variety of reasons, I believe it is logical to think so: because she identified with her own linguistic group, because she was often thrust into situations in which she experienced the deep and bloody hostility of other groups, because the particular social stratum in which she moved shows a preference for communicating in Euskara, because it was her mother tongue, and because language is the basic component of that common Basque identity that was so important in her life. For all these reasons I am persuaded that the answer to that question is affirmative, that Basques did prefer to speak to each other in Euskara and not in Castilian.

Moreover, since the degree to which she both associated and surrounded herself with Basques is a decidedly significant factor in her life, it is likely that such a choice was due in part to the greater ease with which she could communicate in Euskara, probably her dominant language. Vallbona makes a similar conjecture:

> After escaping from the convent at the age of fifteen, during those three years that she travels through Spain dressed as a man, she spends most of that time in Basque regions. We must also keep in mind that in arranging her travel to the New World, during the voyage itself, as well as in her feats and adventures there, she had abundant contact with her countrymen. This information leads us to suppose that her knowledge of Castilian was limited. For that very reason, it is probable that the manuscript reveals the interference of Basque. In addition, we must also consider the possibility that those who helped her write her memories were also Basque.[38]

With the exception of her penchant for associating with other Basques, there are no other indications that would support the idea that she had an imperfect knowledge of Castilian. In fact, one is more inclined to believe the contrary to be true. Even if she possessed an imperfect knowledge of Castilian when she abandoned the convent at the age of fifteen, her travels through Spain and Latin America would have thrust her into continual contact with people with whom she was unable to communicate in any other tongue; therefore, practical necessity would have forced her to gradually improve her mastery of the language.

The Language of the *Autobiografía*

Let us suppose now that it was in fact Erauso herself who wrote all or part of the text of the autobiography. We would then ask, as Vallbona does, if there are dialecticisms or interferences that betray the author's or the copyist's Basque origin, since in texts that date from those centuries it is difficult to know whether the dialectal words can be attributed to the author or to the copyist.[39] Having made a careful analysis of the text, I conclude that it contains no linguistic clue that directly connects the author or the copyist with the Basque territory; neither does it contain forms of Castilian that are typical of this territory, nor structures that are produced as a result of interference with Basque linguistic constructions. I have found neither lexical, nor syntactical nor—of course— phonetic traces. Nevertheless, in her critical edition of the *Autobiografía*, Vallbona echoes an observation made by Roslyn Frank, who points out the possible syntactical influence of Euskara in some of the rather awkward constructions found in the text.[40] The following passage, from the first chapter, is cited as an example:

> *viéronme alli entretanto unos muchachos en reparar, i cercarme, i perseguirme* hasta verme fastidiado [i ...] tuviéronme en la cárcel un largo mes, hasta que él huvo de sanar *i* soltáronme, *quedándoseme a por allá unos quartos, sin mi gasto preciso.*
>
> Meanwhile I managed to attract the attention of some of the town's youths, who encircled me edging up closer and closer, until finally I had had enough . . . I was kept in jail for one long month until the boy I had hit got better and I was set free, my pockets several *cuartos* lighter for the cost of my stay.[41]

It is difficult to know, with any certainty, the origin of constructions of this type, but what is certain is that their presence is sporadic and can be explained without having to attribute them to bilingualism. When he comments on the rather strange constructions that appear in writing by authors of Basque origin, Juan Antonio Frago Gracia rightly wonders whether this kind of grammatical awkwardness is actually due to the author's bilingualism, since in many instances, the grammatical usage "while not elegant, does not approach formal disorder."[42] As an example, in 1589, Alonso Martínez de Lacunza y Urbizu, a wealthy merchant, wrote a letter to his family from Mexico, a letter in which we can find expressions that demonstrate an anomalous word order (en llegando *luego*), the absence of a pronoun ("[la] daría"), the use of the directional *en* ("en llegando luego *en* esta tierra"), and so on.[43] In all cases such as these, when one cannot establish a clear relationship between the Basque constructions that would be generating the Castilian anomalies, it is really difficult to hypothesize that a causal relationship exists, above all if the anomaly produces a construction that might also be possible in monolingual authors. In my judgment, this is the case with respect to the syntactical examples that Roslyn Frank points out in the *Autobiografía*. Moreover, she neither identifies which Basque constructions interfere nor does she say that these anomalies are used in detriment of others more in accordance with Castilian grammar.

On the other hand, there are instances in which one must conclude that the grammatical anomalies are a result of the interference between Euskara and Castilian. Frago offers the case of Gonzalo de Madalén, a rich merchant from Gernika (Guernica) in Bizkaia, whom he judges to be "the author whose Spanish is most affected by an imperfect bilingualism that drove him into continual morphosyntactic mistakes: 'la grandísima pesadumbre me ha dado'; 'sabe Dios si yo quisiera podérsele dar'; 'mis hermanas a *los* cuales beso'; 'quería que v. m. me la [Antonio] ymbiaçe'; . . . 'y a la demás sobrinos (me) encomienda v. m. mucho.'[44] All these examples lead Frago to conclude that in the writings of some Basque émigrés an "idiomatic peculiarity" can be profiled, providing an index of the so called "Bizkaian syntax."[45] Of course, the errors in the agreement of gender (and number) in the examples cited are otherwise difficult to explain, and what is even more significant is that we find them in documents written by Basque émigrés, "especially those who were bilinguals," whose writing clearly reflects the excellent education that they received in Basque schools.[46]

The arbitrary use of masculine and feminine gender in words that refer to Catalina de Erauso has also been linked to her bilingualism, (or that of the presumed author). Since there is no distinction of gender in Euskara, one might be led to believe that the author confused the gender of adjectives and attributes relating to Erauso. Juana Alcira, for example, concludes: "This is what led me to surmise that if her testimony was oral, she must have given it in Euskera . . . she always lived among Basques and it is likely that she communicated with her compatriots in that tongue."[47] In other Basque authors as well, the lack of gender agreement between noun and adjective has been advanced as evidence of "grammatical Bizkaian." For example, in two letters written by the learned Fray Juan de Zumárraga, a native of Durango and the first Bishop of Mexico, one reads "mucho *devoción*," and "se me mandase pagar *del sede bacante*."[48]

At the beginning of the *Autobiografía*, the attributive words referring to Erauso are consistently feminine in gender. At a given point in the narration, Ferrer's version starts to employ the masculine gender, but Vallbona's version, in many instances, continues using the feminine. Although the two editions use the same manuscript as their point of departure, Ferrer's edition made corrections and modifications without annotating them, while Vallbona respects the original text and remains faithful to the fluctuation of gender. Using Vallbona's critical edition, then, I list below the adjectives and attributes associated with Erauso throughout the text.[49]

Chapter 1. There is fluctuation of gender: "le pedí licencia porque estava *mala*"; "a pie y *cansada*"; "*Entrada* en Valladolid . . . y estuve allí bien *hallado* siete meses." As the chapter goes on, both genders appear: "hasta verme *fastidado*"; "bien *tratada* i *vestida*"; "bien *vestida y galana*"; "no dándome por *entendida*." **Chapter 2**. The attribute is masculine: "por ser *nuevo* en el oficio." **Chapter 3**. Vacillation: "*llegada*, me *recibió*"; "*advertido* de las personas, fui *restituido* a la Iglesia de donde fui *sacado*." **Chapter 4**. Only the masculine appears: "me lleva *acido*"; "*Acogido* allí." **Chapter 5**. Vacillation: "*Partido* de Truxillo"; "*acostado* en sus faldas"; "Hallávame *desacomodada* i mui *remota* de favor." **Chapter 6**. Only the masculine appears: "mal *herido*, i *pasado* de tres flechas"; "Estávame *quieto*"; "teníame en particular *acido*"; "Prometiendo premio a quien me diese *preso*"; "quedé un poco *suspenso*"; "Yo quedé *atónito*." **Chapter 7**. Vacillation again: "cargada de arcabuz"; "ya se ve mi aflicción, cansada, descalza, rendida en aquel suelo"; "iba por allí tan apartado y me hallaba rendido y muerto de hambre"; "Viéndome totalmente *falto*"; "Vistióme muy galán"; "Yo me mostré mui *rendido* al favor."

Antiguo San Sebastian / Fuente de la Muralla

Fountain at the wall of the church of San Sebastián el Antiguo. Etching by A. Pirala, from the collection of F. Altube.

Entrance to the church San Sebastián el Antiguo. Etching by A. Pirala,
from the collection of F. Altube.

In the first eight chapters the vacillation is almost constant and, in my opinion, cannot be attributed to any discernable aspect of the narrative content. From Chapter 8 through Chapter 16, the masculine gender is consistently used; no feminine adjective or attribute appears. **Chapter 8**. "*Partido* de Tucuman"; *Vuelto* al Potosí." **Chapter 11**. "*Salido* de este aprieto"; "*Advertido* de mi amo que me guardase." **Chapter 12**. "Llegado a Piscobamba"; "hálleme afligido"; "Llegado allí"; "fui mandado soltar." **Chapter 13**. "*Partido* de allí"; "*Llegado* al río"; "Íbamos de ello algo *consolados*" (referring to Erauso and another woman); "llegué a la Plata, bien *fatigado* y *cansado*"; "En San Francisco, *recogido* con caridad i asistido en la curación por aquellos padres, estuve *retraído* cinco meses." **Chapter 15**. "donde me estuve *quieto* algunos días"; "*herido* me prendieron y yo allí *guare-cido*." **Chapter 16**. "me hallé *ageno* totalmente de culpa, si bien mal *opinado*"; "i me tuvo preso cinco meses, bien *afligido.*"

In Chapters 17 and 18, again we see only the feminine gender. **Chapter 17**. "Yo, *cogida* de repente, no sabía que decir, vacilante y *confusa.*" **Chapter 18**. "Quedando *herida.*" Another shift to the masculine in **Chapter 19**. "*Partido* del Cuzco"; and in **Chapter 20**. "hallóme afligido, me puse *tamañito.*" Immediately after she reveals her female identity, we find "yo *llana* estoy"; "caí allí *enferma*"; (in the title) prende*lo* en el Piamonte, lleva*nlo* a Turin." Next, she uses the masculine gender in a self-reference, something she had not done since she revealed her identity: "*Partido* de Barcelona"; "quizá por verme *solo*"; "de que me vi *cercado.*" From this point on, the gender is always masculine. Vallbona suggests that this is because she had again definitively adopted male garb, and because she had taken the name Antonio de Erauso: "me hallé *abierto*"; fuese *combinado* y regalado"; "*Ciu-dadano Romano*"; "que ser *Español.*"[50]

In Vallbona's view, this gender vacillation can be explained by the interference of Euskara in Castilian syntax, but she also gives a second interpretation: that the narrator uses it as a disguise while playing a masculine role in certain situations. When she is relat-ing an amorous adventure with Solarte's sister-in-law, she adopts the masculine gender, and "in passages of courtship, flirtation, and romance, she uses the masculine form, as she does in those referring to war and duels. Nevertheless, when the context is neutral, the narrator-protagonist reverts to feminine usage."[51] Clearly this explanation is incon-sistent with one that posits an interference of Euskara, in which there is no grammatical distinction between masculine and feminine gender. Personally, I think it improbable that the gender fluctuation can be explained by grammatical interference.

Why is there no confusion in any other instance? Fluctuation or errors of gender do not appear in relation to any other noun in the text; for most of them the gender is rather arbitrary and not associated with sexed beings, which would make such distinc-tions more difficult for a non-native speaker. If the fluctuation only appears in relation to the gender of a protagonist who conceals her sexual identity throughout the story, I believe that, rather than grammatical interference, it reflects uncertainty with regard to how she should be classified. This demonstrates how difficult it is to assign one gender or another to the character: a biological gender or a social gender, a natural gender or a constructed one. Unlike numerous "manly women" of that epoch, Catalina de Erauso does not don a temporary male disguise and then resume her "true" gender; rather, she transforms herself fundamentally into a man. We know that she was born a woman, but later we learn that she became a man and identified totally with a man's life. She both crosses over and spans that duality. If we exclude the gender confusion involving the protagonist, we find only one or two isolated instances of constructions that show a similarly forced syntax as evidence of the possible influence of Euskara in the Castilian of the text. I am not convinced that the linguistic evidence supports the theory that the author is of Basque origin. Although the author may have been Basque, that fact cannot be determined on the basis of unequivocal dialectal signs.

The linguistic facts in and of themselves neither confirm nor deny the possibility that Erauso was in some way related to the authorship of the text. We might, for example, assert that she is not the author of the text because no dialectal traces can be found in it, but this would be the same as saying that her mother tongue must necessarily have influenced her use of Castilian, leaving visible imprints of that interference. Next, I will offer some ideas that cast doubt on the truth of such a hypothesis. I suggest, on the contrary, that if in fact she were the author, the absence of interference of Euskara in the Castilian of the text can be interpreted as proof that her knowledge and mastery of Castilian were comparable to those of a native speaker.

The fact that her Castilian shows no evidence of interference is not so surprising if we remember that for many long years, Erauso regularly, if not mainly, spoke Castilian. Without a doubt, by constantly practicing Castilian over the years she must have achieved a considerable degree of perfection in the language. No matter how much she liked the companionship of her countrymen, these were few in the Americas, and for years the people with whom she had daily contact would be largely from other regions of Spain, and with them she could communicate only in Castilian. Since she spoke to her countrymen in Euskara, and not in Castilian, this would have diminished her exposure to the type of Castilian, which, according to the research, would in fact contain examples of interference caused by bilingualism. On the other hand, it is noteworthy that at no time, and in none of the numerous references to Erauso made by people who knew her and spoke to her, can we find any remarks about the Spanish she spoke. Comments are made about her physical appearance, her clothing, and her disposition, but nothing is said regarding her speech. Bearing in mind that it was customary in that period to poke fun at the incoherent and rude speech of Basques, had there been any trace of that kind of language behavior in her, we can be sure that it would have been reported or recorded by someone. In short, an analysis of the quality of Erauso's voice in the *Autobiografía* has led us to conclude that she possessed a mastery of both languages, Euskara and Castilian; therefore we cannot reject the possibility that Erauso was, in fact, its author.

Now I will consider the literary or narrative voice that is heard in the text in order to determine whether it could have belonged to the historical Catalina de Erauso. In his analysis (1872) of the *Autobiografía*, Diego Barros Arana deals with the problem of authorship. I will cite his general conclusion because, except for some nuances, most of the scholars who have studied the problem are in agreement with him.

> The confident style and the pure and elegant diction reveal a much more experienced pen than that which can be imagined for an adventurous nun, to whom we can attribute neither the practice of writing nor literary taste. On the other hand, the abundance of items of information that conform to the facts and the historical documents, the prolixity of certain details, and the general spirit of the book, completely lacking in any literary pretension and apparently intended to describe true events, in all their simplicity, [all these considerations] indicate that the story is not totally foreign to Catalina herself. After having carefully examined that autobiography, and matched its details with the historical documents published by Ferrer, and with public events to which reference is made, *we have come to believe that the book attributed to the lieutenant nun and published under her name, was written not by her but by one of the numerous geniuses who in that century gave brilliance and splendor to Spanish letters, to whom doña Catalina recounted her adventures in an orderly way.*[52]

Recent scholarship regarding the intellectual life of women brought up in convents during the Early Modern Age suggests that their education was better than it was previously thought to be. In Erauso's particular case we know that she could read and write Latin easily. Another kind of "literary" background she might have acquired would be obtained through oral literature, through the stories listened to and recounted by soldiers in the taverns, stories that were enormously popular during that period. In the narrative episodes that make up the *Autobiografía,* Myers sees a structure that is typical of episodic stories that have a clear ending, a structure very similar to the one that characterized the oral prototype designed for recounting stories in military camps or in taverns.[53] It appears, then, that by reason of her education as well as by the experience she might have acquired as a narrator, we cannot discard Erauso's participation in authoring the text. One possibility is that she is behind the creation of the text, more as the subject who dictates or provides facts to another person who constructs the text than as its direct author. The second option is that she herself is the author of the text. To explore this possibility let us consider another important factor that should be kept in mind in any discussion of the authorship.

In the text of the *Autobiografía* one can detect features that are drawn from various genres: the reports and the chronicles of Spaniards in the Indies, travel journals, literary autobiography, and the picaresque novel.[54] All these literary genres have been pointed out previously when analyzing different parts of the text, but what is the relationship between the historical Erauso and this collage of different genres? Vallbona believes that

> Catalina's original written version (or her own oral retelling of her adventures) lies beneath the text that has come to us, embellished by the interpolation of incredible narrative episodes that we cannot find confirmed in the historical documents of the time or in Catalina's biography. These episodes are what contribute to the fictionalization of the narrative discourse; a fictionalization that is also apparent in the open-ended and cynical conclusion, more in keeping with the model of the picaresque novel than with an autobiographical account.[55]

That is, a number of serialized fictional elements, probably invented by other authors, were later superimposed on the original text attributed to Erauso, a text that captured the essence of her biography and was faithful to historical facts. Examples of these formulaic episodes would be the "number of deaths that the protagonist left in her wake without being punished; the swindles of innocent women by promising marriage; the duel she took part in during which she killed her brother by accident; the fact that for nineteen years no one discovered that beneath the masculine garb there was a woman."[56]

One of the picaresque episodes of the book takes place while Erauso is in the employ of the merchant Diego de Solarte. The text portrays a scene in which she is with her employer's sister-in-law; she is lying between the folds of her skirts, and running her hand up and down between her legs. The sister-in-law urges her to go to Potosí, get rich (on silver, it is assumed) and come back to marry her. The employer, Solarte, unexpectedly comes on the scene and immediately fires her. How could we believe that Catalina de Erauso would consent to being portrayed this way in her *Autobiografía*? We should not forget that the scene being described depicts a woman, a transvestite, seducing another woman. Writing this would have cost her dearly, since there are recorded cases of men in the New World who were burned at the stake for engaging in similar behavior. In addition, and more importantly, at this time Erauso had submitted her *Pedimento* to the king; in it she requests a pension in recognition of the service she had rendered to the Crown, she claims to be of noble blood, and asks that he take into account the "simplicity and honesty with which she has lived and lives."[57] Inasmuch as she is requesting money from the king, it stretches the imagination to believe that she would incriminate herself by engaging in conduct that, at the time, would not only be socially unacceptable but also illegal. This is not an isolated episode; there are also two proposals of marriage to women whom she abandons. It is, therefore, hard to believe that Erauso herself would have included episodes that by their very nature would have seriously endangered her own self-interest.

What, then, are we to believe? With respect to the question of Erauso's authorship, the answer is both yes and no. If there is a historic Erauso who created the text, whether directly, by writing it herself, or by dictating it to a second party, both hypotheses are correct. So great is the wealth of historically authentic details that one has to believe that they were narrated by an eye witness. But then, the story takes flight. And in these flights, there are, in all probability, other voices and other hands that are not Erauso's. Since we have no text that dates from the sixteenth century, the path followed by the text is unknown. But it is very probable that there was an original version of the text in which only one authorial voice could be heard. At a given moment that text began to be filled with other voices that enriched its literary value, but added elements that were far removed from the vital context of the historic Erauso. This, then, would become the fictionalized autobiography of Catalina de Erauso. My hope is that new documents will be found and that this will not be the last word on the matter.

Cartography of Donostia-San Sebastián by Pedro Texeira. Seventeenth century (circa 1622).

CHAPTER THREE

"*Euskaldunak emen badira?*"
Basque Solidarity throughout History

In this chapter we listen to voices that describe the nature and the extent of the special ties that bind Basques together, ties which have unified and strengthened them from time immemorial. Some of these voices are Basque, others are not. Since Catalina de Erauso lived in the New World in the seventeenth century, we will pay particular attention to testimonies relating to that place and time. When she leaves the walls of the convent behind her in her native Donostia-San Sebastián, Erauso also leaves behind a protective circle of family and friends; she forsakes what has until then been her life, and enters a world that she could only have heard about. And she does it alone. The need to continuously conceal her sexual identity must have intensified her sense of loneliness and isolation. Nonetheless, as we read her autobiography carefully, what we will perceive, time and again, is that this loneliness is actually quite attenuated, because whenever she finds herself in the company of a Bizkaian, she also finds, over and over again, protection and unconditional support.

In drawing on the historical evidence that documents this tradition of association and mutual assistance, it is my intention to present the vicissitudes of Erauso's life through the prism of her own participation in this long and well-documented historical reality, hoping thereby to contribute to a better understanding of the course of her life. In a more general sense, I hope to show the degree to which membership in a given group could affect life during that historical period. We will see that the support of her countrymen is a factor that determines entire chapters of her biography; this fact cannot be ignored if we wish to understand the choices she makes in life together with the possibilities that are open to her in Spain, as well as in Latin America, simply by virtue of her membership in a given ethnolinguistic group. Documents that record this mutual support among Basques date back to the thirteenth century; they give evidence of a social phenomenon that, as will be seen, endured with undiminished strength into the early twentieth century up to the coast of New York City.

The Basque Colony in Andalusia (from the Thirteenth to the Seventeenth Centuries)

As early as the fourteenth century, Basque seaports in close proximity to each other signed agreements of mutual assistance—for example, the coalition in 1339 between Donostia-San Sebastián, Getaria (Guetaria), and Mutriku (Motrico). The three ports united "against any people of another nation," and the alliance was invoked in the name of "the bonds of affection, blood lineage and kinship" among the people of these maritime cities. These alliances also reflected long-standing hostilities and rivalries, above all the conflicts among the warring lineages and their camps that continuously plagued Basque geography, and reached a horrific level of intensity in the fourteenth and fifteenth centuries.[1]

Outside the Basque Country, the first written testimonies regarding group solidarity were provided by a group of Basque émigrés in Andalusia.[2] King Ferdinand III had granted concessions to the Basques in return for their naval assistance in the battle against Arab invaders; as a result, by 1247 Basque maritime interests were already well-established in Seville.[3] With reference to these thirteenth- and fourteenth-century Basques, as well as to the later émigrés to the New World, Luis Navarro García remarks that they demonstrate traits that will characterize them from that time on: they maintain ties with their home villages; they tend to associate with people of their own ethnic origin in professional endeavors (with the tendency to a certain degree of endogamy); they form organizations that preserve their union and assure mutual assistance. "Early on, certain patterns of conduct emerge . . . the maintenance of family ties, soon strengthened by additional ties dictated by self-interest, a concept of life that makes existence outside the group unthinkable—[these] will soon materialize throughout the Americas as the Basques begin to swell the current of Spanish emigration to the New World."[4] Thus, as early as the thirteenth- and fourteenth-centuries, the Basque colony in Andalusia had already manifested all the key concepts that typified group solidarity: the preservation of their ties with their home villages, the identification with the collective group and its destiny, and the acceptance of the obligation to help their countrymen. Also noted was the Basque associative tendency in entrepreneurial ventures, as a method of defense and to consolidate their power. Without a doubt, language played an important role in all this. Many of the young people from the Basque Country who arrived each year spoke only Euskara, and the process of their adjustment must have begun by having to learn or master Castilian.

Later, during the sixteenth and seventeenth centuries, commerce with the Indies brought important benefits to the Bizkaian and Gipuzkoan colonies in Seville, groups that would grow and prosper but not assimilate. In general, Basques married within their group, and in commerce as well as in shipping, sectors in which they had a heavy involvement, they demonstrated a pronounced and aggressive ethnic solidarity.[5]

As we will see, once in the New World, the number of testimonies increased and their emotional tone intensified. In the colonial period, those writings that described

Basques always highlighted the following features: the notion of group; the love of their common land of origin, as well as the language and its frequent use; the spirit of solidarity, support, and mutual aid; loyalty; and a strong sense of responsibility and of justice.[6] In the entry he devotes to Catalina de Erauso in the *Enciclopedia General Ilustrada del País Vasco*, Bernardo Estornes Lasa uses expressions like "cosa nostra" or "Basque mafia" to characterize the associations formed by the Basques during the conquest and colonization of the Americas. The comparison was intended to emphasize the powerful meaning attached to belonging to "a family," and to all the rights and obligations that that membership implied.[7]

The Basque contingent was present in the colonial development of all the societies of the Americas. The first to arrive were Basque soldiers and clerics, followed by the bureaucrats and merchants. A significant number of these émigrés achieved such a high degree of success and distinction that it often caused conflicts with rival groups from Spain, who were jealous of their achievements and of the assistance they provided to each other. During the colonial period, the ethnolinguistic solidarity of the Basques led to a coalescence of their common interests, which in turn facilitated easy access to credit, giving them an advantage in creating commercial networks and in establishing other powerful connections. As a result, they would later be in a better position to influence decisions made by the municipal or town authorities: "The Basques in the New World acted, at least on occasion, as a self aware ethnic group. This awareness was translated into collective action, mutual assistance, a common stance toward outsiders, and a perception on the part of outsiders that the Basques were set apart from other Hispanic and Creole (New World born persons of European descent) groups."[8] According to Julio Caro Baroja, the concept of "a community of interests" that united the Basques goes beyond a shared history and extends to the kinds of occupations that united them: "Among the inhabitants and the natives of the former Pyrenees region as well as those of the three territories, there is a growing awareness that a 'community of interests' also unites them, both under and within the Spanish Empire. This is not only true with respect to the zeal they show in maintaining their *fueros* (special privileges and freedoms), but also with respect to the kinds of occupations that unite them during eighteenth century."[9] Similarly, William A. Douglass and Jon Bilbao observe that

> from the earliest years of Spain's New World venture Basques tended to cluster with their fellows in particular areas, where they proceeded to convert, or possibly to subvert, objectives of the Crown into a favored position for Basque interests . . . Secondly, in the Basque activities of northern Mexico we find evidence of the importance of kinship ties as networks that facilitated Basque immigration into the New World.[10]

This solidarity has been perceived as the most important characteristic of the Basque settlements in the New World, where their associative tendency helped them secure a privileged social position and defend themselves against other Spanish peninsular groups.

Marriage within the ethnic group, and even endogamous marriage to near relatives, both functioned as mechanisms for consolidating the power attained. As the worth of the estate to be inherited and protected increased, kinship ties became more important. For example, "In general, consanguinity responds to careful calculations and has a clear intent: when the heir is a woman, foreseeing that there may not be a male heir in the next generation, the line of succession to the inheritance is strengthened through the closest line of cousins, if possible, through the paternal line."[11] Within these dense networks of family relationships, mention must be made of the continual social and economic support extended by the families who emigrated to those who remained in the Basque Country, who represented a pool from which new employees or business partners were chosen whenever they were needed.

Nevertheless, for the Basque community to develop self-awareness, its uniqueness could not only be sensed by Basques themselves; it had to be recognized by others.[12] First, there must be an ethnic consciousness that manifests itself in different ways, particularly in a shared attitude toward others; in addition, others must also perceive the distinctiveness of that group. The group's acknowledgment of self-identity should go hand in hand with the acknowledgment, by others, of that group's singularity as an entity. It is obvious that the Basque language, Euskara, played an essential role in making other groups recognize the Basque "difference." The use of a radically different language thus emerged as the most outstanding cultural signifier for those who spoke it as well as for those who did not.

In their study of collective ethnic consciousness as seen within the context of the New World, Douglass and Bilbao describe numerous episodes in which the Basques displayed ethnic self-awareness. During Columbus' first voyage, the Santa María (the flagship) was Basque-owned and the crew was composed largely of Basques. When the boats had sailed for 800 leagues with no sight of land and Columbus was determined to sail on, the Basque crew of his ship threatened to throw him overboard. It was only after the officers of the other ships intervened that a compromise was reached.[13] In yet another example, we find that the first European colony in the New World, founded by some of the men Columbus left behind on the island of Hispaniola, was destroyed by the Indians. The massacre occurred because the colonists had split into two camps along ethnic lines; apparently the Basques seceded into one camp, and the rest united in another. Bartolomé de las Casas, author of a history of the Indies, states "Certain Bizkaians joined together against the rest." Another historian remarks in a similar fashion, "There was a division among the Christians that was caused by the Vizcayans."[14] Douglass and Bilbao also record an episode which brings to mind the kind of help that Erauso received from Basques throughout her life. Diego de Nicuesa, from southern Spain, was one of two men who had been given the royal mandate to conquer and explore the mainland areas in the Americas. The funding for the expedition, however, came from the Basques, and a Basque, Luis de Olano, was the highest ranking naval officer of the expedition. Nicuesa and Olano set out to explore the coast of Venezuela, but when they reached Darien they had a falling out, resulting in Olano's arrest. "Olano, however, sent word to Martín de Zamudio and other Basques who were stationed at a nearby settlement. These men marched on Nicuesa's position, freed Olano, captured Nicuesa, and forcefully put him on a boat for Hispaniola."[15]

The biography of the first Bishop of Mexico, Juan Zumárraga (1475–1548) also provides important evidence regarding the magnitude of Basque association in the Americas during the early Early Modern Age. José Mallea-Olaetxe, who examined the bishop's personal correspondence, concludes that his Basque origin was a fundamental factor in his life, a fact which had been largely overlooked in the studies devoted to this historic figure. In a way, his case was similar to Catalina de Erauso's. Numerous studies have been devoted to both of them, but all those studies—even though they briefly mention some episodes or a few specific persons—overlook the significance of the single factor that determines the chain of events in their respective biographies: their shared Basque origin.

Mallea-Olaetxe's study provides clear evidence of the protection that Zumárraga always extended to his relatives as well as to Basques in general, with whom he always surrounded himself during the years of his bishopric. His personal assistants, as well as those who frequented the Episcopal houses in the capital of Mexico, were Basques. In several testimonies the bishop was accused of favoring his countrymen. When he needed help with legal, commercial, or craft matters, he always wrote to Durango (Bizkaia), his home village, to offer the work in question to a countryman or a relative. Zumárraga's documents also show that he had a very close relationship with numerous Basque merchants and ship-owners. The oldest known letter in Euskara (1537) was penned by this bishop.[16] On one occasion Zumárraga wanted to get a report critical of the Audiencia (high court) delivered to the Emperor Charles V, and faced with the danger that his letter would be intercepted, he decided to travel to Veracruz where he knew there was a significant Basque community. Suspecting the bishop's intentions to deliver this damaging document, the authorities decided to step up surveillance of the port. Nevertheless, the bishop succeeded in getting the help of a Basque sailor who hid it in a buoy and later retrieved it when the ship sailed.[17]

In connection with Zumárraga, Mallea-Olaetxe mentions yet another document that provides an additional example of the strong Basque group solidarity during that period. In 1536, a rich merchant from Bilbao made a will in the Episcopal palace of Mexico. Three out of four of the executors of the will were from Bizkaia; seven of the eight persons mentioned in the will were Basque, and it is possible that the eighth person was also Basque.[18] Both the merchant and Zumárraga designated significant sums in their respective wills for the maintenance of Basque churches or for the construction of orphanages in the villages where they were born. Thus, even when they were in Mexico these two individuals chose to surround themselves with Basques, and designated Basques as beneficiaries of their wills.

As I noted previously, those who did not get along well in their homeland helped each other nonetheless when they were in the Americas. Basque interrelationships would, by necessity, change with emigration to the New World. Families who had competed with each other, and among whom there was considerable commercial rivalry, were forced to reconsider their relationships when they were in the colonies. There the former hostility and rejection that characterized rival towns or families was transformed into alliance and mutual assistance. From the beginning of the Early Modern Age, the use of the generic term "*vizcaíno*" ("Bizkaian") to refer to anyone of Basque origin gives proof of the appearance of a Pan-Basque identity in which shared cultural traits trump any differences of status, origin, or family ancestry that might have been important in the traditional Basque Country. Because of the colonial experience, Basque identity took on a new dimension, bringing with it a new definition of the individual as a citizen of the Spanish Empire. Spanish citizens in the colonies enjoyed economic and legal rights that they did not have in Spain, rights which broadened their business opportunities and offered new horizons for individual development. For example, the compensation given to a young Basque man for defending the Spanish border against the French in 1522 or in 1638 pales in comparison to the substantially higher sum he could expect for "pacifying" territories in northern Mexico or southern Peru.[19]

The associative tendency of the Basques also materialized itself in the New World. Numerous associations of mutual aid—brotherhoods, confraternities, and mutual aid societies—were founded during the seventeenth and eighteenth centuries, following the models of those established in Seville and Cádiz at the middle of the sixteenth century. Basque mine owners in Potosí organized the first Basque brotherhood in the Americas at the beginning of the seventeenth century; later these mine owners were very much involved in the bloody clashes that took place between the various national groups.[20] These brotherhoods had many aims: to worship Basque patron saints, to do charitable works for Basque natives (for example, visiting prisoners in jail or providing them with legal and economic assistance), to help all the recently arrived Basque émigrés, to find husbands for Basque women who had been orphaned, and to provide endowments for those who devoted themselves to the church. The brotherhoods established specific places of worship (chapels or churches), held funerals for deceased members, and arranged for them to be buried in the church's crypt. Members of the brotherhood, their descendants, as well as any persons of Basque origin, were all eligible for these benefits.[21] Since these organizations enjoyed complete economic and religious independence, they could maintain their autonomy; they neither begged for charity in the cities, nor did they solicit the economic help of other groups. They accepted donations only from Basque natives or persons of Basque descent, and they tried to secure the protection of the Crown.[22]

The Nineteenth and Twentieth Centuries

This quick summary brings us to the nineteenth and twentieth centuries. Pierre Lhande provides the following summary of the circumstances that produced the legendary Basque "team spirit":

From the beginning, Basques understand one thing: that they have to support each other, and, consequently, organize themselves. Isolated by their language, by their patriarchal history in an enclosed valley, by their personality, they realize that if they do not form a compact and resistant nucleus, they will be lost, absorbed in the whirlwind. Team spirit is born of this instinct. They possess one resource lacking in many other foreign settlements; that is, that spirit of solidarity that moves those who enjoy a strong position to extend a helping hand to their poorest countrymen.[23]

This feeling explains the foundation of numerous societies "whose purpose is to lend support to their members, first economic, and then moral, thus creating around the émigrés a little bit of that feeling of their homeland, whose privation they have endured during the first tough years of their emigration."[24]

In their classic study regarding the Basques in the Americas, Douglass and Bilbao assert:

Taken as a whole, they provide a fascinating example of an ethnic group elaborating a series of institutions that reinforce a sense of ethnic cohesiveness among a population that is small and lightly sprinkled over an enormous territory. Through its regional festivals, the network of Basque hotels, preferential endogamy, the kinship system, sense of funerary obligations, social clubs, dance groups, the travels of Basque chaplains, and Basque radio broadcasts, the Basque community has been able to create and to project one of the most viable ethnic heritages in the American West.[25]

The authors describe the importance of Basque boardinghouses or hotels that appeared wherever Basque emigrants clustered in the American West. In those establishments, the recently arrived émigrés would find a welcoming environment, a place where they could speak to people who shared their own language and culture, a place that prepared traditional Basque food, and provided the kind of support they needed. Douglass and Bilbao sum it up eloquently:

By 1910 one of the boarding house operators, Valentín Aguirre . . . established a hotel called the Casa Vizcaína and a travel agency. His hotel and travel agency are today legendary among the Basques of the American West . . . Elderly Basques residing in the American West today still retain vivid memories, spanning more than half a century in some cases, of getting off the boat in New York City filled with trepidation, only to hear the welcome words, "*Euskaldunak emen badira?*" ("Are there Basques here?"). Aguirre's agents were sent to meet every vessel arriving from Europe. Within a short time, the new arrivee was ensconced in a Basque establishment, regaled with familiar food, immersed in conversation in the maternal language, and given the opportunity to work out the tensions of the voyage on a nearby handball court. No longer need he fear for the future . . . Aguirre frequently had standing requests for new herders and could place the man whose major concern was his lack of guaranteed employment.[26]

Just as we witnessed agreements of mutual assistance among Basque fishing ports during the fourteenth century, we now document similar networks of support six centuries later on the coast of New York City.

Anti-Basque Sentiment: Clashes with Other Nationalities

Caro Baroja associated the Basque tradition of emigration, of leaving the territory, with the feeling of distrust that the Basques awakened in other groups. Many Basques who left in the sixteenth and seventeenth century came to occupy important administrative and commercial positions in the government. This had a dual effect: on the one hand the Basques who emigrated became a source of prosperity for the Basque Country, since the riches of a well-positioned family represented wealth for the Country; but on the other hand, for the other nationalities, this success generated mistrust. The role of the Basque "living abroad" caused discomfort that manifested itself in many ways. Juan Vicente Llorente, a nineteenth-century historian, stated that the importance assigned to the *fueros* (concessions granted to the Basques) had been exaggerated because of the prominent position of Basques in the central government administration, in the most important tribunals of justice, and in the offices and secretariats. This topic will be examined in greater detail in Chapter 7, which focuses on the hostility that existed among the various Iberian national groups. In general, it was the prominent role played by Basques in the Spanish social order that generated apprehension, but in addition, "something that becomes gradually more pronounced is the opposition and antipathy felt in many parts of the realm with respect to the autonomy of the Basque Country, its special laws, the distinct character of the Basque territories when compared with the other lands of the monarchy."[27]

We see "the dark side" of this associative tendency, when other émigrés voiced their complaints about the special consideration Basques gave to each other, especially those who occupied positions of responsibility in government administration. The other regional groups believed that Basque success was achieved at their expense, and this resentment gave rise to numerous violent intra-Iberian conflicts in the New World, for example, the wars that erupted in Potosí between the camp of the *Vicuñas* (a group made up of Peninsulars and Creoles) and the Basques; or the rebellion of the Andalusians in Laicacota "given the ill will that Doctor Don Álvaro de Ibarra professed toward those of this nation [Andalusians]."[28] These rivalries were reflected in widely circulated pamphlets that appeared in the seventeenth century. *El Búho Gallego* (The Galician Owl, 1620), for example, expressed a bitter criticism of the disproportionate role played by Basques in the collective social and political life of Spain. This treatise was answered in 1638 with *El Tordo Vizcaíno* (The Basque Thrush), another pamphlet where the Basques responded and defended themselves from these attacks. While *El Tordo Vizcaíno* does not represent an objective view of the Basque Country, it is a very valuable "historic document for understanding the political mindset of a seventeenth-century Bizkaian, and the commonly held ideas about the history of Biscay."[29] *El Tordo Vizcaíno* identified the following elements in the Bizkaian collective consciousness:

> Basques possess an admirable spirit of brotherhood. When it comes to unity, affection, love, favoring and respecting one another, not as countrymen but rather as people suckled at one and the same breast, there is no nation in the world that can compare with them. That love of language, of the motherland, that piety, that warm welcome, that brotherhood, that readiness to shake hands—all are based on sharing the same pure blood. When a true Basque sees that a fellow Basque is down on his luck, he will not scorn him; rather, he will help him, favor him, stretch out his hand, assist him, sponsor him, vouch for him and assure his path; because he knows that when the same blood is shared, those who share it must have a great deal in common.[30]

In the preceding pages, I have gathered general beliefs expressed by individuals from diverse backgrounds, published in different places and in different historical periods, regarding the spirit of cohesiveness that characterizes the Basque population. These beliefs certainly became an integral part of their collective conscience. Any interpretation of Catalina de Erauso's life that fails to address the relevance of these factors would be incomplete. As we seek to understand the essential features of her life story, we will have occasion to point out the specific ways in which these general notions of Basque solidarity come into play. While I do not suggest that these ties are universal, nor that they exist exclusively in the Basque community, the fact that this reality has been repeatedly observed and analyzed throughout history leads me to believe that for one reason or another, this convergence of Basques to advance their collective success and assure their material, social, and spiritual well-being constitutes a continuous and stable trait that they have demonstrated throughout history. Nevertheless, Douglass and Bilbao caution against the danger of exaggerating this ethnic cohesion, and offer, as an example of the individualistic and competitive spirit among the Basques, the ill-fated rebellion of Lope de Aguirre and his followers, known as the *marañones*.[31]

When Caro Baroja discusses the difference between the Basque Country and its people, he emphasizes the importance assigned to kinship or lineage from the earliest times. Over time, this way of connecting people to a sturdy family tree has grown less important, "but we know that in the Middle Ages men were strongly bound together by relationships, which perhaps are the same ones that still survive today." Among these forms of relationship, the concept of *vecindad,* or neighborhood, is fundamental in traditional rural life—"The concept of neighbors, *auzoak*; the concept of neighborhood work, *auzolan*; and the belief that neighbors must perform a series of rituals for each other, regardless of the distance which separates them: [all these beliefs] have governed life until the beginning of the [twentieth] century."[32] It is important to keep these concepts in mind as we search for the origins of that spirit of group loyalty that I have discussed in this chapter. If we take a historical view of the Basques, we will see them as a cluster of individuals who come from the same linguistic and ethnic group, who considered themselves relatives, and who shared a common national identity. The *vecindad* or "neighborhood" (the nearest human group in terms of proximity) is the foundation on which a series of rights and obligations rests. When a Basque emigrated and left this "neighborhood" behind, to what degree did he leave behind that feeling of obligation and membership in a well-defined human group? The distinctive notion of solidarity attested to in the New World can thus be understood as the continued existence of a traditional Basque way of understanding membership in a certain human social community. I believe that in Catalina de Erauso's life we perceive echoes of that primordial reality transplanted to the new situations that emerge in the changing world our protagonist had to face.

View of Seville in the sixteenth century. Painting by J. Vauzelle.

CHAPTER FOUR

On the Road: Catalina de Erauso's Travels

There are three requirements for being an authentic Basque: to have a sonorous last name that tells of your origin, to speak the language of the sons of Aitor, and . . . to have an uncle in America.

Pierre Lhande, *L'Emigration Basque* (1909)

In order to explain the life path chosen by Catalina de Erauso, I will begin by exploring traditional Basque migration and its special connection to the sea and to specific kinds of work. I will then show how her choices corresponded to those previously established patterns. Erauso was not blazing new trails in her journeys through Spain and the Americas; she was following itineraries already established by her countrymen from time immemorial. Both in her departure from Spain and in the destination she chose, her journey fits into a clearly established and historically consistent migratory tradition.

The Tradition of Basque Emigration

When Erauso abandoned the convent at the age of fifteen, she followed the footsteps of many of her countrymen who preceded her, crossing the frontier of her small country to travel first through Spain and then through the Americas. There is no doubt that Erauso was acquainted with this tradition; documents show that her parents, her grandparents, and all her forebears had been in constant contact with their countrymen in Andalusia, that they had dealings with seamen who traveled to Norway or to Newfoundland, fishing for cod or hunting whales, not to mention all the relatives and neighbors who were in the Americas. In all certainty, while they were in the convent, Erauso and her sisters must have listened to stories about their three brothers, all soldiers, who for years had been living in the New World. In the steps that led her afar, she followed a trail forged by thousands of her fellow countrymen, and in so doing identified herself (in this respect as in so many others) as a representative figure of her time and her ethnic origin. It has been pointed out that Erauso could have learned about the Americas through her education in the convent, which was run by Dominican nuns. We know that this order (along with the Franciscans) devoted itself to the indoctrination of the natives in the new territories. "They were missionaries par excellence, and to that end their members were educated, to the degree that was possible, about the lands in which they would have to travel . . . To an already imaginative Catalina, all that could have given wings to her dreams, making her long to be a soldier in those distant lands."[1]

The Basque tradition of migration had always been associated with their connection to the sea, with the scarcity of land, and with the Basque laws governing the inheritance of the family estate. Although that migration was driven mainly by the lack of financial means, there were also other contributing circumstances that, in different historical periods, came into play. During the Early Modern Era, another cause of migration was the unsustainable demographic growth that occurred in the Basque territories. This high population density was the result of the absence of epidemics and the bioclimatic disasters that caused havoc in the rest of the Iberian Peninsula during this period. Consequently, the Basque Country experienced a high degree of demographic saturation, and a large number of its inhabitants were forced to abandon their places of origin and search for other modes of economic survival.

Traditionally, Basque emigration occurred as a consequence of the formation of family groups that had become interrelated through marriage. In these groups, "one son is chosen by the parents to inherit the farmstead, and to marry in order to guarantee the succession. The other children who wish to marry have to emigrate and make lives for themselves outside the family."[2] Traditionally, each family owned (or rented) a farmstead and subsisted by cultivating it. That plot of land represented the basic social unit in rural Basque society, and it was thought that it should not be divided either through sale or inheritance. This led to the institution of *mayorazgo* or primogeniture; that is, inheritance by one individual. This practice, guaranteed by Basque foral law, required that one single heir be chosen from among the descendants. When the patrimony was transferred to the heir, he had to settle accounts with the rest of his brothers and sisters who also had rights. If the siblings left the home or married before this occurred, they received their share in advance. The economic and social status of the non-heirs was precarious, and so it is understandable that this system encouraged the Basque migratory tradition.

The scarcity of land available for cultivation was another contributing factor. This was due as much to the topographical configuration of the land in the Basque Country as to the limitations posed by the institution of primogeniture. If measured by an abundance of grain and livestock, which was the criterion for wealth in the societies of the ancient Mediterranean world, then the Basque Country "is fundamentally and essentially poor; beleaguered by constant instability; [a country] that is forced to import food, a need that causes constant concern, as can be seen in the proceedings of all their meetings."[3] To the low productivity of Basque agriculture and the weakness in the livestock sector, one must add the absence of any industry that could absorb the oversupply in the rural labor force, as well as the economic crisis that affected the shipyards and foundries in the last decades of the sixteenth century.[4]

In the observations he recorded as he traveled through Spain (1524–26), Andrea Navajero identified the two previously mentioned factors (the scarcity of land and the system of *mayorazgo*) as forces that drove the Basque from his homeland. "The Basques go to sea because they have many ports and many ships, which they can build cheaply, given the abundance of oak trees and iron ore that they possess; on the other hand, given the small size of the region and the great number of its inhabitants, if they want to make a living they are forced to leave."[5] The land's unsuitability for producing what was necessary to sustain the population, and the high demographic density that had been a historical reality in the Basque Country, pushed some of its people to emigrate and make a life beyond its borders, where they might find more favorable conditions.[6] This situation, born out of need, together with the "entrepreneurial spirit" of the Basque people and their willingness to move beyond their geographic area when it became necessary, explained why there were many Basques who, from the very beginning, traveled to the New World and participated in its development.[7]

In general, economic considerations (the lack of money, the search for a better life, the desire to make a fortune) are what essentially drove Basques to abandon their homeland and start a new life in the New World. Others, however, crossed the Atlantic in search of a life full of danger and adventure. The stories they heard about countrymen who made their fortunes easily and quickly, who sent for their relatives or sent large sums of money to them, or the return home of these newly wealthy émigrés—all these reports were like promotional advertisements, luring those who had remained at home to do the same thing. The "relative in the Americas" is the first link in the chain that led many other Basques to the new continent. For many, the following process unfolded: first, a relative left home, succeeded in his venture, and then summoned a brother or a nephew to assist him with the daily tasks of doing business. This gave rise to family networks that also promoted active, significant business ties. These connections helped to consolidate the "ethnic Basque consciousness" that was later translated into collective action characterized by reciprocity.[8]

For the reasons mentioned, and others that we will address next, we can speak of a continuous mobility of the population away from the traditional Basque territory. In Caro Baroja's opinion, the large number of Basques who live and work outside the Basque Country forces a necessary distinction between the Basque people themselves, and the territory they occupy, the Basque Country.

> The Basques, known for their mobility from medieval times, and for the navigational skills that led them to sail an expanse that stretches from the northern seas to the eastern edges of the Mediterranean Sea, expand these activities [during the Early Modern Era]. As a result (and again we must differentiate the people from their land), we find that there are large numbers of individuals who are Basque in nationality, but who tend to play out their lives, almost always, *outside their Country*.[9]

Casa del almirante Oquendo.

House of Admiral Oquendo. Steel engraving by Gomez, from the collection of Alejandro Fernández.

San Sebastián: la vieja Iglesia de San Sebastián, «El Antiguo y sus alrededores, 1890»

Donostia-San Sebastián: The old church of San Sebastián el Antiguo and surroundings, 1890.
Steel engraving by J. Comba, from the collection of Alejandro Fernández.

The Basques' close relationship to the sea also explains why many of them were to discover their destinies far from their homeland.

The American Adventure

During the colonial period, Basque emigration to the Americas was considerable. Voluntary migration to the New World, and the military demands made by the Spanish Crown in order to maintain its power, were factors that produced a sociodemographic imbalance. A document dated 1629 acknowledges that "Vizcaya is suffering from a lack of inhabitants, because so many of them leave to serve his royal Majesty in His armies and navies, and the shortage is especially acute in the seaports." This state of affairs was so critical that in the mid-seventeenth century, Bizkaia issued several public calls that sought to repatriate Bizkaians who were living "in the Indies, Flanders, Italy and other provinces." At this time, three out of four inhabitants of Bizkaia were women.[10]

Erauso's departure for Latin America fits into the larger context of the great migratory movement that occurred after the conquest of the New World. During the sixteenth and seventeenth centuries, emigration to Latin America was largely masculine, and involved adolescent and young men, usually unmarried, who signed up for the American adventure hoping to make their fortunes in those far-off lands. In the group of Spanish colonists who settled in the New World during the fifteenth and sixteenth centuries, only 3.8 percent came from Basque provinces. Nevertheless, it is reasonable to think that the actual statistics surpassed the official ones, since the latter do not take into consideration the fact that ships engaged in maritime traffic between Spain and Latin America were manned by crews made up largely of Basques. This would have represented an advantage for any of their countrymen who might want to risk making an illegal crossing. Without doubt, there were also crew members who stayed in the Americas just as Erauso did after she gave up her job.[11] The official figures also do not include the great number of Basques who, after registering as official residents in Seville, Cádiz, Huelva, and Jerez, sailed for Latin America.[12] In short, during this period, as the text of Erauso's autobiography clearly reveals, not only were there many Basques in Latin American lands, but their economic progress and their privileged social position were also evident. It appears certain that Basque emigration continued to increase over the centuries, reaching its largest numbers in the seventeenth century. The documentary evidence seems to corroborate a change in the patterns of migration during the seventeenth century; it registers a decline in the number of émigrés from the southern regions of Spain, along with an increase in those from the north, especially the Basques. This is understandable, since, as we will see, the Crown gave preference to Basque ships and crews from 1582 on.

As we have previously mentioned, numerous documents were found that underscored the shortage of men in the Basque territories during the same period. The increase in the number of Basques who migrated occurred at the same time that the general flow of migration decreased because of the high cost of transportation, the dangers to navigation posed by pirates, and the restrictions imposed by the Crown. Given these factors, the ease with which the Basques eluded official procedures as they engaged in their commercial and maritime activities was noteworthy. In a similar fashion, the administrative reforms instituted by the Spanish Bourbon monarchs during the eighteenth century created new opportunities in the field of administration and a demand for functionaries, especially those required for the establishment of new commercial and mining centers. These opportunities represented powerful incentives for many Bizkaians, inducing them to spend short terms or to live permanently in the New World.[13]

The Basques and the Sea

As has been noted, although Bizkaia and Gipuzkoa were considered poor rural areas, from the twelfth century on they gradually attained significant economic importance because they provided a large share of the country's sailors, fishermen, and metallurgists.[14] Due to its strategic location between France, Castile, Aragon, and Cantabria, the Basque Country became a crossroads for international mercantile transactions, and by the end of the Middle Ages commerce had already become a basic component of the Basque economy. Besides generating considerable income, commerce also provided the foundation for the subsequent development of the industrial sector.

Basque seamen devoted themselves primarily to cod fishing and whale hunting, activities they began in medieval times and brought to their peak between 1500 and 1700.[15] According to the evidence provided by Lhande, in the twelfth century whale hunting was already well-developed in Bizkaia, and it is likely that ship building and whale hunting had already been important for two centuries:

> Under relentless hunting pressure . . . these animals modified their annual migrations, avoiding Basque waters in favor of an open sea route to the Asturian/Galician coasts. The Basque whalers responded by constructing larger vessels capable of traveling to these new hunting areas . . . It was this demand for larger boats in the whaling trade that created the basis for a Basque shipbuilding industry.[16]

The whale is so important that it appeared as a symbol in several seals used in maritime ports; for example, the ancient seal of Hondarribia (1297) depicts a whale being hunted from a small rowing vessel. The symbol still exists in present day Bermeo, Getaria, Lekeitio (Lequeitio), Mutriku, and Ondarroa.[17] The coat of arms of Lekeitio, one of the most important whaling centers, bears the following inscription: *Horrenda cette subjectit*, or to those who "dominated the terrifying cetacean."[18] Since ancient times the whale was native to the Basque coasts, and the ones that ran aground on the beaches were always exploited. With the passage of time and the improvement of their techniques, the whalers headed west, to the coasts of Cantabria, Asturias and Galicia, and the whaling industry began to develop on a grand scale. As Basque whalers acquired a reputation as experienced sailors, skilled in the use of the harpoon and the boning knife, their fame in the art of fishing and sailing became well-known in the principal seaports of Europe. As early as the fifteenth century, Basques established themselves in European seaports, where they engaged in a number of commercial activities such as the exportation of wool and iron, transportation, fishing, and even piracy.[19]

In these ports, Basques first heard the accounts of the voyages made along the coasts of Canada by the Venetian, John Cabot, and the Portuguese Corterreal brothers. According to a long-held belief, one hundred years before Cabot's expedition and those of the Norman and Breton fishermen, Terranova was discovered in the fourteenth century by a Gipuzkoan (some accounts claim it was Juan de Echayde; others, that it was Matías de Echebeste), who later led his countrymen there.[20] Whatever the truth may have been, Basque fishermen pushed northward in search of the cod that had become legendary throughout European coastal areas. They reached Iceland and Greenland, and from there sailed on to the Canadian coasts. While they were searching for cod, they discovered and hunted the first whales of Terranova. By the 1530s the whaling campaigns reached a level that exceeded those previously attained on the Iberian-Atlantic coast. "Throughout the North Atlantic, from the Isle aux Basques on the coasts of Labrador, to Port des Basques in Newfoundland, to the Bay of Basques in Spitzbergen, the Basque whalers are regarded as the masters of the trade."[21] Basque whaling reached its peak in the sixteenth and seventeenth centuries, and Basques were considered the best whale hunters in all of Europe. Among the numerous Basques who traveled to Newfoundland to hunt whales were two of Erauso's relatives: Antonio and Miguel de Erauso. Once again she and her family appeared entwined in the fate shared by their collective ethnic group.[22]

The Basque Naval Industry

From the thirteenth century on, medieval chronicles referred to the participation of Basque navigators in the imperial enterprises of Castile; for example, in the conquest of Seville, in the African campaigns, in a number of political initiatives, and in its conflicts with other Christian kingdoms. What in most historical accounts is called "Castile's navy" largely refers to the fleet of Basque and Gipuzkoan ships that sailed from small ports and was of prime importance in the colonization of the Americas.[23] Historians of naval shipbuilding constantly refer to the activities of the Basques, and acknowledge their superiority in coastal traffic. They were considered to be outstanding in maritime commerce, using ships that sailed "not too far from the coast, from port to port, with heavy, deep, wide vessels, suitable for carrying out the tasks of mercantile shipping."[24] This skill in coastal seamanship enabled the Basques to sail to the shores of the Eastern Mediterranean, to Constantinople, to the Netherlands, England, Germany, Scandinavia, and even, as we have noted, across the ocean for whale hunting. The Cantabrian navy was already important by the fourteenth century, a period when the sea played an important role in colonial development. Sometimes the ships had to cease their mercantile operations because they had to go to war; sometimes Basque ports had to defend themselves against the leagues organized by large European seaports. During the fourteenth and fifteenth centuries the Basques were considered the best shipbuilders in Europe, and their dockyards experienced a boom. In documents dating from this period, the English complained that the Cantabrian sailors sought to control the seas because they were making incursions on the very coast of England, as far north as the Isle of Wight.[25]

This maritime-commercial tradition explains the significant Basque contribution to colonial development, both in terms of the special skills they possessed and the large number of participants who were involved. Although there were a few Andalusian seamen who had sailed the Atlantic, most of the mariners who had experience on the high seas came from the Basque Country and the Cantabrian Corniche. In addition, the Bizkaians, the Gipuzkoans, and the Cantabrians had an established tradition in shipbuilding and metallurgical industries, which from the outset had received support from the Spanish Crown. From the end of the fifteenth century through the late eighteenth century, the best shipyards in Spain were located in Pasaia, Orio, and Bilbao, and Basque and Cantabrian vessels transported most of the supplies needed for the colonization. At the close of the fifteenth century, in his *Crónica de los Reyes Católicos*, Antonio de Nebrija writes, "The natives of the County of Bizkaia and the province of Gipuzkoa are skilled in the art of navigation, and valiant in naval battles, for which they possess the ships and equipment; in these three matters, which count the most in naval battles, they are better prepared than any other nation of the world."[26]

The discovery and colonization of the New World provided an immediate stimulus to the Basque economy. There was great demand for the metals produced in Basque foundries, and in particular, there was a pressing need for ships built in Basque dockyards. From 1492 on, the shipyards of Bizkaia and Gipuzkoa constructed vessels for the imperial fleet as well as for those used in commercial traffic bound for the New World. As had been the case in the iron manufacturing sector, the protectionist ordinances and decrees of the Crown contributed to the technological development of the shipbuilding industry, and thus to the creation of a society that was well developed in its economic, labor, and administrative sectors.[27] In this period there was no clear distinction between the merchant navy and the military navy; as a result, many of the ships that had been constructed in the Basque dockyards by Basque shipbuilders for commercial and industrial purposes were the same ones on which the Monarchy placed an embargo in order to use them for war purposes. The pressures experienced by the ship owners, the shipbuilders, and the seamen gave rise to periodic crises and tensions. Caro Baroja points out that Basque naval power itself explains why foral rights were at times scrupulously respected by the Crown. "If there is no compliance with the foral rights, the shipbuilding industry stops."[28] The technical skills of the Basque shipbuilders and seamen played a key role in maintaining the naval strength of the Crown, both under the Austrian and Bourbon dynasties.

In 1529 Charles V authorized the seaports of Bilbao, Donostia-San Sebastián, La Coruña, Bayona, Avilés, and Laredo to engage in free commerce with Latin America, with the single condition that upon their return voyage the ships had to stop at Seville to pay the required taxes. This concession stimulated the massive growth of Basque dockyards and ironworks.[29] According to Pierre Chaunu, in terms of its maritime strength,

The industrialization of cod fishing in the Basque territories. The salting process.

Preparing the cod for treatment and packing the cod.

Bilbao was more powerful at the beginning of the sixteenth century than either Seville or Cádiz. Although the commercial monopoly of traffic to the New World had been conceded to Seville by the Spanish Crown, it was northern Spain, especially Bizkaia, that enjoyed a monopoly of the merchant marine, since it supplied almost all the ships involved in trade with the Indies. Basque interests also provided the capital, the equipment, and the goods for commerce, as well as a considerable number of the personnel.[30] In fact, a royal concession specified that only ships built on the Cantabrian coast were to be used in the "transatlantic run" to the Indies. Later, many Basques found employment as captains, gunners, masters, and cabin boys, including Catalina de Erauso.[31]

The Basque Mining Industry

Since ancient times, a large number of iron foundries had operated in the Basque territories. Now, with the colonization of the New World, industries related to ironworks and shipbuilding experienced considerable development. This boom was driven as much by the war and the need for the manufacture of arms as by an increased demand that was a result of the technical changes that were taking place in agriculture, in architecture, and in the development of the shipbuilding industry.[32] From the beginning of the colonial period, Basque iron found an excellent market in the Indies. According to the *Fuero de Vizcaya,* its natives had been granted exclusive rights for the exportation of iron products, and the monarchy depended on Bizkaian iron for its ventures in Spain and in the Americas. Many towns in Gipuzkoa and Bizkaia involved in arms production (a technical sector related to the iron industry) experienced pressure from the Crown similar to that experienced by the shipbuilding industry. During the reign of the Catholic Monarchs, for example, decrees were issued that not only allowed for the confiscation of arms, but also required an increase in the production of certain kinds of arms, regardless of the wishes of the armorer. In short, pressure was brought to bear on the arms industry so that it would meet the specific needs of the Crown.[33]

Because of its excellent quality, the ease of its extraction, distribution, and transport, Basque ore enjoyed a privileged place in the international market. Even before the colonization of Latin America, Basque iron had enjoyed considerable success in European markets, but what took the iron industry to a much higher level of production was the emergence of the Latin American markets, especially as they directly reflected the demands of the Crown. In one of the chapters of the *Recopilación de las leyes de los reynos de Indias,* it was ordered "that they not be allowed to transport iron if it is not from Bizkaia." As a result, the entire mineral product which came to the New World during that period was Basque. In the sixteenth century there were already three hundred ironworks in Bizkaia and Gipuzkoa—a not inconsequential number—and by the close of that century Basque iron production represented 16 percent of all the iron produced in Europe.[34]

Iron ore had been associated with the Basque Country since ancient times. In his *Natural History,* Pliny refers to enormous iron ore mines that, according to Caro Baroja, must have been those of Bizkaia.[35] Early medieval documents from Navarre, Araba, and

Bizkaia mention workshops in small villages in which iron was worked for domestic and local uses.[36] The number of ironworks began to multiply, supported by a series of privileges and exemptions granted by the Crown, to whom the iron industry was crucial. In the technical development of this industry, the proprietors of Basque ironworks collaborated with their European counterparts. Documents show that at the beginning of the fifteenth century, German mining technicians were present in Navarre, having come there to discover the possibility of deposits, iron ore mines, and other minerals.[37] Subsequently, and extending into the nineteenth century, the mining technology used in New Spain was based on practices imported from the Basque provinces and Germany during the seventeenth century.[38]

From the Middle Ages on, the wars which took place between various factions and clans in Bizkaia and Gipuzkoa also reflected the importance of the mining sector in the Basque economy. One of the most terrible aspects of the factional conflicts was the deliberate destruction of ironworks and factories which could produce wealth for their adversaries. For that reason, in the *Fuero de Vizcaya*, in the logbook of the Hermandades de Vizcaya (The Brotherhoods of Bizkaia), and in other legal codes, we repeatedly find a detailed description of the punishment which should be meted out to those who would destroy foundries or ironworks, or mistreat ironsmiths—in other words, all those persons who might have diminished the benefits brought by this industry.[39]

With respect to the relationship between the Basque mining sector and Latin America, the impact of the conquest of the Americas in the Basque mines was twofold: first, it accelerated the development of an already firmly established industry; second, it opened the door to the founding and development of Latin American mining. From the peninsular perspective, the discovery of the Americas and the appearance of unlimited colonial markets, the arrival of an abundance of precious metals, the development of plans for construction, industrialization, and navigation in the New World—all these factors provided the impetus which the Basque iron industry needed for its full expansion and consolidation. For the Latin American economy, iron was a basic necessity.[40] The mining sector generated a large demand for iron products, inasmuch as it needed quicksilver, hand tools, etc. The textile and naval industries were also in constant need of iron, which was provided principally by the Basque Country. Thus, as new Latin American markets were created, there was a conjuncture of events that accelerated the development of Basque foundries and catapulted them into modern industrialization. For almost a millennium these foundries had represented the basis of the local industry; they had expanded with their sights set on exportation, since this was the only way they could compensate for the land deficit which forced them to import grains and other products needed for subsistence. The high degree of technical development, the quality of their product, their privileged geographical location—all these factors placed Basque iron in an advantageous position with respect to other European producers during the first centuries of the Early Modern Era. It is understandable that the Spanish Crown protected this rich source of income and reserved Bizkaian and Gipuzkoan iron for Spanish and Latin

American markets.[41] Catalina de Erauso came into contact with this Basque mining tradition when, dazzled—as were so many others by the riches of the land—she decided to stay in Potosí and work for a wealthy Basque miner. "I moved on to La Plata and found work with Captain *Francisco de Aganumen, a very rich Basque mine owner*; I was with him for a few days, until some unpleasantness broke out between me and another Bizkaian, one of my new master's friends."[42]

The Erauso Family as Part of the Basque Migratory and Maritime Tradition

Catalina de Erauso's family fits into the context of the patterns we have outlined. First, it had participated fully in the maritime tradition for generations; second, it was also deeply affected by the conquest of the New World. In his detailed study of Erauso's life, José Ignacio Tellechea Idígoras clearly demonstrates the deep Latin American and maritime tradition of the Erauso family.

In his research, Tellechea discovered that when Catalina de Erauso was a year-and-a-half old, her father Miguel de Erauso was implicated in a trial related to the record of the estate left at his death by her grandfather Miguel de Erauso, El Viejo (the elder). There was considerable discrepancy between the calculations of the worth of the estate presented respectively by her father and by Juan de Erauso, grandson of Miguel de Erauso el Viejo, (that is, the son of his other son Juan de Erauso). Many citizens of Donostia-San Sebastián were required to appear in court to make declarations regarding what they knew. From these declarations we can construct the history of a noble family closely connected with the sea. Margarita de Unanberro, "a very close friend" of the family of Miguel de Erauso el Viejo, recalls that Catalina de Erauso's grandfather "was thought and reputed to be the richest of those who at that time *owned ships, fitted them out, and sailed them to Terranova*, and she had heard it widely spoken about many different times."[43] And so, her grandfather figured among the shipowners who sent their ships as far as the Canadian coast; he thus connected himself with a fundamental part of Basque fishing and maritime history.

Tellechea's account as he recorded the statements offered by the witnesses is telling. Echazarreta, a seaman, said that "Miguel de Erauso, el Viejo, bought two ships, one while his wife, Graciana de Aya, was alive, and another after her death, before marrying his third wife. He sold the first vessel to Juan de Erauso in Seville; the second one, which he bought in partnership with Pedro de Barrena, was embargoed for the Royal Armada [fleet] and served in Seville." This quotation reflects the economic and naval axis on which three elements revolved: Basque ships, the Crown, and Seville. Still another witness, Joanes de Gayangus, provided specific information about Miguel de Erauso's vessels.

> During Graciana's life, [Miguel] bought three vessels from some Frenchmen; one (300 tons) made three trips to Terranova, two for whale hunting, and one for cod fishing;

another (120 tons), went cod fishing. He [the witness] saw both of those vessels, as well as a third one in Seville, where they were sold . . . After Graciana's death he purchased one-third share in an additional vessel, as well as another smaller one (80 tons) in partnership with Pedro de Barrena, and made one voyage to Terranova, another to Rouen, and a third to La Coruña. To Rouen they transported sacks of wool; to La Coruña provisions for the Crown, the first with a good profit. Later he sold them in Seville.[44]

The maritime and commercial activities of the Erauso-Aya family were considerable; in pursuing whale hunting and cod fishing they exemplified the activities in which Basque ships engaged. In their commercial activities, they gave evidence of the close relationships they maintained with the Basque colony residing in Andalusia. Moreover, we also see that the needs of the Royal Armada played an important role in the construction and utilization of the ships built in the Basque dockyards.

Catalina de Erauso had additional relatives who provided further evidence of the close connections of her family to the New World. Her father, Captain Miguel de Erauso, probably served in the Latin American colonies. Her oldest brother, Miguel, went to the Americas when she was two years old. Three other brothers (Domingo, Francisco, and Martín) would follow Miguel, and all four of them would die there.[45] In 1626 Catalina de Erauso filed two petitions with the *Consejo de Indias* (Council of the Indies), seeking compensation for her military service to the Crown. In these documents she briefly recounts her heroic deeds; first, she stated that she had been in the service of his Royal Majesty for nineteen years; second, she argued that she should also receive credit for the services rendered to the Crown by two of her brothers. She mentioned the valiant deeds of her two brothers: Captain Miguel de Erauso, who served in the Armada de Lima with Rodrigo de Mendoza; and Domingo de Erauso, who sailed with the Armada that went to Brazil and perished when the *Almiranta,* the ship on which he was returning, burned on the Cantabrian coast.[46] These facts are not taken from the *Autobiografía*, but from historical archives which contain petitions and other litigations before the Crown. Nevertheless, the *Autobiografía* does expand on her family connections as they relate to her transatlantic voyage and her search for fortune in the Americas. For example, as soon as she arrived in the New World, she unexpectedly met her brother Miguel, who helped her find a comfortable position. In addition, she departed for the Americas on a galleon commanded by one of her uncles.

We see that as her persona took shape, it emerged from the firmly rooted traditions we have described in the preceding pages. The narrative portrays a noble family that adheres to a social and economic path closely tied to the Basque historical reality of that period. Although at first glance her biography may seem atypical, the family tradition into which she was born outlines the context within which she is forced to make her choices. We have addressed a few of them; many more will emerge.

People Who Accompanied, Helped, and Protected Erauso throughout Her Travels

Upon examining the very diverse settings in which the events of Erauso's life took place, and the way these events were affected by her association with her countrymen, I propose that the section dedicated to her travels was dictated by the plot of her *Autobiografía* itself. It is important to remember that we are dealing with the life of an adventuress, who was constantly on the move. From the moment she abandoned the convent, traveling became a *modus vivendi* for Erauso. None of her jobs lasted very long, and when they ended, she was forced to move on. Just in Spain alone, and over a period that spans less than three years, she traveled through Bilbao, Vitoria-Gasteiz (Araba), Valladolid, Lizarra, Donostia-San Sebastián, Cádiz, and Seville. Once in the Americas, the distances she covered increased, encompassing territories which today belong to Panama, Ecuador, Peru, Chile, Bolivia, and Argentina. Upon her return to Spain, she took to the road again: Madrid, Barcelona, France, Rome, and Naples. In Naples her story ends. We know, however, that later she returned to Latin America and worked transporting cattle and merchandise from one place to another until her death. As travel itself assumed importance, so did the necessity for "knowing how to get along" on the road; that is, knowing how to find a helping hand that would provide shelter and make life easier in those places where she knew no one, and no one knew her.

From Donostia-San Sebastián to Cádiz: The Basque Colony in Andalusia

As a traveler, Erauso did not choose her itinerary by chance. It was determined, rather, by the factors which shaped the social and economic history of her own family. It was not by chance that her steps led her to Seville and Cádiz. During her years in Donostia-San Sebastián she had undoubtedly heard stories about ships that sailed for Seville, ships owned not only by her own family but by many other families of her native city, families that had enjoyed a long-standing tradition of maritime and commercial relationships with Andalusian seaports. It is, furthermore, easy to imagine that while she was being raised in the convent, she was told stories about the New World, where her four brothers had been living. Her final destination would be that frequently imagined New World, but in order to get there, she would have to go through Andalusia.

By royal decree, there was only one official port of entry and departure for traffic between the mother country and the colonies: first it was Seville, and from 1717 on it was Cádiz. For this reason it is understandable that Andalusia became an obligatory place of residence for captains, masters, and businessmen; in short, for all those who in some way or other played a role in the Latin American adventure. Among them were many Basques; as we previously noted, navigation and the transportation of goods were activities undertaken largely by people from northern Spain.[47] Because of its maritime tradition, the Erauso family was linked to Andalusia by necessity. To Seville they sent ships loaded with merchandise to be sold, also selling the ships themselves at times. "And [they send] one or two [ships] to Ruan [Rouen] with sacks of wool, and two others to Seville with iron."[48] Because Seville was directly involved, both with respect to the use and the final destination of each one of the ships owned by Miguel de Erauso, the city came to play an important role in the commercial activities of this well-known family from Donostia-San Sebastián.

The Basque connection with Seville, however, dates back to the Middle Ages. Ships that sailed from the Basque seaports of the Cantabrian coast played a decisive role in the conquest of Seville in 1248. From that time on, over the centuries, Basque navigators maintained an uninterrupted association with Andalusia.[49] Basque maritime interests had established operations in Cádiz and Seville through their old involvement in Mediterranean and African trade; in addition, starting in the early fifteenth century, a navigators' guild named *El Colegio de los Pilotos Vizcaínos* (the College of Basque Navigators) was headquartered in Cádiz.[50] In that same century, the Bizkaian presence on the Andalusian coast became prominent. "The reasons for it were many: Seville was one of the principal mercantile cities of the kingdom; the seaports of Lower Andalusia were obligatory ports of call in the Bizkaian routes along the Mediterranean; and quite apart from the important Basque role in commercial transport within the larger maritime international traffic, the Bizkaians went to Andalusia seeking specific products: two in particular, oil and wheat."[51] It is important to underscore this particular aspect of Basque activity—commercial transportation—since, as García Cortazar observes, "above all else, the Bizkaian is a transporter, the maritime transporter par excellence of the fifteenth century."[52]

In the broadside *El Tordo Vizcaino*, comments regarding a Basque brotherhood refer specifically to the Basque colony in southern Spain.

> This brotherhood has flowered most in the rich and populous city of Seville, to which the Peruvian and Mexican chapters belong; Bizkaia's greatness is reflected there, because [in that brotherhood] her sons have always held the best positions, coming from lineages of the purest blood, showing themselves to be honest and truthful, establishing the best credit and the safest treasury . . . The two are sister Provinces as they were in previous centuries. So it is that one can say with truthfulness: in Seville there is something of Bizkaia, just as in Bizkaia we find something of Seville: and if Bizkaia possesses certain grandeurs, they can also be found in Seville—and if Heaven endowed [Bizkaia] with the strongest and most invincible iron, it endowed [Seville] with the two most precious metals, and many others allied with iron; so that invincibility is assured there, and pomp and grandeur is assured here.[53]

By 1540, the Basque community in Seville was of sufficient magnitude, numerically and socially, to warrant a specific place of worship where they could celebrate mass and bury "all those who belong to their nation." After making several requests, they succeeded in persuading the Franciscans to cede them "a chapel which the Convent had at the entrance to the church." The vitality of the Basque language in the community created a need for priests who could confess "those who did not know the Castilian language well."[54]

As Andalusia's role in the new economic order of Spain grew, so did the size and importance of its Basque community. In both Cádiz and Seville, Basques were named to administrative positions in municipal government and in ecclesiastical councils. A quick review of the rosters of individuals holding important administrative posts in the *Casa de Contratación* (Board of Trade) during the sixteenth and seventeenth centuries reveals that a disproportionately large number of the chief justices, judges, district attorneys, treasurers, and accountants were of Basque origin, a fact which undoubtedly afforded them the opportunity to wield influence. In this connection, José Manuel Azcona Pastor offers the example of Bernardo Díaz de Argandoña, the best known district attorney of Seville, whose role was decisive in protecting Basque interests in Andalusia in relation to businessmen from other Spanish provinces, and who also took part in commerce with the Indies. In 1593, the Basque community persuaded Philip II to prohibit ships built in Seville, Cádiz, Puerto de Santa María, or Huelva from taking part in the convoys that sailed to the Americas.[55] In the ecclesiastical sphere of influence, a Gipuzkoan, Cristóbal de Rojas y Sandavol, held the highest position in the Archdiocese of Seville during the sixteenth century; in that same century and the following one, Basques held positions in the Council of Trent. In addition, it was the Basques who, in collaboration with international businessmen, launched the first banking ventures of sixteenth-century Atlantic coastal Andalusia. A hundred years later, they would try their luck as buyers of precious metals: they would purchase the silver that came from the Americas, refine it, and transform it into legal tender in La Casa de la Moneda (The Royal Spanish Mint). For the buyer, this business could easily lead to either riches or ruin. By the second half of the seventeenth century, only six individuals were engaged in buying gold or silver, and all were Basque, further proof of the Basque preeminence in this type of industry.

The historical evidence summarized here leads us to the conclusion that during the sixteenth and seventeenth centuries (and above all favored by the commercial activity with the Indies) the Basque colony residing in Andalusia was large and highly successful. This bustling and productive colony would soon be visited by Catalina de Erauso. When she met the Basque captain Miguel de Berroiz in the port of Pasaia, a seaport very near Donostia-San Sebastián, and learned that he was planning to depart on one of his ships bound for Seville, she asked him to take her. "I begged him to take me, and we settled on a price for forty *reales*. I went on board, we set sail." When they arrived at San Lucar, she disembarked. "I went off to see Seville, and though I liked the place, and thought about staying for a while, in the end I was only there for two days, and then returned to San Lucar." There she again met up with a countryman who would take her to the New World. "I met up with Captain Miguel de Echazarreta, a native of my own province. His ship was escorting the galleons of General Don Luis Fernández de Córdoba, part of the royal armada which set sail for Punta de Araya in 1603, under the command of Don Luis Fajardo."[56] Captain Miguel de Echazarreta was a Knight of the Order of Santiago and General of the galleons assigned to the Indies.[57] In describing him, Erauso underscored their shared identity, referring to him as "a native of my land." So the question arises of whether or not she used this designation only for those born in Donostia-San Sebastián, while referring to Basques from other places as "Bizkaians."[58] An official document (1630) confirms Captain Echazarreta's role in Catalina de Erauso's life.

On July 4, in a manuscript which records Seville's daily events, the following statement is found:

> Thursday, July 4, the Lieutenant Nun was present in the Iglesia Mayor. She was a nun in San Sebastián, she fled, and in the year 1603, dressed as a man, she went to the Indies. She served as a soldier for twenty years, and was thought to be a eunuch. She returned to Spain: she went to Rome and Pope Urban VIII gave her leave to go on wearing men's clothing. The king conferred on her the rank of lieutenant, calling her The Lieutenant Nun Doña Catalina de Arauso, the same name that is used in her documents in Rome. In years past, Captain Miguel de Echazarreta took her to the Indies as a cabin boy, and now, as the general of the convoy he takes her as a lieutenant.

Thus, it was a *donostiarra*, first a captain and later (Admiral) General of the Sea, D. Miguel de Echazarreta, who took her to Latin America the first and the last time, the latter in 1630, on July 21, bound for Mexico or New Spain. Her passage through Seville in 1630 is confirmed by the documents previously included.[59]

A third Basque captain was the commander of the galleon on which Erauso sailed to the Americas. Erauso joined a specific network created by a well-established Basque colony, where she could seek help, and where she could at least find the language and the cultural patterns that were most familiar to her. And clearly, that is exactly what she did.

The Transatlantic Crossing

Each year two fleets sailed for the Americas. One, that went to Cartagena, Portobello, and Nombre de Dios, was escorted on the return trip by eight galleons because it carried gold and silver from Peru, Quito, Nueva Granada, and Venezuela; for that reason, this fleet was referred to as *Los Galeones*. The other fleet, which went to New Spain, was escorted by only two galleons and was called *La Flota*. Erauso traveled with the former, which usually consisted of five or eight warships, other smaller faster vessels called *pataches*, and merchant ships.[60] Under the command of her uncle Estevan Eguiño, Erauso made her first transatlantic crossing on one of those galleons. As was the case with many other relatives who protected her and came to her aid, her uncle did so without knowledge of her true identity. "I found work as ship's boy on the galleon of my uncle, Captain Estevan Eguiño, a first cousin to my mother, who now lives in San Sebastián. I went aboard, and we set sail from San Lucar on Holy Thursday, 1603."[61] Rima R. Vallbona verifies that Eguiño was still living in Donostia-San Sebastián in 1629, because his name appears as a witness in the document in which Erauso renounces her rights to the properties to which she was entitled by inheritance, and transfers them to her sister Mariana.[62]

When Erauso boarded the ship, her uncle was unaware that she was his niece, but he recognized her place of origin, and this was sufficient to guarantee that she would receive preferential treatment. "The work was new to me and I had a hard time of it at first. My uncle, with no idea who I was, grew fond of me and took me under his wing, especially when he heard where I was from, and the names of my parents, which I concocted for him."[63] As can be seen, Erauso did not wish to reveal her identity, and although she did not give her true surnames, she invents others that are also "Bizkaian." For her uncle, simply the knowledge of where she was from, along with the false names she provided, was reason enough to afford her protection. Either because she could not disguise her speech, which would betray her ethnic origin, or because she was well aware that telling the captain she was his compatriot would work to her advantage, she invented surnames that identified her as a Basque. We must suppose that she spoke to Eguiño in Euskara, as she had, after all, only recently left the convent where, as we previously noted, in all probability Euskara was the dominant language. Speaking in the "Bizkaian tongue" to her fellow travelers would constitute an undeniable demonstration of her ethnic identity.

There is no documented evidence regarding Erauso's first trip to the Indies.[64] Since it is impossible to verify the factual details of her embarkation, we do not know whether she sailed under a false name, sailed without legal authorization, or whether the record of the embarkation was lost. The Casa de Contratación was established in 1503 to regulate the flow of emigrants to the Americas; the most important measure adopted during that period stipulated that all passengers had to obtain permission prior to sailing. These boarding licenses have been useful in determining the volume of emigration and the regions from which the emigrants came.[65] Azcona Pastor explains that this license had to include the following documents: (1) an application filled out by the passenger; (2) a notarization of the same; (3) a copy of the royal decree authorizing the emigration; (4) "proof" regarding *limpieza de sangre* (literally, purity of blood, but meaning anyone who could prove they were free from Jewish or Moorish ancestry) which included declarations by three witnesses and could be accompanied by a baptismal certificate; (5) if the emigrant was married and was traveling alone, documentation of his wife's consent; (6) a note indicating that the emigrant had boarded; (7) a note indicating that the emigrant had paid for the boarding licenses; (8) to facilitate the authorization, letters from relatives already established in the Americas stating they were sending for them. The Crown's dispositions also included a list of prohibitions regarding those persons who were not authorized to migrate to the New World: Jews, Moors, Gypsies, and anyone who was not a Spaniard. Most women were also prohibited from traveling to the Americas. During the reign of Philip II, unmarried women not accompanied by male relatives were not permitted to travel. Married women had no legal status, so they themselves could not even apply for permission to emigrate; they could only travel if accompanied by their spouses, or they could be sent for by their spouses once the latter were already settled in the Americas.[66]

Nevertheless, these restrictions were not always enforced because, among other reasons, the emigrants figured out many ways to evade the law. Strict control over the identity of those who had legal permission to emigrate to the Americas decreased over time. The documentation required for leaving Spain diminished in terms of the quality and the level of information given. For example, any person who had been assured a job could travel without presenting proof of *limpieza de sangre*, an exemption that was extended to the entire family. The case was similar for servants who accompanied state functionaries—it was sufficient for the master to declare that the servant was who he claimed to be, and that he was unmarried. This, along with a cash payment, met the requirements for stating their ancestry and Christianity. This proved to be an ideal way to elude administrative control; it also explains the high percentage of people who, from the middle of the seventeenth century, claimed to be going to the Americas as servants.[67] Other ways of evading the law included enlisting oneself as a soldier or a sailor, and then deserting upon arrival; or purchasing, on the black market, the boarding licenses authorizing travel.[68] In documents dating from the fifteenth through the seventeenth centuries, we find frequent references to illegal and clandestine embarkations.[69] During the sixteenth and seventeenth centuries, reports of these illegal embarkations multiplied, but they could not be stopped, in spite of a decree (1607) that stated that any officer transporting unauthorized passengers to the Indies would be punished by death. Over time, the punishment was reduced to the payment of a fine.[70] The falsification of permits and later the policy of free trade are factors which make the research of this phenomenon even more difficult.

Vallbona asks, with respect to Erauso's embarkment, "How could Catalina de Erauso have gotten through without duly identifying herself? Was she perhaps a stowaway? Did she use false documents? Or was it perhaps that those strict laws regarding emigration were simply not enforced just as (according to what has been proved) the decrees that prohibited recreational books were also not enforced?"[71] In her account of the arrangements she made for her first trip, Erauso explained that she contacted her uncle, Captain Estevan Eguiño, and agreed to sign on as a cabin boy on the galleon under his command. What were the terms of that agreement? Possibly, Eguiño certified Erauso and by so doing complied with the requirements regarding her Christianity and her ancestry. As was previously noted, since the crews were largely made up of Basques, it is not unlikely that a large percentage of the illegal emigrants were persons of Basque origin who, to assure their passage to the New World, made good use of their contacts with their seagoing countrymen.[72] It is obvious that in Erauso's case, her relationship to the captain who transported her across the sea to the other continent was a significant factor; he being Basque like her, "made much of her on learning where [she] was from," and in him she "found a protector."[73] All this was very helpful in getting her to the Americas. Since it is highly improbable that she would have had the money needed to pay for her passage to the New World, we can assume that when she enlisted to work under the captain's orders, it was agreed in that negotiation that she would work in exchange for the cost of the trip. At the beginning of the seventeenth century, the price of a trip to the Americas was about fifty silver ducats; with the additional taxes, the total cost came to seventy ducats. This was not an inconsiderable sum; to finance it, the would-be passengers were sometimes forced to sell property, take out loans, ask parents for an advance on their inheritance, work as servants for someone who could pay the cost, or write to relatives in the Americas requesting money for the trip.[74]

Although Erauso received favorable treatment on the trip, this did not prevent her from ignoring the official ordinances against leaving the ship, and once in the New World she jumped ship and decided to stay in the Americas. Shipboard passengers were forced to take an oath that they would not leave the ship in any of the ports of call en route to their final destination. Abandoning the ship was exactly what she did, but not without first robbing her uncle of all the money she could: "I played a rare trick on my uncle by pocketing five hundred pesos belonging to him." The sum is truly a considerable one when we bear in mind that later, while in the employ of Diego de Solarte, she earned an annual salary of six hundred pesos.[75] From the first moments of her American experience, Erauso chose to inhabit a space in which orthodox belief, and even the law, were constantly challenged.

From Cuzco to Guamanga

When Erauso arrived in Cuzco, she stayed "for a while at the house of the treasurer, Lope de Alcedo." During that stay, she became involved in a confrontation with another soldier, nicknamed the "New Cid," who tried to steal some money from her while they were sitting together at a gambling table. The incident turned into a free-for-all between the New Cid, his followers, and Erauso, who was aided by two Basques who happened to be passing by "hastening to the noise, and seeing me engaged single-handed against five, took my part."[76] After the bloody encounter, in which she killed the New Cid and she herself was badly wounded, some charitable persons carried her, half dead, to Alcedo's house, where she had been staying. From there she was later taken to the church of San Francisco, to the cell of Father Fray Martín de Aróstegui, "one of my friend Alcedo's kinsmen." After spending four months recovering from her wounds, fearing arrest by the constables and reprisals from the dead man's relatives, she decided to depart.

> By this time I was on the mend, and could see that my days in Cuzco were numbered. And I also figured that the dead man's many friends were bent on killing me, and taking all this into account, with the help and the advice of some friends of my own, I decided on a change of scene. Captain Don Gaspar de Carranza gave me a thousand pesos; Lope de Alcedo, the treasurer I mentioned earlier, gave me three mules and some weapons; and Don Francisco de Arzaga gave me three slaves—and so, in the company of two trusty Biscayan friends, I left Cuzco one night and headed for Guamanga.[77]

The "help and advice of my friends" to which she alluded refers to the money, the mules, the arms, and the slaves, all given to her by three Basques to facilitate her departure from Cuzco, as well as the company of another two Basques who remained with her until she safely crossed the border. Erauso was not alone; there were people who watched over her and protected her. And it is undeniable that her entire support network was Basque, beginning with the Treasurer Lope de Alcedo who provided her with lodging upon her arrival in Cuzco, followed by Father Aróstegui who hid her in his cell, the three friends who gave her money and everything she required for the trip, and the two Basques who fought and traveled at her side until they were certain she was out of danger.[78]

From Cartagena Back to Spain

After having roved through Latin America for two decades, Erauso again found herself bound for Spain. This lieutenant who returned, crowned with glory, was a very different person from that adolescent girl who set out on her first ocean voyage, and later learned to adapt herself to a man's life. "In Tenerife, I learned that the armada of General Tomás de Larraspuru was about to set sail for Spain. I embarked in the captain's flagship in the year 1624, and I was well-received by the general, regaled, invited to dine at his table, and things went on like this for more than two hundred leagues, well past the Straits of Bahama."[79] Tomás de Larraspuru, from Azkoitia (Gipuzkoa), was well known for his pursuit of buccaneers and corsairs on the Indies run.[80] In his *Compendium*, Lope Martínez de Isasti, a seventeenth-century Gipuzkoan historian, confirms the facts regarding Erauso's voyage to Spain on board the ship *Capitana*. "General Tomás de Larrazpuru, [was] a Knight of the Order of Alcántara [he had been the commander of two districts of the Order of Santiago, never changing his habit]. He was a General of the galleons that made the Indies run; participated in [that activity] for more than thirty years, was a member of the War Council, was appointed first commander of his Order and [was] Captain General of the Armada that protected the Indies' coasts."[81] In the same text it was stated that Larraspuru "served twice as General of the galleons carrying silver in the year 1621."[82] In documents found in the archives of the Council of Indies, on which Vallbona bases her edition, this captain's name appears as Tomás de la *Raspur*, a spelling that conceals his Basque identity.[83]

During her return voyage to Spain, Erauso recounted that one day, while she was playing cards, the predictable (for her) happened: she got into a quarrel with another gambler. In the fight, she cut his face with a knife, "and the general was obliged to shift me and transfer me to another flagship, the *Almiranta*, where there were men from my part of the country."[84] It is interesting to note that she said that the general "was obliged" to transfer her to another ship on which there were other Bizkaians. This implies that the measure taken by the general (placing her on a ship that carried other Bizkaians) was the most logical and reasonable one. Once again, as was the case in the episode in which she killed the New Cid, her gambling squabbles seemed to be colored by the feelings of rivalry that existed among the various regional groups that made up the Spanish monarchy. In this particular episode, the general's decision seemed to suggest that after figuring as the principal player in a violent episode involving persons from other regions, Erauso would need the security, the peace of mind, and perhaps the protection that only her countrymen could provide.

Back Again in the Old World: The Ill-Fated Trip to Rome

When Erauso returned to Europe, she had two purposes in mind: to obtain a pension from the king as a reward for the services she had rendered to the Crown, and to obtain papal dispensation that would allow her to continue her life dressed in a man's clothing. In order to accomplish the second objective, a few months after her arrival in Spain, she set forth for Rome. Unfortunately, the trip ended badly. In Turin, they accused her of being a spy of the Spanish Crown, arrested her, took her money and the clothing she was wearing, and kept her in jail for fifty days, after which they sent her back to Spain. These events are corroborated by historical facts. In the hopes of obtaining financial compensation, Erauso went before a notary to make an official declaration about the series of disasters which had befallen her on this unsuccessful trip: "The misfortunes she endured were viewed as meritorious deeds, especially when seen within the context of that fierce war, referred to as the War of Thirty Years, in which France and Spain were bitterly locked."

What is of particular interest in this legal proceeding is the identity of Erauso's traveling companions. Again, Tellechea, who examined the documentary evidence, provides a list of the persons who testified about the ill-fated trip, some of whom were accompanying her. "Pedro del Río, a native of Marcilla [Martzilla, in Navarre], twenty-eight years old; Juan de Arriaga, a soldier from the Pamplona Citadel, thirty-six years old; Martín de Enbiza, a servant of the Baroness of Beorlegui, twenty years old; Juan Pérez de Biquendi, from Pamplona, thirty-four years old; Juan de Echevarría, a native of Abadio [Abadiño], Biscay, twenty-eight years old." Juan Sanez de Sillero, a priest, testifies that he accompanied her as far as Donibane Garazi (Saint-Jean-Pied-de-Port, Low Navarre in Iparralde or the Northern Basque Country) and then returned to Iruñea (Pamplona), leaving her in the company of his servant, Pedro del Río. The aforementioned priest had known Erauso for seven months, "being in the same house with her during said time, and having seen and spoken to her daily." Also testifying were the two pilgrims, Biquendi and Echevarría, who were headed for Rome for the Holy Year Jubilee, and whose company Erauso joined following the departure of the priest. The other two witnesses, Arriaga and Martín de Enbiza, were not Erauso's traveling companions, but they provided statements regarding their knowledge of the facts, either through hearsay or through what she herself told them before and after the trip. After her return to Spain, Erauso settled in Iruñea, and all the people she summoned to testify in her favor were Navarrese (natives of Navarre). As Erauso and her servant traveled to Rome, every one of the persons in their traveling group was Basque.

Why did she always surround herself with Basques? Perhaps the common language played an important role; and yet, when Erauso met Biquendi and Echevarría, these two pilgrims were accompanied by a third traveler, "a Catalonian named Miguel," so we must assume that they did not communicate with each other in Euskara, at least not in any sustained manner. At this juncture, Erauso had returned from the Americas, where she had lived among people from other territories of the Crown, as well as among groups indigenous to the New World: Indians, Creoles, mestizos. It was not just her preference for the Basque language, customs, and overall culture that caused her ethnic origin to become such a determining and powerful force in her life; it was also because Basques possessed a group consciousness in which mutual protection and help were cardinal values, especially when members of that group found themselves competing with people from other regions of Spain, people with whom they shared no common interests.

In the preceding pages, we traced Erauso's path as she journeyed to the New World and then returned to Spain. Her escape from dangerous situations in the Americas was witnessed. On her return, her embarkation on an ill-fated trip to Rome was documented. In all those travels, one common denominator stands out: the presence and intervention of other Basques, in whom she placed her trust, and whose fate she was willing to share. It is important to note that, upon reviewing the itinerary she described in her narrative, the episodes in which the Basque presence came into play were not singled out; all of Erauso's significant movements from one place to another were examined, at least all those which are reported in the *Autobiografía,* as well as those in which proper names appear or references are made to the birthplace of individuals.

This feature of the *Autobiografía* is noteworthy not just in and of itself, but because seeking out and finding compatriots was "the norm" in Erauso's pattern of conduct. We might say that for Erauso, her association with Basques was a neutral choice, one that we would have expected her to make in normal circumstances. Certainly this was a representative part of the individual and collective history of the Basques in the Indies. In this sense, the narrative of Catalina de Erauso's life demonstrates in a very concrete way why Basques bonded with each other, and for what purposes; it clearly illustrates that being able to rely on assistance from her countrymen was an invaluable asset during those difficult times and in those far-off places where she played out her life. An analysis of her biography thus leads us to conclude that her ethnic identity was a key determinant in her life; it was an element which shed light on its very meaning. And as this was true in her case, it points out the need to reconsider the way in which ethnic group awareness may have played a role in shaping the historical world in which the Spaniards of the sixteenth and seventeenth centuries fulfilled their destinies. This additional perspective may contribute to a deeper understanding of that complex world.

CHAPTER FIVE

Catalina de Erauso: A "Jack of All Trades"

Catalina de Erauso's employment history was varied and extensive. In both Spain and colonial America, she took jobs for which her education had prepared her, doing them well, according to Erauso, until she found herself in the military. When it was discovered that she was a woman, her life as a soldier came to a halt, and she returned to Spain in 1624. After returning once again to the Americas in 1630, she made her living as a muleteer and a merchant.

The preceding chapter demonstrated how Erauso's wanderings from place to place were facilitated by Basques. If these movements were necessary for her survival, getting a job that would provide her a livelihood was even more so. We can clearly observe the repeated and systematic assistance provided to her by her compatriots in the succession of jobs that Erauso took on in the New World, and especially in the ways she obtained them. Time and time again, the only credential she need offer was her surname and her place of birth, both of which clearly identified her as a Basque. These simple facts assured her a job. And these facts assured that when she left one post to go on to another, her employer would pave the way for her by recommending her to another Basque who in turn found a place for her. This network of connections between Basques virtually guaranteed her subsistence. One might ask whether similar protective social networks existed within the other regional groups that comprised the Spanish Crown. Although the answer to that question goes beyond the scope of this study, it nevertheless is a topic that merits serious research.

Next we will examine the series of jobs that Erauso took on, as they are described in her *Autobiografía*. This chapter will focus on those textual passages that refer to the assistance she received, the persons who provided it, and the reasons that justified it. Most of the activities that Erauso performed fell within the professions traditionally associated with the Basques—that is, those connected with the commercial and mining sectors, as well as the so-called "*oficios de pluma*," professions that involve keeping written records of bureaucratic and administrative services. As early as the Middle Ages, the Basques had already acquired a reputation as mariners and soldiers outside their traditional geographical context. Later, at the beginning of the sixteenth century, when Spanish colonial expansion took place, they are also characterized as heavily involved in government and ecclesiastical administration. In her sojourns through Spain and Latin America, Erauso will at some point participate in all those types of activities. She will be a page, a sailor, a soldier, and a merchant.

Before Sailing for the New World: Labors of the Pen

Erauso's first three jobs, those she performed immediately following her departure from the convent and those she took on the in the New World, all involved "labors of the pen." In his characterization of his countrymen, Esteban de Garibay notes that in addition to being warriors, sailors, blacksmiths, and men of action, they also were given to "labors of the pen." Caro Baroja explains that in the sixteenth century, that phrase referred to the knowledge and skills required in business management: that is, accounting and calligraphy, and he emphasizes the fact that it was precisely in the Basque Country, a territory that did not have universities, "where what we would now call primary education was most emphasized."[1] We know that during the years she spent in the convent, from the time she was four until she was sixteen, Erauso benefited from that kind of instruction. Her *Autobiografía* describes her first steps in the world of work.

She gets her first job as a page or secretary in the household of a professor from the city of Vitoria-Gasteiz.

> I entered Vitoria without the least idea where to put up, but it wasn't more than a few days before I met a certain doctor of theology, don Francisco de Cerralta, who took me in without a fuss, despite the fact that he didn't know me, and even gave me some new clothes. He was married, as I soon discovered, to yet another of my mother's sisters but I didn't let on as to who I was. I stayed there what must have been some three months, and the doctor, seeing that I read Latin well, took a fancy to me, and got the idea in his head that I should continue my training as his student. When I let him know I wasn't interested, he pleaded and insisted, and finally went so far as to lay his hands on me. With this I decided to leave—and that is exactly what I did.[2]

From there she goes on to the Royal Court in Valladolid, where she works for Juan de Idiáquez, the king's secretary and an important figure of that period. "The Court was in Valladolid at that time, and it wasn't long before I found work as a page with the king's secretary, don Juan de Idiáquez, who immediately dressed me up in a new set of clothes. There I went by the name of Francisco Loyola, and for seven months I did very well for myself."[3] In the city of Lizarra, in Navarre, she again found employment as a page. "I found work there as a page to don Carlos Arrellano, who belonged to the Order of Santiago, and I remained in his employment for two years, well-fed and well-clothed."[4]

As we can see, Erauso was able to get these first jobs because of her literacy, her ability to read and write. Her stints as page and secretarial assistant offer a concrete illustration of occupations that, beginning in the fifteenth century and extending into her lifetime, Basques characteristically came to occupy. An important social phenomenon emerged in the Basque Country during the fifteenth, sixteenth, and seventeenth centuries: the appearance of Basque calligraphers and secretaries. Beginning in the middle of the fifteenth century, we see the emergence of a bureaucratic middle class in the Basque Country, represented, for example, by the pedagogues Juan de Iciar and Pedro de Madariaga (from Durango and Arratia, both in Bizkaia, respectively). By the sixteenth century, the superiority of Basques in "labors of the pen" was so well established that it became a literary cliché, and being a Basque seemed to be the essential requirement for obtaining a position as secretary in the king's court.[5] Perhaps the need to learn Castilian as a second language was a factor that promoted a better formal study and mastery of the language. During a certain period of her life, Erauso fit the stereotype, as described by Caro Baroja, of that young lad who would venture forth to the Spanish Court or to an unfamiliar city

> armed only with his little ink well, his skill in calligraphy, and his knowledge of mathematics. He, too, starts off as a page. And by virtue of his special kind of knowledge, he comes to occupy positions that taken together constitute an entire body, an entire system, within which (as is shown in the often-quoted passage from *Don Quixote* and in accordance with the widely shared belief of that time), one can hardly imagine a *secretary*, or an accountant, or one of those men to whom we entrust large business enterprises, who is not a Basque. As a result ... during the sixteenth, seventeenth, and eighteenth centuries, a significant part of the [Spanish] bureaucracy is comprised of Basques, who find themselves scattered in far-flung places: in the Americas, throughout the Empire of Charles V, and in Flanders. They go everywhere.[6]

As a result of the civil legislation regarding *mayorazgo* (primogeniture) that was applied in the Basque Country, those persons who were excluded from family inheritance had to find their fortunes elsewhere. The *Fuero de Vizcaya* (1526), confirmed by the Emperor Charles V, recognized the universal nobility of all Basques, regardless of the modesty of their origins. They could therefore aspire to all types of privileges and honorary posts. This noble status was a great advantage to those who wanted to obtain jobs in civil, military, and religious administration. Armed with a mastery of written and oral Spanish, and a tradition of excellent calligraphy, these disinherited Basques would become the best secretaries and functionaries of the Spanish Kingdom.

During the reign of the Habsburgs, a significant number of Basques came to power as royal secretaries.[7] From the end of the Middle Ages, and above all in the Early Modern Era, thousands of Basques felt drawn to the opportunities available in the governmental machinery of the Empire, and they succeeding in getting rich in those bureaucratic careers. A multitude of clerks, functionaries, ecclesiastics, technicians, construction workers, sailors, soldiers, and businessmen, all of Basque origin, made their presence felt in Castile and in the Indies. Under Charles V, a majority of the secretaries were Basque, and it is said that the Emperor himself learned some Euskara.[8] Juan de Idiáquez, one of Erauso's employers, was a secretary to Phillip II and Phillip III, and earned a reputation for his efficiency and professionalism. Juan de Idiáquez was the son of Alonso de

Idiáquez, who had served as advisor and secretary to Charles V. The Idiáquez family represented an outstanding dynasty of illustrious secretaries and royal counselors.[9] In the New World we find a comparatively high proportion of Basques occupying posts as influential public clerks.[10] The literary sources studied by Father Lagarda show them filling important posts in the kingdom and in the Royal Court, in disproportionately high numbers when compared to the general population. Underlining its political and social importance, Caro Baroja notes the emergence during the Early Modern Era of what he has labeled "the bourgeoisie of the bureaucracy," a group that represents Basque spheres of influence. The other nationalities of the Spanish Crown were very conscious of the privileged positions held by the Basques throughout the realm of Castile, and felt threatened by them; for this reason, they repeatedly criticized the disproportionate number of Basques occupying powerful administrative posts in many Spanish institutions. This criticism is reflected in the books and pamphlets of that period, and as Caro Baroja points out, "There is even a satire written by Quevedo in which, referring to these secretaries, accountants, admirals, etc., he depicts them as demanding human beings, and refers in a hostile manner to what he calls the 'Cantabrian pen pushers'; that is, their participation in those tasks involving administration and record keeping."[11]

Now we will see how this state of affairs was reflected in Erauso's employment experiences. As has been noted, her first employer was Cerralta (or, according to the spelling in Vallbona's edition, Zeralta). None of the editors of her *Autobiografía* provide information regarding this doctor. Cerralta's wife was a cousin of Erauso's mother, but of course, Erauso does not reveal this, nor did the doctor seem to recognize her. This would be a repeated pattern throughout her life; she would be aided in one way or another by relatives who did not recognize her. It was a pattern that reached its high point in her relationship to her brother, Miguel. Erauso tells us that Cerralta took her in with ease. I think it is reasonable to suppose that this gentleman was a Basque, since he lived in Vitoria-Gasteiz and was married to one of Erauso's relatives. But Cerralta wanted more than Erauso was willing to give; he beat her, and she left. From there she set out for Valladolid, which in 1600 had again become the seat of the Royal Court. Phillip II had moved it to Madrid; but two years after acceding to the throne, his son Phillip III moved it back again to Valladolid, where it would remain until 1606.[12] Erauso's second master was a distinguished representative of this Basque collective performing important roles in administration. As has been previously mentioned, Idiáquez was a secretary to the Crown. We know that he was the secretary of both Phillip II and Phillip III. We also know that he was a very good friend of Miguel de Erauso, Catalina's father. In his edition, Ferrer includes the following note:

> D. Juan de Idiáquez, son of D. Alonso, of whom we shall speak elsewhere, was a native of this city and a state secretary to Phillip II and Phillip III, a Knight Commander of the Order of Leon, President of the Council of Orders, Ambassador to the Republics of Genoa and Venice, a man of great probity and good habits. He died in Segovia on the 12th of October in 1614, and his body was transported to the Convent of San Telmo in San

Sebastián, where it rests in a marble urn next to the main chapel, and facing the urn where his father D. Alonso rests.

Indirectly, Erauso must have been aware of the identity of this well-known family. In addition to the fact that Juan de Idiáquez was a personal friend of her father's, the Dominican convent of San Sebastián the Elder in which she was brought up was founded in 1546 by Juan's father, Alonso de Idiáquez. The latter was a member of the Royal Council and also a secretary to Charles V:

> He accompanied the Emperor in his Expedition to Tunis. In 1540 he was a witness to treaties between Spain and France after the Imperial Army went to Paris; and on his return, the Emperor sent him to Spain as an envoy to confer with Prince Phillip II regarding the marriage of the Infanta Doña María to the Duke of Orleans, for which she would receive as dowry two states in Flanders. When this illustrious citizen of San Sebastián was returning to Spain from Germany, he was killed on June 3 by the Lutherans as he was crossing a river in Saxony, and according to Garibay and Sandoval, the assassins were duly punished. His body was brought to San Sebastián and is found interred in the sarcophagus of the Main Chapel of the Convent of San Telmo, which he founded, as he did the convent of the Dominican nuns in San Sebastián the Elder.[13]

The same source tells us that his son, Juan de Idiáquez, died in Segovia in 1614, and that his body was also taken to the convent of San Telmo, on which occasion "with all funereal pomp, the entire city came out to receive him, from as far up as the hill of Oriamendi . . . Don Juan always loved his native San Sebastián, and promoted its greater prosperity during his ministry, especially with respect to the construction of its public fountains and the new plan for fortifying the Castle on the Mota [River]."[14]

The conclusion that can be drawn from these sources is that Erauso lived and worked in the household of an important personage of the Royal Court. Without recognizing her, he employed her, clothed her, and treated her well. Erauso disguised her true identity by using the name Francisco de Loyola. As will be the case with many of the fictitious names she subsequently used, she selected a name that clearly pointed to her Basque origin. I believe she chose this name either because she thought a Basque surname would work in her favor, or because she found it difficult to hide her true identity. Perhaps she did it for both reasons.

Idiáquez is followed by Carlos de Arrellano. Information about him is scarce, but since he was from Lizarra (Navarre), it is safe to assume that he was also Basque. For some two years, she lived with him in Lizarra, working for him, once more as a page, using the skills and knowledge she had acquired while she was in the convent. As was previously pointed out, the education she received there was far superior to the one provided to women who were raised outside the convent walls during that same period. In the sixteenth century, Antonio de Guevara lamented women's lack of knowledge, and referring to upper-class females he observed that they "are so ignorant that hardly one of them knows how to read."[15] With respect to women in the Basque territories, if we examine law suits dating from the sixteenth and seventeenth centuries in which their names appear, we find proof that very few women of the middle and lower classes knew how to sign their names. The situation was much the same for women belonging to the nobility, as Erauso's own family demonstrated. Her grandmother, María López de Barrena, did not know how to sign her name, despite the economic status represented by the Erauso-Barrena marriage, an alliance of two rich families. When she made her will in 1570, she had another person sign for her;[16] neither could the second wife of Catalina's grandfather, Miguel de Erauso, write her own name, although she too was from a wealthy family.[17] Catalina de Erauso's own mother, María Pérez de Galárraga, did not know how to write, even though she brought a considerable dowry to her marriage: "the bride, so well endowed, could not sign her name."[18]

The situation was very different for the male side of the Erauso family. In his careful examination of the documents and registers in which information about Erauso might be found, José Ignacio Tellechea Idígoras discovered that in 1589 a certain Miguel de Erauso was the mayor of Donostia-San Sebastián. Since this fact is never mentioned in the voluminous records of the lawsuit in which Miguel the Elder was involved, it is unlikely that this person was her grandfather, so this Miguel de Erauso must have been her father. We also know that on June 15, 1587, a certain Miguel de Erauso enlisted as a seaman on the galleon María San Juan, commanded by Captain Sebastián de Echazarreta; that galleon was one of the ships of the Spanish Armada, and formed part of the Squadron under the command of Miguel de Oquendo.[19] What is surprising, says Tellechea, is that: "He claims to have served from June of [15]88 until July of [15]89 . . . as a clerk."[20] It is very likely that this Miguel de Erauso who is mentioned in all these documents is in fact Erauso's father: "a man, therefore, of the sea, of the pen, and at some time in his life, a mayor."[21] In this characterization, he emerges as the embodiment of all the characteristic Basque economic activities during that period.

The summary of Erauso's work experiences in Spain ended at this point. Next we will trace her steps as she embarked on a ship with her uncle Esteban de Eguiño, and later settled in Latin America. Her knowledge of accounting and calligraphy continued to be assets in her struggle to earn a living until that juncture at which her civilian life ended and her military career began.

Erauso in the Americas: Commerce and the Military

During the fourteenth century, the lineage system ceased to govern Basque society. Urban centers began to emerge, and commerce became an important activity in the Basque Country. As the former agrarian base of that society was weakened, a new class of merchants, strengthened by their economic power, came into ascendancy.[22] With the new possibilities opened by the conquest of the New World, this merchant class would later be in a position to play a key role. In the Americas, mercantile activity was the economic sector that the Basques developed par excellence. Their long-established tradition of commercial activity and the advantages afforded them by the special *foral* privileges granted by the Crown for overseas trading, were now combined with their capacity for hard work, their entrepreneurial spirit, and their taste for adventure. All these factors converged during the period of colonial expansion.[23]

According to the *foral* system, the inhabitants of the Basque provinces were exempted from paying taxes for any merchandise that was imported, "and these taxes were collected only at border crossings into Navarre, Castile, or when crossing the borders between provinces."[24] This exemption favored the Basque maritime provinces because of the increasingly growing commerce with the Americas, and because there was a surprising degree of freedom in commercial transactions of all kinds that were not subject to the rigid central authority of the Crown. Customs officials seemed powerless to curb frequent smuggling and the illegal exportation of money, both of which had adverse effects on the economy of Castile. Given this state of affairs, and the ethnic solidarity characteristic of the Basques, they became, in David A. Brading's words, "a semi-hereditary and virtually endogamous commercial and entrepreneurial elite."[25]

Juan Javier Pescador points out that in many cities, towns, or villages of the Basque Country, migration to the New World was a logical extension of the local mercantile activities. Many Basques that were transplanted to the New World engaged in economic activities that were very similar to those they had practiced in their native land; this was especially the case with respect to the production and manufacture of iron, as well as all the sectors related to shipbuilding. In a similar manner, farming, mining, cattle-raising, and sugar production required both practical and technical knowledge, and in all these areas Basques had more experience than emigrants from other parts of the Iberian peninsula. Because of their traditional agrarian roots, these emigrants had extensive practical experience with sheepherding, with construction using various materials, and with the systematic exploitation of forests. In the Americas these skills proved to be crucial; because of their technical expertise in iron mining, for example, many Basques held privileged positions in that sector. While natural resources were protected by communal laws in the Basque Country, in the Americas this was not the case. And, since the colonial economy was dependent on the exploitation of natural resources, those who knew how to clear a forest, or make iron and coal, enjoyed a clear economic advantage in the New World. Those Basques who had engaged in the production of iron also possessed a solid knowledge of mercantile activities, a knowledge they would subsequently use in the New World in organizing the transportation of minerals or in determining the division of labor within the mines. In short, the colonial economy offered Basque emigrants the opportunity to apply their prior competence in management, in the organization of labor, in obtaining loans or credit, and in the exchange of goods. It is, therefore, not surprising that the Basque contingent would be highly successful in the capitalization of colonial resources.[26]

Now let us turn to the series of masters that employed Erauso in commercial activities:

(1) "I signed off as ship's boy and became my uncle Captain Eguiño's cabinboy."

(2) "Once the rest of the fleet departed, I found work with a certain *Captain Juan Ibarra, the treasury agent for Panama,* who is still alive . . . He wasn't a particularly generous man, and the little he gave me was soon gone, as well as whatever I had pilfered from my uncle, all spent, so that now that I was penniless, I set off to look for a living elsewhere."

(3) "After much asking around, I heard of *a Trujillan merchant Juan de Urquiza,* and I signed on with him and did very well for myself the three months we were together in Panama."

(4) "*At my master Juan de Urquiza's bidding,* I presented the letter to *Diego de Solarte,* a wealthy merchant who is today the chief consul in Lima. He received me in his house in a most gracious and kind manner, and a couple of days later put me in charge of his shop with a yearly salary of six hundred pesos, and there I worked much to his satisfaction and content."

It comes as no surprise to learn that her four masters were Basque. Although they occupied a disproportionately large number of positions of power, the Basques were far from being a numerically large group in colonial America. Her pattern of finding masters of Basque origin could not be accidental; it happened because she actively sought them out.

Juan de Ibarra was Erauso's first master in colonial America. He was the treasury agent of Panama; that is, he was responsible for a local branch of the royal treasury. The historian Lope Martínez de Isasti mentions him among the Knights of the Order of St. John who were natives of Gipuzkoa, stating that he was "the son of the Secretary Juan de Ibarra, a native of Eibar."[27] The Ibarra family typified the preeminence of "Bizkaians" (that is, Basques) in key administrative and bureaucratic posts. He was the second distinguished secretary for whom Erauso worked. As we noted previously, in Spain she had worked for Juan de Idiáquez. She did not last long in Ibarra's employ, apparently because the pay she received left much to be desired. "He was not a particularly generous man, and the little he gave me was soon gone, as well as whatever I had pilfered from my uncle." Given that situation, she decided to leave him and seek her fortune with another master: "After much asking around, I heard of Juan de Urquiza, a Trujillan [from Trujillo, present-day Peru] merchant, and I signed on with him."

Juan de Urquiza represented that group of colonial wholesale merchants who distributed imported goods; they in turn were clients of the shippers who had transported merchandise in transatlantic fleets. In the distribution chain, Erauso was the link that connected to the merchants; she functioned as a sales agent, who brought the merchandise into the cities. Urquiza and Erauso, the merchant and his agent, illustrate how commerce was organized in colonial America.[28]

The mutual esteem felt by Erauso and Urquiza is clearly evident in the *Autobiografía.* Urquiza was not just her master; he was also a friend and a benefactor. In those times, ties of friendship were sometimes stronger than those that existed between husband and wife. During the sixteenth century, one of the consequences of the consolidation of mercantile and industrial capitalism is that the social status of women was diminished.[29] They became increasingly identified with inactivity and indolence, while men, on the other hand, were educated with a view to developing their intellectual and economic power. This distinction between men and women had the effect of strengthening the ties between men and their masters, while it simultaneously weakened marital ties. The close bond between Erauso and Urquiza could well exemplify this kind of servant-master relationship.

In my view, the high point of Erauso's experiences in her employment history came during the periods when she was employed first by Urquiza and later by Solarte. Military honors aside, the successful management of the shops owned by these two men gave her a strong feeling of satisfaction, which is clearly reflected in the text of the *Autobiografía*. The description of the work she did for Urquiza is rich in detail, and this is noteworthy in a text in which details are notorioulsy absent in the narrative discourse. Pivotal moments in Erauso's life are dispatched laconically; for example, when she left Spain for the first time and embarked alone on a ship bound for an unknown land, we are told little more than the names of those who were on board with her. In a similar manner, upon her arrival at the first seaport in the Americas, when she decided to jump ship, we are given no explanation for her reasons for making such a crucial decision; nor are we told how she felt about doing it. We will also see that the account she gave of the most important battle in her military career, for which she received her only decoration, takes up only ten lines in the narrative. The terseness with which she related such dramatic events stands in sharp contrast to the details she provided when she was describing her work in managing the shops owned by Urquiza and Solarte.

In the descriptions of her management of Urquiza's shop, repetition abounds, another clue that signals the degree to which the narrator is emotionally involved in the narration. Erauso took pains to give us a precise account of the procedures she used in her work:

> In Manta, we [Urquiza and Erauso] managed to find passage on one of the king's galleons, for a princely sum, and we headed for the port of Paita, where my master found his shipment as expected in a vessel belonging to Captain Alonso Cerrito. He then charged me with the task of sending on the shipment in numerical order, and went on ahead. I set myself to the task I had been given, unloading the goods and sending them on in the proper order. All the while my master was receiving the stuff in Saña, some sixty leagues away. And when I finished unloading everything, I set out from Paita with the last few items to rejoin him.[30]

With respect to the passage quoted, Vallbona observes, "It is obvious that the narrator, eager to relate the events, gives attention to the meaning and neglects the form." In my view, however, this "neglect of the form" should be interpreted as a sign of involvement with the narration.[31] Erauso was proud of her work. "When I arrived in Saña, my master gave me a warm welcome, delighted with the work I had done." Urquiza showed his gratitude by giving her some clothing that she described in detail: "Straightaway he gave me two new outfits, one black and the other brightly colored." Few passages in the memoir—if any—offer such detail, especially with respect to human relationships. In my judgment, this was Erauso's true calling, rather than her military experiences. In fact, as we will see, she enlisted in the army only when she had lost her job and could find no other means of earning a living.

Urquiza was grateful for her work, and as we have noted, he rewarded her by giving her two suits, gifts she did not fail to appreciate. He also showed his confidence in Erauso when he later left the business in her hands during his absence, allowing her to assume full responsibility while he was gone:

> He set me up in one of his shops, placing in my care a great deal of property in the form of goods and cash, all in all more than one hundred and thirty thousand pesos worth, and then he wrote down in a book the various prices of items and how I was to sell them. He left me two slaves to assist me, and a black woman to cook for me, and indicated I was to spend three *pesos* on daily expenses, and having done this, he loaded up the rest of the goods and took them on to Trujillo, some thirty-two leagues away.[32]

At this point in her narrative, Erauso immediately went into a detailed description of her management of the shop. As the repeated use of possessive adjectives ("my shop, my ledger") signals, it was a shop and a labor that she considered her very own. "I remained behind in Saña in my shop, selling the goods according to the guidelines he had given me, collecting the money, and making notes in the ledger as to day, month, and year of the sale, the item, quantity, the name of the customer, and the prices—and doing the same with all of the purchases on credit."[33] Our protagonist performed her duties with such zeal that when she observed that Beatriz de Cárdenas, her master's mistress, was taking a large quantity of fabric from the store on credit, she felt obligated to write to Urquiza to corroborate that he approved this transaction. She noted his response: "He wrote back that that was perfectly all right, and that so far as the lady's penchant was concerned, even if she asked for the whole shop, I should give it to her. So I put the letter safely away, and carried on with business as usual." Erauso knew that she had to keep a record of decisions for which she may have later been held accountable; she made it a point to let us know that she was doing this, thus showcasing her managerial skills.

Shortly thereafter, she got into a fight with Reyes (referred to in Chapter 1). As a result, she was forced to leave Saña, and—still in Urquiza's employ—go to Trujillo. In the memoir, she continues relating all the details pertaining to the business, and she again mentions the ledger and her records.

> [My master] said I should go to Trujillo and set up shop there—and that is exactly what I did. I moved on to the city of Trujillo, which is under the authority of the bishop of Lima, where my master had set up a shop for me. I started to work, conducting business as I had at Saña, with another ledger like the one I had used there, containing information about the stock, the prices, and the accounts on credit.[34]

Even in her account of what was a bloody encounter with Reyes, she took the trouble to mention the exact amount of a note she was cashing, and the fact that she carefully obtained a receipt for it. "It must have been two months later, when one morning around eight, as I was cashing one of my master's notes for some twenty-four thousand pesos, a Negro came in and told me that there were some men at the door who appeared to be armed. This put me on my guard. I awoke the accountant, got my receipt, and sent word for Francisco Zerain, who came directly."[35] As was previously noted, these specifics stand out in bold relief when they are contrasted with the paucity of detail provided when she narrated episodes that by all logic would merit a more vivid and detailed description. But instead, she chose to remember and set down the minutia of a relatively peaceful interval in her life, during which she was very competently managing a shop for a master for whom she felt respect and high esteem.

Unfortunately, that peaceful interval in Trujillo was short-lived. Reyes and his friends arrived, and a sword fight ensued in which she killed a man. Erauso ended up taking refuge in the sanctuary of a cathedral.

> Once inside, I sent word to my master in Saña. He arrived shortly thereafter and tried to settle the matter, but made no headway because, in addition to the murder they had charged me with God knows what else they didn't rake up, and the only way out of the whole mess, it seemed, was for me to slip off to Lima. I turned in my books, my master furnished me with two suits of clothing, two thousand six hundred *pesos,* a letter of introduction—and off I went.[36]

When she arrived in Lima, with Urquiza's recommendation in hand, she went directly to the home of the Consul Diego de Solarte (referred to as Olarte in the *Primera Relación*), another rich Basque merchant.

Solarte installed her in a shop, and fixed her salary: "There I worked much to his satisfaction and content." Everything went well until, one fine day, as Erauso was frolicking with the two young sisters of Solarte's wife, his master found her "lying with her head in the skirt" of one of those ladies, "running her hand up and down her legs." Solarte fired her. Without work and penniless, Erauso decided to sign on as a soldier, for which she received a salary of eight hundred pesos. When Solarte learned of her intention to enlist, he was saddened and worried. "He offered to speak to the company officers and get my enlistment annulled and to repay the money they had given me." But Erauso refused, saying that "she had a mind to travel and see a bit of the world." Despite the problems with her master because of her behavior, Solarte continued to show concern for her welfare. Diego Bravo de Sarabia, a Basque, was the Chief Commander of the regiment in which Erauso started her military career.

Lieutenant Catalina de Erauso: A Soldier's Life

Immediately following her enlistment, as she prepared to go to her first post in Paicabi, she met her brother Miguel. It is the most dramatic and moving episode of her memoirs.

She tells us how overjoyed she was when she heard the name Miguel de Erauso and realized that it was her brother. Although she did not know him, since he had left for the Americas when she was only two years old, she says that, nevertheless, she "had had news of him even if [she] didn't know his whereabouts." The conjecture we made earlier is confirmed by these words; that is, that the stories about her brothers' adventures in the New World had penetrated the walls of that convent within which, virtually isolated from the world, she grew up. All those stories, and the images they created in her mind, must have played a role in helping her envision the framework of possibilities that might have been open to her. Those stories probably guided her very first steps when she crossed the threshold of the convent; and, later, they inspired her to embark on the adventures we have been retracing.

Erauso's encounter with her brother occurred when she disembarked in the port of Concepción. There Miguel de Erauso appeared, acting in his role as the secretary to the governor Alonso de Ribera. Again, another Basque, in this case her own brother, was occupying a position as secretary to a key person in the government administration. When he read the soldiers' roll book, Miguel recognized Catalina's surnames and birthplace. And once again, these determined her fate. This particular passage in the text offers perhaps the most eloquent proof of the element we have been underscoring: the feeling of solidarity, the keen awareness of common identity that made Basques bond with each other. The scene that describes the reunion between the siblings possesses a heightened emotional quality that is uncharacteristic of other parts of the text.

> He took the roll book and went walking up and down the line, asking each of us our names and where we were from, and when he came to me and heard my name and country, he dropped his pen, threw his arms around me, and asked for news of his father and mother, his brothers and sisters, and his beloved little sister, Catalina, the nun. I responded as best I could, without giving myself away, or arousing his suspicions. And so he went on with the roll call, and when he had finished he invited me to have supper at his house, and we sat down to eat.[37]

The description of Miguel as he methodically and impartially performed his official duties, one by one, creates a feeling of growing suspense leading up to that moment when he comes to her name, and suddenly drops his pen. The suspense then reaches its climax when the two siblings embrace; the detailed enumeration and his affectionate reference to his "little sister" serve also to convey his emotion at having encountered someone from his homeland.

During this historical period, Erauso's native Donostia-San Sebastián had a population of slightly more than three thousand inhabitants. Since, according to the historical records, the Erauso family was well-known, it is reasonable to think that Catalina would have been able to give her brother news regarding the city and its prominent citizens. She could not, of course, give him information about Catalina "the nun," because of the four Erauso daughters raised in the convent, she was the only one who did not finally profess; her sisters Mari Juana, Isabel, and Jacinta did, in 1605, 1606, and 1615, respectively.[38] We leave them seated at the same table, at the start of a friendship that, in its initial stage, would last three years.

Following his first effusive reception, Miguel intervened to change his sister's assignment, for which he sought the aid of the governor in whose service he was employed.

> He told me that the garrison we were assigned to at Paicabí was a soldier's worst nightmare, and that he would talk to the governor to see if he couldn't get me a new post. At one point in the meal, he went up to see the governor, taking me with him, reported the arrival of the new recruits, and begged him as a favor to reassign to his company a greenhorn from his own province, saying he hadn't seen any of his own countrymen since leaving home. The governor had me brought in, and when he saw me—I cannot say why—he said there was nothing he could do. My brother was crushed and left the room, but then a little while later the governor called him back and told him it should be as he requested.[39]

Can we believe that during all those years, Miguel de Erauso had not seen a Basque person? I think not. As was pointed out previously, it is possible that when he used the descriptive phrase "from my homeland" he was referring only to natives of Donostia-San Sebastián. In any case, he did not hesitate to ask a favor of his superior to assure that his countryman would remain close at his side, and get an assignment that would be more benign than the one he had been given. In fact, the only reason given by Miguel to justify his request to the governor was that a soldier from his homeland had just arrived, and he had not seen anyone from there in a long time. And the governor respected this reasoning. Erauso remained a solider in her brother's military company for three years.

Her relationship with her brother did have its ups and downs. The first altercation occurred when Catalina, disobeying her brother, secretly visited Miguel's mistress. The siblings had a brawl and Catalina, fearing the governor, took refuge in a church. Miguel interceded again on her behalf, but this time he asked the governor the opposite favor he requested the first time; that is, he asked him to send Catalina to Paicabí. His request was granted.

In Paicabí she endured hard times. "So there I was in Paicabí, for three years of misery, and after having always led a good life. What with the swarms of Indians in those parts, we ate, drank and slept in our armor."[40] From Paicabí she went to Valdivia, where she would perform her most glorious military deeds, for which she was promoted to the rank of lieutenant. The narrative text in which she described how the flag was lost to the Indians on the battlefield and then rescued is as dynamic as the action itself; yet the only emotional note she registered concerns her brother, who appeared after she was wounded. "A few men came to my side, among them my brother whom I hadn't seen in a while, and this was a great comfort to me."[41] These words betray a restrained emotion and afford a brief glimpse of her emotional life.

> We were quartered in the plains of Valdivia, on open ground, five thousand men, with everything but discomfort in short supply. The Indians sacked Valdivia and took the field. Three or four times before, we had marched out to meet them and engaged them on the

field, always gaining the upper hand and butchering them—but in the last battle reinforcements arrived and it went badly for us, and they killed many of our men, captains, my own lieutenant, and rode off with the company flag. When I saw the flag being carried off, I rode after it, with two horsemen at my side, through the midst of a great multitude of Indians, trampling and slashing away and taking some wounds in return. Before long, one of the three of us fell dead, and the two that remained pressed until we overtook the flag. But then my other companion went down, spitted on a lance. I had taken a bad blow to the leg, but I killed the chief who was carrying the flag, pulled it from his body, spurred my horse on, trampling, killing and slaughtering more men than there are numbers—but badly wounded, with three arrows in me, and a gash from a lance in my left shoulder which had me in great pain—until at last I reached our own lines and fell from my horse. A few men came to my side, among them my brother, whom I hadn't seen in a while, and this was a great comfort to me. My wounds were tended to, and we stayed quartered there for nine months. At the end of that time, my brother brought me the flag I had rescued, a present from the governor, and I became the lieutenant of Alonso Moreno's company.[42]

In spite of the heroic deeds recounted in this episode, in it we do not perceive the same satisfaction and pride she conveyed when she detailed her work as a merchant. Nor do we perceive in this account the same degree of personal involvement and true calling that seemed to inform her performance as a shop manager. It would appear, rather, that since she had no money, wanted to see the world, and sought adventure, Erauso had no other choice but to enlist as a soldier. Both before and after her military stint, she worked as a merchant and a muleteer, activities for which she seemed to display much more affinity.

After the battle at Valdivia, Erauso continued to serve for five years as a lieutenant. She took part in the battle at Puren, where her captain was killed; as a consequence she was left in command of the company for six months, a period during which she "had several encounters with the enemy and received several arrow wounds." While in the valley of Puren, Erauso, along with eight hundred mounted men, "were on a rampage for six months or so, slashing and burning Indian croplands." Following that, the governor gave her leave to return to Concepción. The interval that elapsed between this point in her employment record and her next job in Potosí is punctuated by a number of vicissitudes that befell her: she accidentally killed her brother, outwitted the plots of women who wished to marry her, and endured the hardships of travel through the desert. But first we must note an addition to her military record: the post of sergeant major, an appointment she mentions only later in her *Autobiografía*. After helping to put down the mutiny of Don Alonso Ibañez in Potosí, Erauso explained that "because of some role I might have played in the uprising, or perhaps because of something I had done earlier, I was given the position of attaché to the sergeant major, a post I held for two years." Vallbona doubts the veracity of this assertion: "This piece of information is erroneous, because all the official documents state that she only obtained the rank of lieutenant."[43] In any case, Erauso tells us nothing about the two years she spent in this assignment. At a later point, we will devote more detailed attention to the rebellion of Alonso Ibañez, since it was one of the episodes in the civil wars that plagued the New World and that, particularly in Potosí, was characterized by a high degree of violence and carnage.

In the chronology of her multiple employments, we must make a leap ahead to describe Erauso's next and final military engagement. The event was the attack on Lima by a Dutch naval squadron.

> I arrived in Lima in the days when don Juan de Mendoza y Luna, the marquis of Montes-Claros, was the viceroy of Peru. The Dutch were laying siege to Lima with eight warships that had been stationed off the coast, and the city was armed to the teeth. We went out to meet them from the port of Callao with five ships and for a long time it went well for us; but then the Dutch began hammering away at our flagship and in the end she heaved over, and only three of us managed to escape—me, a barefoot Franciscan friar, and a soldier— paddling around until an enemy ship took us up.[44]

A number of historians give an account of this battle, among them Friar Joaquín Martínez de Zúniga, who authored a history of the Philippines, published in 1803. Drawing on this source, Ferrer states:

> He mentions a Dutch fleet, composed of four warships and two tenders, which had recently come from Europe through the Strait of Magellan and appeared at the mouth of the Mariveles [River]. Given the coincidence in time, there is no doubt that this squadron from Spilberg is the same one that engaged the squadron of Don Rodrigo de Mendoza just outside the Callao of Lima. This Dutch squadron probably was also one of the several to which Father Mariana refers in his history of Spain (1617), in which he assures that a few years before, numerous [Dutch] vessels had traveled to the Indies through the Strait of Magellan, wreaking great havoc in the Southern Sea; they sailed up the coasts of Peru and New Spain without stopping before heading out to the Philippines and the Moluccas Islands.[45]

Ferrer registers his surprise at the fact that Erauso does not allude to this naval battle in her petition to Phillip IV seeking recognition for her military service. This is especially puzzling since in that same petition she mentioned the services of her brother Francisco de Erauso "who served with Don Rodrigo de Mendoza in the Armada of Lima."[46]

Erauso's Later Occupations: Cattle Driver, Merchant, Judge, and Page

When, following years as a lieutenant in the military service, Erauso reached Potosí, she obtained a position as a cattle driver for Juan López de Arguijo, a *corregidor* (alderman or sheriff) of the city of La Plata: "I found work with him as his *camarero* (or steward) at a fixed salary of nine hundred pesos a year. He put me in charge of twelve thousand head of llama and eighty Indians, and I left with them for Charcas, where my master was also bound."[47] The size of the herd and the number of Indians both suggest that Erauso had been given an important responsibility. This was the profession in which she chose to end her days when she returned to the New World after visiting Spain and Europe. The Capuchin monk Friar Nicolas de Rentería, a fellow Basque, described this last period of her life. According to his statement, when he was still a layman he traveled to Veracruz

(1645) on the galleons of Pedro de Ursua; there he claimed to have seen Erauso (who was going under the name Antonio de Erauso) several times.[48] It is not clear whether she was working only as a cattle driver or whether she was at the same time a clothing merchant: "She owned a pack of mules with which she, with the help of a few negros, carried clothes all over, and on those mules and with those slaves, she transported the clothes to Mexico for him."[49]

In Charcas, after being absolved of the crime of murder for which she was accused, and yet again in need of a job, she reconnected with Juan López de Arguijo. The assignment she then accepted must have been similar to the one she had previously done for him, but this time, her description was much more detailed.

> There I met up again with Juan López de Arguijo, the alderman—and he gave me another ten thousand head of llama to drive and a hundred-some-odd Indians. He also gave me a great deal of money to buy wheat in the Cochabamba plains. My job was to grind and get it to Potosí, where the scarcity of wheat made for high prices. I went and bought eight thousand bushels at four pesos a barrel, hauled them by llama to the mills at Guilcomayo, had thirty-five hundred ground into flour and took them to Potosí. I then sold them all at fifteen and a half pesos a bushel. I went back to the mills, where some of the rest had been ground, found buyers for it at ten *pesos* a bushel, and brought the cash back to my master in Charcas, who liked the deal so well he sent me back again to Cochabamba on the same errand.[50]

This description is comparable to the one Erauso offered of her work as a shopkeeper during the periods when she was employed by Urquiza and by Solarte, although in this one she provides even greater detail than she did before. The power of images to communicate meaning and feeling resides in their ability to evoke scenes, and it is partly because of details that the reader is enabled to imagine a scene with greater or lesser vividness.[51] The inclusion of detail lends authenticity to what is narrated, contributes to the development of the story, and plays an important part in the author's self-characterization. The truth is that those moments in the *Autobiografía* that abound in detail, revealing a high degree of the author's emotional involvement, are not the pivotal moments of her life. As I have observed before, she devotes only a few words to the description of her first trip to the Americas, to her leaving an entire life behind her; nor does she tell us very much about her military life, her wanderings through so many countries, or her return—as a celebrity—to Spain and Europe, where the crowds gathered just to see her dressed as a man. On the other hand, we are given specifics about prices, ledgers, types of fabric, and the commercial itineraries connected to the jobs she performs. Vallbona also registers her surprise at the degree of detail that is offered in the episode that describes her management of Urquiza's shop. It would seem that behind those details we perceive the voice of a real person who wanted to talk about her skills and her successes, to reveal her most private qualifications.

Of course, Erauso's experiences in Potosí included references to mining in American soil, which we referred to in the previous chapter. During her time, the silver mines of

Potosí and Huancavelica, respectively, provided the two bases of economic support for the administration of colonial government in Peru. The geographic area in which those mines were located was also the one that she chose in her wanderings.

Basque Mining in the Americas

Following the rebellion of Alonso Ibañez, Erauso departed with a company of soldiers headed for Los Chunchos and El Dorado, "a district rich in gold and precious stones." After several bloody battles with the Indians of that district, they reached the Dorado River, and there the governor ordered them to draw back, which they did "but with little relish for it, seeing how the men had found more than some sixty thousand pesos' worth of gold dust in the huts of the village, and an infinity more of it along the banks of the river, and they filled their helmets with it. Later on we learned that when the river fell there was gold for the taking, three inches deep, along the banks."[52] In view of this discovery, the soldiers asked the governor for permission to conquer that area; he refused, and they decided to desert the company and go their separate ways. The subject of mining was thus introduced at this juncture in the *Autobiografía*.

During the first decades of the seventeenth century, the city of Potosí had almost 150,000 inhabitants, a population that exceeded that of Seville, one of the largest cities of Europe at that time. Spain's financial resources were based on the extraordinary riches of Peru; this wealth along with its commercial activity and large population placed the Viceroyalty of Peru in the foreground of the Spanish Crown.[53] It is easy to understand the lure of this region, with its promise of overnight wealth, for a miscellaneous group of itinerant miners, merchants, soldiers, and adventurers in search of fortune. The population of the city was comprised of this heterogeneous group, as well as a substantial number of natives who worked in the mines and lived in neighborhoods with their families. Potosí was a rich and diverse urban center, but it was also turbulent and restless, a place where vice, crime, gambling, and prostitution thrived.[54]

The presence of Basques in these New World silver mines dates back to their very beginnings. It was they who discovered the mines of Zacatecas, which would become the most important mining region of Mexico. Three of the four founders of Zacatecas were Basques: Cristóbal de Oñate, a native of Vitoria-Gasteiz; Juan de Tolosa, a native of Gipuzkoa; and Diego de Ibarra, a native of Eibar. Not too long after this celebrated discovery occurred in 1546, the Basque miners, equipped with the mining heritage they brought from Spain, would gain control of the most important silver mines of the New World.[55] The bloodiest conflicts that occurred between the various nationality groups that comprised the Spanish Crown were related to the exploitation of silver and the kind of society that it spawned; I am referring to the civil wars of Potosí, a topic that will be examined in more detail in Chapter 7. Peter Bakewell has made an in-depth study of Zacatecas, its mines and its society, during the colonial period. In his view, the prominent role played by Basques in the founding of Zacatecas is emblematic of the manner in which they dominated the entire exploration and colonization of Northern New Spain during the sixteenth and seventeenth centuries. He attributes their preeminence to the kind of relationships the Basques had with each other. "More than was the case with other Spanish groups, Basque emigrants tended to band together with those who shared their language and place of origin."[56] This observation is significant for two reasons. First, it asserts that the tendency to associate is stronger among the Basques; and second, it refers to the linguistic basis of that association. In order to compare the Basques to other national groups, it would first be necessary to examine the internal workings of each of the groups that made up the Spanish Crown during this colonial period. With respect to language, Bakewell's observation only underlines, once again, how salient it was in the perception of Basques by members of the other nationalities. Bakewell explains that at no time did Basques outnumber other Spanish nationalities in Zacatecas. Basque families were influential, but they were few in number. The fact that a minority group should possess such a disproportionate degree of power and money probably contributed to fueling the resentment felt by other collective groups.[57]

When she arrived in La Plata, Erauso's Basque contacts helped her find a satisfactory job ("I found work with *Captain Francisco de Aganumen, a rich Bizkaian mine owner*. I was with him for a few days"), and they also forced her to leave him ("until some unpleasantness broke out between me and another Basque, one of my new master's friends"). We see that although the relationships among Basques might not always be cordial, there were certainly many of them to be found in her master's circle. Although Basque cohesion is undeniable, it is dangerous to assign too much importance to it, inasmuch as these same Basques were in many ways individualistic and fiercely competitive. This is an important nuance, and we will revisit it when we examine the disturbances between the different nationalities and the way in which these conflicts reinforced Basque solidarity, that under different conditions might have not have been so pronounced. Erauso's dispute with another Basque—a dispute that caused her to leave her job—serves as an example of these internal conflicts.

Erauso as Judge and Business Manager

Still in the employ of López de Arguijo, Erauso started her work as a financial and commercial agent, investigating and calculating what was owed to her master.

> From La Plata, I headed for the city of Cochabamba to settle some business between my master *Juan López de Arguijo* and one *Pedro de Chavarría, a native of Navarre* . . . We settled the accounts, which showed a balance of something like one thousand *pesos* in favor of my master, Arguijo. Chavarría handed over the money *in a cheerful, businesslike manner and asked me to his house for dinner, and put me up for a few days.*[58]

The debtor, Chavarría, is "a native of Navarre." It is noteworthy that throughout the entire *Autobiografía*, the regional origin of a person is mentioned only if he was a Basque. Perhaps Chavarría treated her "in a cheerful and businesslike manner" and invited her to stay at his house for two days because she was a compatriot. With these comments she is calling attention to the kind of treatment she received, a treatment that in her view deserved mention. She may have wanted to signal that in her business dealings she was well-received; or, perhaps, that her competence was appreciated by others. Both possibilities find precedence in her life narrative.

Soon after, Erauso was thrust into in an unexpected adventure. Chavarría's wife, María Dávalos, was caught *in flagrante delicto* with her lover, and fearing her husband's wrath, she threw herself on top of Erauso's horse and implored her help. Erauso fled with her, and took her to safety to the convent where her mother, María de Ulloa, lived. Attributing questionable intentions to Erauso, Chavarría attacked her, and both were wounded in the skirmish. Following her convalescence, we find Erauso again searching for a job. It was Doña María de Ulloa who obtained one for her: a commission to Piscobamba and the plains of Mizque "to investigate and punish certain crimes that had been reported in the area. They set me up with a notary and a constable and we set off together."[59]

Erauso departed for Piscobamba where she arrested Lieutenant Francisco de Escobar, who was accused of having killed two Indians whom he intended to rob, and of burying them under his house. Erauso ordered a search for them: "We dug around and found the bodies." She pursued the case against the lieutenant until it was closed, and then, she said, "I called the parties before me and sentenced the defendant to death."[60] The accused man filed an appeal, and the case went before the Court of La Plata, but there the sentence was upheld and "Escobar was hanged." After discharging the job she had been given on the plains of Mizque, she returned to La Plata. Ferrer speculates that her commission to Mizque was probably for the purpose of "making a count of the Indians, or some other business pertaining to the royal treasury; these [commissions] were usually very lucrative for the commissioners, and so they were given to individuals whom the magistrates wanted to favor."[61] Ferrer also observes that we should not be surprised that Erauso would be given the job of arresting Francisco de Escobar, since this criminal case involved the prosecution of a Spaniard in "an Indian village, whose mayor would not be considered capable of carrying it out." What does astonish Ferrer is "the disposition and intelligence of this extraordinary woman, who can perform so many and such diverse roles in the world."[62] Indeed, we have no evidence that Erauso had previous experience as a judge, but we have seen her doing a great variety of jobs: managing a shop, making practical business decisions involving what is commercially viable and what is not, settling accounts and collecting them, as well as having slaves, servants, and thousands of heads of livestock in her charge. In this latest of her many and varied employments, she claimed to have "tracked down every last detail of [the] case"; that is, she had meticulously observed all the regulations in a legal proceeding; and as she had done before, she made it very clear that she knew how to follow the rules of whatever system was in play (commercial or judicial), and successfully carry out the assignment at hand.

A Page Once Again in Spain

We have traced the series of occupations by which Erauso managed to earn a livelihood. We now come to the very last one she described in her *Autobiografía*. On her return to Spain, she became a page once again, as she had been before her departure to the New World. Fate led her back to the Basque Territory, to Iruñea (Pamplona), and to a master who was also a Basque, the Count of Javier. "[From Seville], I went on to Madrid, where I managed to go unnoticed for some twenty days. In Madrid, I was arrested on order of the Vicar—I don't know why—and later set free by the Count of Olivares. I found work with Count Javier, who was bound for Pamplona, and went there with him, and remained in his service for what must have been about two months."[63] After being robbed in the Piedmont as she was traveling from Iruñea to Rome, she returned to Madrid to present the record of her services to the king. He granted her an income of eight hundred *escudos* a year, an amount that satisfied her. She set out for Barcelona; then she traveled on a galley to Genoa and to Rome, where Pope Urban VIII granted her permission to continue her life dressed as a man. The text of her *Autobiografía* leaves her in Naples, again seeking a job, but now with the permission of the king and the pope to continue being the person she had become.

CHAPTER SIX

Erauso in Danger:
How She Manages to Save Her Own Life

In exploring the way in which Erauso's Basque identity might have affected the trajectory of her life, I have tried to trace those narrative threads of her biography in which networks of Basque mutual assistance figure importantly. First, I detailed her movements from one place to another, noting the identities of those who help her or give her refuge during her wanderings, initially through Spain and Latin America, and later in France and Italy (Chapter 4). Next, I addressed her many occupations, giving special attention to the kinds of jobs she held, how she obtained them, and by whom she was employed (Chapter 5). As I have shown, most of the occupations in which she engaged fit into the general categories of economic activity associated with Basques during this historical period. I also pointed out that those who employed her or intervened on her behalf were, for the most part, Basques. In her memoir, Erauso customarily commented on how well she was treated and mentioned the specific gifts she received. With careful detail, she described the work she did; this is particularly true with respect to her commercial endeavors, which, it would seem, represented her true calling.

In this chapter I give attention to still another way in which that same factor came into play in her life. I will examine those situations where Erauso had scrapes with the law and managed to get out of them and save her neck, thanks to the intervention of her compatriots. After examining this third theme, I will have completed my review of the many instances in which individuals of Basque origin intervened directly in her hectic and adventurous life. In addition, I will highlight those references to the Basque foral laws in force at that time, a factor that directly affected Erauso's legal status.

As we review Erauso's scrapes with the law, we should bear in mind that seventeenth-century Spanish society was in decline; it was a society characterized by the indiscriminate use of violence. In the opinion of some authors, violent behavior ruled the streets. With respect to the Basque Country, Beatriz Arizaga points to some ordinances in Donostia-San Sebastián in which the seriousness of the crime committed was in inverse proportion to the punishment meted out for it. For example, a person who attacked another person with a sword would be fined fifty *maravedís* and have to spend three days in prison; however, a person who "maliciously" pulled another person's hair would be fined one hundred *maravedís* and be locked up in the tower for eight days.[1] This penal standard makes sense if we consider that there was such a high incidence of minor crimes in the city that the ordinances were intended to suppress them by significantly increasing the penalties. These ordinances describe all manner of possible attacks: with arrows, crossbows, sticks, riding whips, fists, and hands. In reading the trial proceedings of that period, one is struck by the number of murders committed in homes, entrance halls, and streets. Another surprising fact is that the fights occurred between individuals who belonged to very different social classes:

> . . . [between] the magistrates and their lowliest servants, between magistrates and constables, between clergymen, women and soldiers. The High Constable of Castile killed his servant and ordered the rest [of his servants] to attack a councilman; the Marquis of Cañete was killed by a footman; the Duke of Pastrana's coachman struck his master, declaring that he was his equal; and all these crimes caused noisy disputes and created serious disagreements among the legal authorities, or among the social classes of the state.[2]

One of the episodes in Erauso's memoir exemplifies this kind of street violence. When she was in Bilbao, a group of young boys attacked her and she defended herself by throwing rocks at them. She injured one of them and wound up spending a month in jail. In Erauso's case, the weapon was a rock and the sentence was a month in jail. Prior to this event, and while she was still in the convent, Erauso was the victim of physical abuse when she got into a quarrel with one of the sisters: "She was a big robust woman, I was but a girl—and when she beat me, I felt it." Later she will leave her first master for the same reason: "He pleaded and insisted and finally went so far as to lay his hands on me."[3] And these episodes were only the first of Erauso's numerous experiences with physical violence; subsequently countless gambling quarrels and altercations were a recurring motif throughout her *Autobiografía*. Given the context of urban violence at that time, the violent conflicts we will next consider, more than revealing an extraordinarily hot temper, seem rather to reflect the social reality of that era in the streets of Spain and the Americas.

Quarrels of Honor

In an episode to which we previously referred, "a certain Reyes" was seated in front of Erauso in the theater, blocking her view, and when she asked him to move, a nasty exchange occurred. Even though she had been threatened and insulted, since she was unarmed, she could not challenge him to a duel; and so she had no choice but to leave. She confronted him the next morning. She went looking for him, found him strolling down the street, slashed his face and attacked his companion.

> "Ah, señor Reyes!"
>   He turned and asked, "What do you want?"

I said, "This is the face you were thinking of cutting up," and gave him a slash worth ten stitches.

He clutched at his wound with both of his hands, his friend drew his sword and came at me and I went at him with my own. We met I thrust my blade through his left side, and down he went.[4]

What happened next is what routinely occurred in similar episodes: Erauso sought refuge in a church where she waited until the storm blew over. In this particular instance, however, the affair was complicated by the fact that the *corregidor* dragged her from the church. "He carted me off to jail—the first I was ever in—and clapped me in irons and threw me in a cell."[5] How did she get out of this predicament? With the help of her most beloved master, Juan de Urquiza. She notified him; he came immediately and spoke to the sheriff, persuading him to let Erauso return to the church. Three months later, she was able to leave a free person. To avoid any more problems with Reyes and his friends, Urquiza suggested to Erauso that she "should go to Trujillo and set up shop there," and she agreed with this solution.[6] It is clear that this employer, in addition to providing her with a job and treating her well, looked out for his compatriot's welfare, whether it concerned her bloody fights or her tangles with the law.

But as we have seen, the Reyes affair did not end here. After she was established in Trujillo, one day a black person came into the shop where Erauso was working and warned her that "there were some men at the door who appeared to be armed."[7] Alarmed, she sent word to her good Basque friend, Francisco Zerain, and a fight ensued between Reyes and his gang and Erauso and Zerain. The sheriff, Ordoño de Aguirre, arrived on the scene and with his two deputies "grabbed hold" of her.[8] The sheriff was curious about her background. "He asked me who I was and where I was from."[9] These inquiries reveal that the peninsular origin of the colonists (whether they were from Castile, the Basque Country, or Andalusia) was a determining element in the internal functioning of that society. Erauso had this same experience many times. As we observed when we summarized her jobs and travels, her surname and place of birth served as a kind of passport that guaranteed that she would be afforded preferential treatment. When the sheriff learned that Erauso was a Basque, his immediate reaction was to protect her from the legal authority he himself represented. The linguistic code they shared allowed them to cover their complicity. "He said to me in Basque that when we came to the cathedral I might consider loosening the belt he was holding me by. I took the hint, did exactly as he said, and darted into the cathedral." She did so, while the sheriff "stood outside bellowing for help."[10] Then, her master Urquiza—to whom she has again sent word— "arrived shortly," but since he found the matter too difficult to settle, he decided it would be better if she would slip off to Lima.[11] First, however, he gave her clothing, money, and a letter of recommendation. It becomes abundantly clear that without the intervention of Urquiza, Zerain, and Aguirre, respectively, Erauso could not have gotten out of these scrapes unscathed.

Butron Castle, Gatika (Bizkaia). Naval Museum, Madrid.

View of Bilbao in the seventeenth century. Naval Museum, Madrid.

...tiróme una estocada y apartéla con la daga y tiréle otra, de tal suerte, que se la entré por la boca del estómago...

"... 'You dog—still alive?' and he thrust at me with his blade. I forced the blow off the side with my dagger, and with a bit of luck managed to find the unprotected soft of his belly with my blade, pushed it clear through him, and he fell to the ground, begging for a priest."
Lieutenant Nun: Memoir of a Basque Transvestite in the New World. Michele Stepto and Gabriel Stepto, 56. Drawing by P. Tillac.

IN HOC SIGNO VINCES.

St: SEBASTIAN.

Per varios casus, per mille pericula rerum, Promissam, tandem tendimus in patriam.

Wers wilde Meer der argen Wellt
Durchschwimmt, und Ritterlich sich hällt

In allem Kreütz, dem will Gott gebn
Die Cron der Ehrn, das Ewig Lebn.

Coast of Donostia-San Sebastian. Engraving from the seventeenth century.

Like most of the soldiers and adventurers who populated the towns of the New World, Erauso was an inveterate gambler. Wherever she went, she found no lack of crowded gambling houses, where the police also frequently made their appearance because so many of the quarrels ended in violence. Erauso played the leading role in a number of them. She tells us, for example, that one day, accompanied by a fellow lieutenant, she decided to go into a gambling house. Problems soon arose. "We began to play and the game was going along smoothly, when a small misunderstanding came up, and my companion, with plenty of people around me to hear it, told me I lied like a cuckold. I drew out my dagger and ran it into his chest." A huge brawl ensued and Erauso found herself alone, fending off her many attackers. Francisco de Párraga, the local judge, arrived and tried to question her, but she refused to answer: "I told him I would make my statement before the governor." At this point, her brother made a dramatic entrance: "My brother came in and told me, in Basque, to run for my life." For the second time, Erauso refers to the linguistic code used in the interchange. Why? If, as we might surmise, she customarily spoke to her brother in Basque, why should she call attention to it in this particular circumstance? I believe she does so because she wants to make it clear that Miguel is speaking only to her and to any other Basques who might be present, and could be supposed to be her friends and accomplices. The use of a "secret" shared code allowed the speakers to disassociate themselves from one group and strongly identify with another. For the second time, the Basque language functions as a safeguard in protecting Erauso.

In fact, it seems that every time Erauso sat down at a gambling table, the game ended in a knife fight. Just after her arrival in Piscobamba, she began playing a card game with a Portuguese man, and a verbal exchange took place. Although they both drew their swords, the other players held them apart and no blood was shed. Three days later, the Portuguese man tried to ambush her, but in the fight—which no one saw—she killed him. The next morning the sheriff arrived, arrested her, and threw her in jail. Witnesses made false statements against her, and she was sentenced to death. This time it appeared that no miracle would save her. She refused confession, even at the gallows with the rope literally around her neck: "They started pushing me up the four rough stairs . . . I had to stand on tip toe while they gave me the *volatín*, which is the thin rope they hang you with, but the executioner was still having trouble getting it around my neck." What could possibly save her now? As always, it was the action of a fellow Basque.

> In the middle of all this a messenger rode up from La Plata, dispatched by the secretary under orders from the president, don Diego de Portugal, and *at the urging of Martín de Mendiola—a Basque* who had heard about the squeeze I was in. With the town clerk looking on, he handed the sheriff a court order postponing the execution and shifting both prisoner and trial to the Royal Court, some twelve leagues away.[12]

She subsequently explained that those men who had testified against her were themselves about to be hanged for other crimes, and they had been bribed to give false testimonies.

The court, spurred by Martín de Mendiola, was moved by this tragic story, and sent a stay of execution. Who was this Martín de Mendiola? We do not know, and it is possible that Erauso herself did not know him personally. But what we do know is that her Basque origin was important. Without a Martín de Mendiola, without an Urquiza, what would her fate have been?

Of all the numerous gambling fights recounted by Erauso, the most celebrated, and the one she described in greatest detail, was that which she had with the New Cid. When she arrived in Cuzco she put up at a friend's home, and it was not long before she started gambling. One day, while she was playing cards, a tall, hairy giant of a man called the New Cid stuck his hand in Erauso's winnings. She let him do it once more but the third time, she took out her dagger and skewered his hand to the table. Once again, two Basques came to her rescue, reacting almost instinctively. In these life-threatening situations, Erauso's survival was almost guaranteed because she belonged to a group whose members were keenly aware of their well-defined rights and obligations. Among these was the defense and protection of any compatriot who was in danger, especially when the threat came from hostile groups.

False Accusations

But Erauso had to extricate herself not only from the predicaments for which she herself was responsible, she also had to defend herself when she was falsely accused of crimes. One such episode involved two high-born ladies in the city of La Plata who got into a quarrel about who should have the first pew in the church. One of them then struck the other with her clog. The next thing we know is that as one of the aforesaid ladies (doña Francisca de Marmolejo) was walking down the street with her husband, an Indian ran by and slashed her face. It was an act of revenge plotted by the other lady, doña Catalina de Chaves, and carried out by an Indian, who was one of her servants. But when the latter was questioned by the authorities, he swore that he had seen Catalina de Erauso "leave the house dressed in Indian clothes and wearing a wig, all of which his mistress had given [her]; and that it was the Basque barber Francisco Ciguren who had furnished the razor; and that he had seen [Erauso] return and heard her say, 'The deed is done.'"[13] Why did the Indian accuse Erauso? Since the authorities had threatened to put the Indian on the rack, we might surmise that he accused her just to save his own skin; but I believe that there was another reason as well. Erauso was a Basque, and what the Indian suggested was a Basque conspiracy in which the barber supplied the knife, and Erauso carried out the deed. In fabricating this story, the Indian tried to create a cloud of suspicion. Given the tensions among the various Iberian nationalities that played a part in colonial American society, this would not have been difficult. These tensions were created by conflicts, feelings of mutual distrust, and prejudice. This false accusation alleging a Basque conspiracy brings to mind the bloody civil wars of Potosí, to which I will later refer. On the other hand, the fact that an Indian attempted to cast suspicion on a Basque should not be surprising. Because they were exploited by Basque miners, the Mitayan

Indians identified all Basques, who had seized power and wealth, as oppressors. Miners were ruthless in the methods they used to get maximum productivity from the Indians, and they created resentment. As a result, the Indians, mulattoes, and mestizos sided with other Spanish national groups who challenged the Basques. And so this Indian from La Plata simply reflected a widespread attitude toward the Basques at that time.[14]

Following this accusation, Erauso and Ciguren were arrested and incarcerated. She took pains to inform us that they were kept "far apart from each other, and far apart from everyone else, too." Does this again suggest the fear that if two Basques were left together they would be plotting something? Erauso was sentenced to ten years in Chile without pay, and the barber got two hundred lashes and six years in the galleys. But once again, the sentence was not carried out because the Basque logistical apparatus was set in motion. She explained it briefly but it appears that she did not know how it actually happened: "We appealed *through our fellow Basques,* and the affair went its course (but how I cannot say) until one day, a ruling came down from the Royal Court saying that I was free to go." It is not known how they did it, but these compatriots to whom she appealed must have done something to rescind such a severe sentence. And the barber is also freed. What was Erauso's explanation of all this? "It goes to show that persistence and hard work can perform miracles, and it happens regularly and especially in the Indies, thanks to intelligent knavery."[15] What she was implying here is the power of money to curry favor with the law. That this was especially the case in the Indies is also likely. Those who returned from the New World always commented about the loose morals and the laxity of laws there. And as we know, there was no lack of money in the Basque community.

Erauso and Basque Foral Law

Now I will revisit the difficult straits in which Erauso and the barber found themselves. They had been incarcerated for two days when a justice of the high court came to the jail and tortured the barber, who before long "admitted that he and another person were guilty." Next they question Erauso; when she denied knowledge about the crime, they prepared to tie her to the rack and torture her. But at this crucial juncture, a lawyer appeared on the scene. "A lawyer stuck in his head and pointed out that I was a Basque, and therefore exempt from torture by the privilege of nobility."[16] This signals the introduction of an important topic: the centuries-old legal codes of the Basque Country, specifically the rights or *fueros* guaranteed to its citizenry.

The law invoked by the lawyer that expressly prohibits the torture of a Basque is found in the description of the rights, exemptions, and freedoms of the Seigniory of Bizkaia.[17] "According to the exemptions and customs, no matter what the crime or wrongdoing, whether it be private or public, regardless of its nature or its gravity, whether the presiding judge may proceed or whether he may not; *no Bizkaian can be tortured, nor can he be threatened with torture, directly or indirectly, whether he be in Bizkaia or in any place outside Bizkaia.*"[18]

Nevertheless, this time the exemption was not observed and the justice ordered that the proceedings go on.

The exemptions or *fueros* recognized the noble status of all Basques, and yet the failure to recognize these privileges, as seen in Erauso's case, seemed to be the rule in the New World. It was not until the seventeenth century that membership in the nobility became an important factor in the colonial society of the New World. Only then were distinctions drawn between the *hidalgos,* or noblemen, and commoners. In fact, certain privileges enjoyed by the hidalgos (for example, honorary titles or the fact that they could not be arrested for debts) were abolished in 1575 because the merchants complained about them. "The privileges, freedoms and immunities enjoyed by the nobility were hardly observed in the Indies, both as they applied to financial as well as judicial matters; respectable nobles were incarcerated along with common criminals, and sentenced by the court, sometimes the nobles did not even invoke their jurisdictional (legal) rights."[19] The failure to respect Erauso's *foral* (the adjective *foral* derives from *fuero*) rights would not appear to have been an isolated case.

The Origin and Nature of the *Fueros*

The *pase foral* can be defined as an institutional mechanism of control that guaranteed and protected the Basque juridical and political heritage from royal decrees. According to its provisions, Basque entities reserved the right to either approve those decrees, or appeal them. In the first instance, prior to their execution and enforcement, all decrees emanating from the king, his councils, and courts of justice had to be examined to determine whether they should be respected or not according to preexisting laws that the king had sworn to conserve. Following this deliberation, the decrees may have been approved (*pase* means to pass). In the event they judged that a decree encroached on their foral rights and privileges, the Basque community had the right to appeal to the king. Such an appeal would presume the suspension and enforcement of the decree that was being challenged.[20]

Foral laws arose as a means of resolving social conflicts. They were elaborated gradually, not as a consequence of evolving legal theories, but as a result of making decisions, case by case.[21] There are two concepts of jurisprudence: "written" law and consuetudinary law, based on custom. Foral law is based on the latter. The general term *fueros* refers to the privileges conceded to certain individuals or groups by a higher authority. The *Fuero Vasco* has a more complex meaning because it is a body of law associated specifically with the Basque territories, arising from a series of customs and practices observed there from time immemorial. These laws that the territories formulated for themselves remained in force until 1841 in Navarre, and until 1876 in Araba, Gipuzkoa, and Bizkaia.

The Spanish Crown was originally respectful of the local rights and the laws of the several kingdoms it absorbed. But as the need to have a centralized government became more important, there was growing doubt about the power of royal officials to change or contravene vernacular laws, customs and practices.[22] During the reigns of Philip IV and

Philip V, a few royal ministers attempted to reform Basque foral laws that they considered abusive, but there were persons in the king's inner circle—many of them Basque and
Navarrese—who successfully blocked these attempts. In 1634, when the Conde Duque
de Olivares tried to introduce the use of stamped letters in Bizkaia, the measure was
viewed as a contravention of their *fueros*, and caused serious disturbances in the population. The fact that the Basques enjoyed a legislative autonomy not granted to the other
regions that comprised the Crown provoked feelings of antipathy or outright opposition
in some circles, causing concern in the Basque territories. It was, in fact, only when there
ceased to be an influential Basque-Navarrese bureaucratic element in Madrid, that the
foral laws became endangered both in theory and in practice.[23]

As was mentioned before, the *fueros* recognized the nobility of every native of the
Basque Country. The historical basis for this distinction goes back to their resistance to
the occupation by Rome and by the Arabs, by performing heroic deeds in the defense
of their homeland. The natives of Gipuzkoa claim to be noble because "in their lineages
they have maintained their purity of blood, without mixing with other foreign nations."[24]
Moreover, "those who are descended from families of Gipuzkoa, Araba, and Bizkaia
[consider themselves to be noble] because in those parts the Christians were free of any
contact with the Moors, as they had been free of any with the Romans, and for that reason they were able to keep their language until this day."[25] In still another history of the
fueros of Navarre, Bizkaia, Gipuzkoa, and Araba, the very same reason is given for the
universal nobility of the Basques; that is, the failure of the Arabs to conquer their land,
"because from the eighth century on, they encountered the unanimous resistance of the
inhabitants." This resistance, according to the Basques, was rooted in their Christian religion, in their love of independence, and in the legal obligation incumbent on all of them
to come "without fail, to repel the enemy; thus the law that prescribes a call to arms in
defense of the homeland existed prior to the Saracen invasion."[26]

Basque universal nobility should not be understood as referring to the upper ranks
of the nobility but to the lower ones; Basques were noblemen not by *cartas ejecutorias*, that
is, documents issued in the name of the king proving a certain person to be noble, but
by birth. The summary of the *fueros* and privileges of the province of Gipuzkoa addresses
the different types of nobility: the theological supernatural, the primary natural, and
the secondary natural. The *supernatural* [nobility] is that of the soul in a state of grace,
for which man was created. The *primary natural* [nobility] is the one that corresponds to
each creature according to its species, and the *secondary natural* [nobility] "is the only one
that applies to humankind, many of whom, by virtue of their personal qualities have
been honored, and have earned the esteem of others, and have brought distinction and
luster to their lineages; others have reclaimed the [nobility] they inherited from their
forebears."[27] The latter is the one that applies to the natives of the province of Gipuzkoa;
it is a type of nobility "commonly known as nobility of blood because men come by it
through their lineage, and because this honor is due them by right and by justice, since
they inherited it from the first parents of humankind."[28]

One disputed issue in the history of the ratification of the *fueros* is whether they exist "from time immemorial," or whether they came into being as a result of privileges granted by the king. In 1588, Juan García, the prosecuting attorney for the Royal Council, cast doubt on the universal nobility of the natives of Bizkaia. In response, the Bizkaians invoked the Royal Warrant of 1591. The Seigniory of Bizkaia registered its complaint with the king who, after consultation with the Council of Castile, decreed that anything in Garcia's book that might offend or cast doubt upon the universal nobility of Bizkaia be erased, and crossed out.[29] In addition, the scholar Juan Gutiérrez rebuts the prosecuting attorney's arguments, and presents proof that the Bizkaians are without a doubt noblemen. It is resolved that Basque nobility derives from its bloodlines and not from privilege; that is, in its remote origins it was not granted by a king:

> Regarding this point there was . . . a very wise discussion, and they concluded by deter-
> mining that there were two kinds of noblemen in Spain: some are nobles by blood and oth-
> ers by privilege; that the only true nobility is that which is granted by the king; but those
> gentlemen whose noble origins are unknown, or for whom there is no written record, nor
> is it known which king granted the title—all these will be called noblemen of blood; this
> remoteness in time is deemed by the republic to be more honorable.[30]

The same concept appears in a compendium of the *fueros* of Gipuzkoa.

> Although some authors assert, not without some foundation, that all titles of nobility were
> originally granted by kings and lords, this general statement does not always apply. The
> true origin of Gipuzkoan nobility, as will be seen, is general and uniform in all the descen-
> dents of its lands; it was not granted by any of the kings of Spain, as is shown by that fact
> that there is no record of it, nor was it acquired by any means described in law, nor was it
> introduced here by any of the foreign nations that occupied the kingdom . . . but rather [it]
> was conserved and transmitted, without infringement, from fathers to sons from the time
> of the first inhabitants of the province until the present day.[31]

The historians Amalio Marichalar and Cayetano Manrique (1868) both conclude that the *fueros* can be traced to the beginning of the eighth century; therefore they predate any approvals by the Castilian monarchs. However they do not agree with "the exaggerated claims of some Basque authors who, citing a passage from Livy that they think supports their theory, try to trace universal Basque nobility back to the time of the Roman occupation."[32]

The *Fueros* of Donostia-San Sebastián and Gipuzkoa

The specific *fueros* that applied to Erauso's city and province were the *fueros* of Donostia-San Sebastián and Gipuzkoa. In 1189, Sancho the Wise, a king of Navarre, used a *fuero* to found the town of Donostia-San Sebastián. Antonio Beristain finds some of the details of this *fuero* to be noteworthy: the attention given to the commercial practices of the area; the broad spectrum of individual rights; the rules governing judicial procedures that guaranteed equality; the right of the citizenry to elect their own judges; the fact that citizens accused of crimes could not be judged outside the territory of Donostia-San Sebastián, nor could they be judged by outsiders or by persons not elected by the citizens. By possessing these legal rights, the citizenry enjoyed a very privileged status. A man from Donostia-San Sebastián "carries his laws with him; not even in the the the king's tribunals can he be judged according to any other code of laws."[33] That is what is affirmed in the following articles of the *Fuero* granted by the king: "Let whoever has a grievance against a citizen of San Sebastián come to San Sebastián to receive justice."[34] Furthermore,

> Wars and duels with outsiders are not permitted for any disputes; rather let two witnesses be named, one Navarrese and the other French ... Let no man of San Sebastián go on trial anywhere but in San Sebastián ... If a man from San Sebastián is abroad, and a man in that place has a grievance against him, let [that man] come with him to San Sebastián and receive justice according to the *Fuero* of San Sebastián, because I would not have him receive justice from a foreign alderman ... I grant the following privilege to the settlers of San Sebastián: let them be judged according to the *Fuero* of San Sebastián wherever they may be, in my land or in my curate.[35]

Furthermore, the "settlers of San Sebastián" were also given tax exemptions: "I grant as a privilege that ships from San Sebastián be free and exempt and that they not pay tolls ... I grant to the settlers of San Sebastián the right to make ovens, baths and mills, which they and all their descendents will own freely, and exempt, and that the king may not levy any taxes on them."[36]

Natives of Gipuzkoa enjoyed many privileges by virtue of their nobility. These laws are clearly advantageous to them. They are exempt from paying taxes; they cannot be called up for military service; they cannot be incarcerated because of civil debts; they are given preference in filling posts in the royal government; and, as we already noted, they cannot be subjected to torture. Following is a list of the privileges that have a direct bearing on the state of affairs we have been describing in the pages of this chapter. Privileges possessed by noblemen according to both common law and the laws of the kingdom:

    I. They are exempted from paying any levies, tributes, and rent, whether royal or personal.

    II. Being noblemen of blood, they are exempted from going to war; therefore, they cannot be forced to do so, nor to form a company, nor to have weapons, or horses, or receive guests in their homes, nor furnish needed clothing and animals ... Noblemen cannot be forced to go to war except by their own will; thus they will be informed of the necessity of war and of their persons, requesting that they present themselves, and hoping that that they will participate willingly.

    III. Those Gipuzkoans who willingly go to war must first be paid a salary according to the privilege granted by King Fernando, as stated in the ledger.

    IV. They cannot be arrested for civil debt unless it is a rent imposed by the king, or derives from a crime or a near crime.

    V: They cannot be tortured; because this right was granted to them of old; three monarchs of the kingdom so state.

VI: They cannot be hanged for a crime that merits the death penalty, rather [they should be] beheaded; nor can they be condemned to the galleys, nor beaten; more honorable punishments should be meted out to them, for example, service in Oran or in some other frontier.

VII. They cannot be forced to retract their statements, according to a law of the kingdom that says that a nobleman who insults another not be condemned to take back his words, and pay five hundred *sueldos*, and two thousand *maravedis*.

VIII. Positions in the government should be given to noblemen rather than to commoners, as can be deduced from the Holy Scriptures.

IX: The king's officers should be noblemen of good lineage, as the laws of the King Alonso the Wise dispose.

X. Let it be known that the noblemen of *blood*, especially those of Gipuzkoa, do not lose their nobility if they perform lowly but necessary services, even if they have fallen into extreme poverty; because the nobility of blood did not issue from them, but came to them from their elders, and it is sufficient that it existed in them, even though presently the reason for it may have ceased . . . But if the nobility is of privilege, called *ex accidenti,* it is lost when the person himself engages in lowly activities, but not if they are done by servants, as a law of the kingdom states. Let it also be known that a nobleman lives nobly even though he may be a man of the country and work with his hands; he does not for such a reason lose his nobility.[37]

In conclusion, the text of the *Autobiografía* reflects important aspects of the particular legal code that defined the rights of native Basques. As a Basque, Erauso enjoyed a juridical status that assigned specific rights and privileges to her by virtue of her place of birth, and these were supposed to be respected in Spain as well as in the Americas. The fact that they were not reflects the historical situation of that period; nevertheless, the references to her foral rights in the text of the *Autobiografía* reveal her own awareness of the importance of this component in shaping her identity and her fate.

CHAPTER SEVEN

Hostility and Conflicts between the National Groups: The Basques against Everyone and Everyone against the Basques

"... the Basques are few but they are united and help each other in their fights as well as in their finances."

(Anonymous account of the Civil Wars of Potosí)

The preceding pages describe the many facets of Basque mutual assistance that were reflected in the life of the Gipuzkoan woman, Catalina de Erauso. Now we must look at the dark side of this ethnic solidarity, a side that manifested itself in the way various regional groups clashed as they competed with each other in colonial Latin America. This competition placed Basques in direct opposition to the rest of those groups. Because the *Autobiografía* reflects that conflict, it represents an especially valuable insight into the complex reality of the Basques as a collective group in American colonial society.

At the beginning of the sixteenth century the Catholic Monarchs, Ferdinand and Isabel, had launched a drive to transform the fragmented Spanish state into one nation. A century later, during Erauso's lifetime, there was still considerable antagonism between the Spanish peninsular groups (Castilians, Extremadurans, Andalusians, Basques, and so on) in American colonial society, a fact that suggests that the efforts to promote national unity had still not produced the desired results. What Ferdinand and Isabel wanted to do was give each person a new identity that was not so dependent on his or her place of birth, but on a more abstract set of values and beliefs. In the final analysis, this new identity would require a person to relinquish the individual ties of home and family which had previously served as the cornerstones of personal identity.[1]

The modern state protects the individual from chaos and insecurity, but this protection by an authoritarian state exacts a price: repression and over-regulation. In the newly formed Spain, identity did not derive from ideas involving regional or tribal loyalty; it was based on a concept that transcended such notions. The "new man" thought of himself as "Spanish" rather than as a Jew, a Catholic, or a Basque. Nonetheless, as we have seen, Erauso's self identification as Basque did have a profound effect on the trajectory of her life. As her narrative shows, it appears that within the context of early seventeenth-century colonial society, it is important to distinguish gradations in the degree to which a "Spanish" national identity actually existed.

The discovery of America in 1492 coincided with the creation of Spain as a nation. The Extremadurans, Andalusians, Basques, Galicians, and others involved in the development of the colonial enterprise intermingled and lived together in the Americas, but they retained a deeply rooted sense of their respective regional identities; in some cases that regional identity prevailed over the much more recently acquired national identity. In the New World, members of each of those groups were drawn into a new social dynamic in which they were forced to coexist and interact with people from the other peninsular regions, in close relationships that had not yet evolved among those same groups in Spain. In addition, it is important to bear in mind that in the New World laws and customs were not as strictly observed as they were in the Iberian Peninsula. As a result, the colonies represented a new social and legal space that differed considerably from that of the homeland.

What were the social consequences of this new coexistence? In all those places where Spaniards participated in the development of the colonies, factions emerged. Since each group had its own laws, customs and practices, it took a long time for them to develop harmonious relationships with each other. Caro Baroja reminds us that when "the 'Spaniards' who had united in a single national identity got acquainted with each other, they were sometimes able to achieve cordial relationships, but in many cases [that acquaintance] also exacerbated their differences and caused mutual distrust."[2]

Clearly, the economic and political success of the Basques, their exclusivity, and their high-handed treatment of others were the principal causes of a wave of anti-Basque sentiment.[3] Viewed from the wider perspective of Spanish society, the Basques were latecomers to the national alliance, and their commitment to it was sometimes questioned. As far as their commercial activity was concerned, the Basques were seen as opportunists, middlemen who exchanged Mediterranean products and Castilian wool for goods from Northern Europe, and who profited at everybody's expense. In addition, the claim of universal nobility by the Basques was a source of tension: Basques were resented by Spaniards who did not possess this status, as well as by those who did possess it but—unlike the Basques—dedicated their lives to preserving its values.[4] It would appear that economic, historical, and sociological factors converged, producing an image of a regional group that was granted a series of undeserved privileges that placed it in a more advantageous position than other Spanish regional groups.

In the seventeenth century, there were already numerous signs of hostility between the distinct groups that comprised the Spanish Crown. Many widely circulated pamphlets appeared in which the Basques were depicted as the compendium of all evils. In all of them, criticism was leveled at the social and political role played by the Basques in affairs outside the Basque Country, and at their excessive influence in the collective national life. Some precedents from the sixteenth century confirmed the rivalry among Basques and Montañeses, particularly as it affected the competing interests between the Basque navy and that of Santander, the neighboring region. By this time the Basque Country had developed a powerful navy, but in the pamphlets that circulated at that time, it was depicted as inferior to that of Santander.

Seventeenth-century broadsides target the Basques with respect to two matters about which they were very sensitive: their loyalty to the Crown, and their universal nobility. Although some of those pamphlets were penned by Castilians, the most important one, *El búho gallego* (1620), came from the northern region of Galicia. These publications reflected a widespread feeling of hostility toward the Basques. Shortly thereafter, *El tordo vizcaíno* appeared, which denied the accusations made by *El búho gallego*, and praised the noble qualities of the Basques. Yet another anonymous pamphlet was circulated in 1624, which referred to one of the most violent civil disturbances that occurred in the town of Potosí. The author complained about the excessively favorable treatment accorded to the Basques by the Castilian authorities in Peru. In addition to these pamphlets, Bizkaians were made the butt of jokes by Castilians, who portrayed them as clumsy, angry, raving fools.[5] At the same time, there was a growing awareness that within the Spanish Crown the natives of the three Basque provinces were united by a "commonality of interests" that expressed itself in the zeal with which they preserved their freedoms, privileges, and rights, and in their establishment of societies and companies from which they derived direct benefits. Catalina de Erauso experienced the outbreak of violence among the different nationalities of the Crown in Potosí. Next we will see what caused that violence.

The Civil Wars of Potosí

At the close of the sixteenth century and during most of the seventeenth century, the mining district of Potosí, located in what is today Bolivia, was the scene of bloody conflicts between the Basques and the "Vicuñas." Members of the latter group (composed largely of Portuguese, Creoles, and Spanish peninsulars from Castile, Extremadura, and Andalusia), were known as "Vicuñas" because "they wore wide hats made from the wool of the vicuña, a four-legged animal found in those and other regions of the Americas."[6] What has rightly been called the "civil" war of Potosí represents an intense manifestation of anti-Basque sentiment in colonial American history.

Alberto Crespo, who has made an excellent study of these outbreaks of violence, notes that the lure of silver attracted many kinds of people to the Cerro of Potosí. The Basques were naturally drawn to Potosí, given their character and their tradition in industry and commerce, and soon outnumbered the other groups. "Their economic power allowed them to wield influence in government spheres, and to get favorable treatment in the courts of justice; they enjoyed a privileged situation that they had obtained as a result of their group solidarity. But, on the other hand, that same power caused people to dislike and distrust them; after a time, a growing legion of malcontents came to feel ill will toward them."[7] The other "nationalities" in Potosí, who had come from Extremadura, Castile, Portugal, and Andalusia, embodied the heroic spirit of the first *conquistadores* or conquerors. They were soldiers rather than shrewd businessmen; they were adventurers who trusted more in luck and heroic feats than in steady daily effort. Other groups who took side with the peninsulars against the Basques were the Creoles, the *mestizos*, the mulattoes, and the Negroes, all of whom considered themselves victims of Basque dominance. In their view, the Basques stood for "the ambition of merchants and traders who took advantage of the abundance of silver in order to sell their goods at inflated prices, and the mean greedy spirit of miners who stopped at nothing to get as much productivity as they could from the Indians."[8]

The Indian support for the Vicuñas was a direct result of the system established for the development of mines. As the quality of the silver deposits worsened, there were fewer Indians available to work in the mines. The production of silver declined, causing a financial crisis. The Viceroy of Toledo then introduced a system known as the *mita* that conscripted selected Indians to work in the mines for a set number of days each year, for which they received a minimum salary. Each year 13,000 Indians came to Potosí for that mandatory service. Since they were accompanied by their wives and children, the total number rose to 40,000. The *mita* required the Indians to abandon their homes and their customary means of earning a living, and toil in the Spanish mines under deplorable working conditions. Chinchón, one of the few viceroys who showed sensitivity to the plight of the Mitayan Indians in the seventeenth century, wrote a letter to the king (1630) in which he describes the conditions endured by the natives in the mines of Huancavelica: "People who are free, innocent, defenseless, poor, and afflicted are condemned to do work in which the risk of death is high; we know this because many of them have already perished; there are fewer of them, and they fear that kind of servitude."[9] We cannot unequivocally establish a connection between this state of affairs and the episode in which Erauso and the Bizkaian barber are falsely accused by an Indian. However, if that Indian was going to accuse someone, it is not unlikely that he would choose two members of an ethnic group that was identified with the power structure that unjustly imposed an inferior status on the Indians. And, in addition, it was the group which at that time was already in conflict with the other nationalities.

As we can see, there were two very different perceptions of the Spanish presence in colonial America. First, there was the heroism of the *conquistadores par excellence*, men who chose the military, who disdained a sedentary life, but who, once the conquest was completed, found they were unemployed and practically without income. In contrast, the Basques represented the utilitarian or pragmatic aspect of the colonial enterprise. They turned their attention to systematically and methodically exploiting the mines of Potosí; then as they became wealthy, they took control of the economic and political power.[10] Thanks to their heritage and to the special privileges in foreign trade guaranteed to them by their *fueros*, Basques assumed preeminence particularly in activities related to commerce and mining. It was easy to imagine the thoughts of those who did not enjoy the same advantages. In his analysis, Crespo includes an account that reflects those attitudes.

> The haughtiness felt by the Basques because of their wealth, was "the worm that gnawed at the hearts of the Castilians who, disheartened and downtrodden, suffering opprobrium and insult, were wandering about in remote places, complaining that their fathers had won these lands so that the Biscayans would be in charge, lording it over them and keeping them down."[11]

As the confrontations worsened, the Castilians, Andalusians, and Extremadurans became more aware of the historical roots of the tensions. They had been the original conquerors, but, over the years, the wealth, the Cerro of Potosí, had passed into the hands of those who had not fought for and won them. It now became a question of recovering what was rightfully theirs.[12] On the other hand, these opposing views regarding the true state of things were only a manifestation of profound changes that were having an equal effect on all parts of American colonial society. During the sixteenth century, social stratification ceased to be as stable as it once had been. Changes in fortune or in personal circumstances could alter an individual's social status, and with respect to families, within a few generations their position could improve. In the seventeenth century this social dynamic became more pronounced, weakening confidence in a stable hierarchy founded on moral values or divine will.

> While it is true that personal merit and lineage still count as factors that command respect and esteem, they do not carry much weight if you compare them to what they once meant during the period of the Conquest, when military deeds and personal courage were enough to elevate many to the top of colonial society. Now money is the best and most effective vehicle for moving up in society; it even enables one to buy a title of nobility or curry the king's favor; it will, in the final analysis, give truth to Sancho Panza's dictum, "There are only two lineages in the world, the haves and the have nots."[13]

The economic and sociopolitical changes that produced social instability created a climate that exacerbated the feelings of animosity between the rival groups, and ultimately led to violent clashes.

The differences between both groups became patently clear when they found it necessary to organize themselves and defend their interests. The Castilians' confidence in individual courage, a quality that previously served them well in the historical enterprise in which they played the principal role, here turned them into "helpless people, scattered about, each one going his own way."[14] Committed as they were to uniting their forces and providing mutual assistance, the Basques reacted very differently to these conflicts; needless to say, they responded as a single group. For many years the Andalusians, the Extremadurans, and the Castilians, each in their separate groups, had confronted Basque dominance. Only when the conflicts turned bloody did they band together and fight as a single group, and that they did "only fleetingly in the streets of Potosí."[15]

The squabbles among the Spanish national groups started with the discovery of silver itself. The first recorded altercations between Extremadurans and Basques occurred in 1582. Shortly after, in 1587, "a fight provoked by the Creoles causes a fire and the destruction of an entire neighborhood. The Basques start to be perceived as the common enemy."[16] A few facts will help us understand the magnitude of their economic power. As far as personal wealth, all persons who had more than half a million *pesos* were Basques; twenty-two of the thirty-eight officials of the treasury were also Basques, as were all the supervisors of the mines.[17] But 1622 is the year that marked the beginning of the true "wars" among the factions. The elections for the town council that year created serious tensions in Potosí, because they placed the Basques in a position of absolute power, in spite of the fact that many of them did not have the legal right to vote because they owed money to the royal treasury. The Basques, supported by the *corregidor*, interpreted the law in a way that changed the original meaning of the royal ordinance and favored them. As a result they were able to continue enjoying an absolute majority of the votes in the town council.[18]

Shortly thereafter, the Vicuñas assassinated the Basque Juan de Urbieta and left his body at the doorstep of the home of Francisco de Oyanume, a rich miner. The perpetrators of the crime, Extremadurans, were arrested and taken to jail where they made their declarations. Among the judges was Domingo de Verasategui, one of the most powerful Basques of Potosí. When they realized that the Extremadurans who had been arrested were not likely to be judged impartially, their fellow countrymen went into the streets to confront the Basques. Violence broke out; in the fracas daggers and swords were drawn, and shouts were heard "praising their own nationality and insulting the other."[19] Once again, we find evidence that the use of the Basque language is the marker that identifies the speaker's nationality: During the night, Basques made rounds through the town crying out in their language, "Whoever does not answer in Basque will die."[20] This cannot fail to bring to mind the episode in which Erauso was arrested after having killed a man in Trujillo. On that occasion, the sheriff, a fellow Basque, told her in Euskara that he would allow her to escape, and advised her to take refuge in the cathedral if she wanted to save her life. This new episode confirmed the central importance of language in the life of the Basque community, and in the creation of a Basque identity in colonial American society.

After these events, an agreement brought peace to the opposing bands. The organizational differences between the Basques and the Castilians again became clearly evident. In the meeting that finalized the pact, two individuals, Domingo de Verasategui and Francisco Oyanume, came forth to represent the Basques, while the Castilians "responded that they did not have a leader; rather they would all, one by one, shake hands, as was done."[21] But the reconciliation did not last long, and a series of bloody reprisals soon began.

It is important to recognize that these serious disturbances never represented a challenge to royal authority. Whenever the colonial officers invoked the king's name, those orders were obeyed. This in spite of the fact the king showed his partiality on more than one occasion.

Erauso and the Civil Wars

All of this is directly related to the Lieutenant Nun. In Chapter 8 of her *Autobiografía* she recounts events that can only be understood in the context of the situation we have just described. Erauso took part in the clashes between the Vicuñas and the Basques, specifically in the uprising of Alonso Ibáñez, which took place while Rafael Ortiz was the *corregidor*. Here is the fragment in which she refers to it:

> It wasn't long after [my return to Potosí] that the Alonso Ibáñez uprising occurred. The sheriff at that time was Rafael Ortiz, a knight of Santiago, and he raised more than a hundred men, myself included, to go up against the rebels. We went out to meet them one night in Santo Domingo street, and the sheriff shouted "Who goes there?" at the top of his lungs. The rebels backed up without saying a word, and again he shouted, "Who goes there?"
>
> "Liberty!" some of them shouted back.
>
> Then the sheriff bellowed out "Long live the king!" with many of the men echoing his words, and he charged toward them, with the rest of us behind, stabbing and shooting. At that same instant, the rebels prepared to defend themselves, but we backed them into an alley and then came at them from behind around the other end, lashing away at them until they were forced to surrender.
>
> Some had escaped but we arrested thirty-six, among them Ibáñez. We found seven of their men dead, and two of our own, with a pile of wounded on both sides. Some of those arrested were tortured and confessed that an uprising had been planned for that night. Three companies of Basques and men from up in the mountains were raised to defend the city, and after fifteen days, all of the rebels had been hanged, and the city was quiet again.[22]

In this description we find that Alonso Ibáñez and one hundred men who served under him attempted a military uprising. The *corregidor* then called up forces to fight against the rebels, a call to which Erauso responded. One night an armed confrontation between the two factions took place, in which the *corregidor* prevailed, and arrested thirty-six men, among them their leader Ibáñez. When we see the composition of the three companies organized by the *corregidor*, Ortiz de Sotomayor, to keep order in the city after the armed conflict ("three companies of Bizkaians and men from up in the mountains"), it becomes clear that in this war between two factions, the *corregidor* favors one of them. Two weeks later, the rebels were hanged and, for the time being, the story ended.

Vallbona states that she was unable to find any historical verification of an uprising led by Alonso Ibáñez, or Yañez, as the surname appears in other versions.[23] However, in his study regarding the wars between the Vicuñas and the Basques, Crespo does mention him. He informs us that in 1612 the aforesaid Alonso Yañez, "playing on the aspirations of the discontented and the resentment of the exploited . . . put together a plot with the intention of destroying the industrial system of Potosí, burning the machines, demolishing the buildings, taking over the town, and then using it as his command post to spread the rebellion throughout Peru."[24] The plot is discovered when an informer tells the authorities about it, and Yañez and his followers are hanged.

With the support of Rafael Ortiz de Sotomayor, the Basques secured their power. An anonymous account of the struggles in Potosí declared, "This nationality became so prominent that the governance and control of the land was in their hands; the will of Verasategui, Oyanume, and Ormache was carried out, and the Castilians were ignored . . . The Bizkaians elected the councilmen they liked best; that is, the ones who were the most generous."[25] It was during Ortiz de Sotomayor's tenure that the resistance to Basque hegemony emerged and intensified; what was until then a silent protest began to take more concrete shape in secret conspiracies and in open attacks. The plot hatched by Alonso Yañez offers a clear example of this unwillingness to accept Basque domination. In a letter (1621) addressed to the king, there is a reference to the uprising by Alonso Yañez, which attributes it directly to the steadily growing tension between the factions. It is stated that Yañez's attempted rebellion "was based, more or less, on the usual pretext of hatred for the Basques; and the *corregidor* made use of [the Basques] to punish the rebels and restore peace."[26] Ortiz de Sotomayor clearly appears to have supported Basque dominance, which immediately provoked a reaction on the part of those who were excluded from power.[27]

In his study regarding the silver mines of Zacatecas, Peter Bakewell sheds light on the complex colonial administration, and in particular on the role played by the *corregidor* that was central to the events we have been describing. The *corregidor* was the highest ranking government official and judge in the city. In Bakewell's opinion, a local government official like the *corregidor,* "if he possessed sufficient skill, could in many cases manipulate the system easily, placing higher authorities in conflicting positions, and in this way preventing or postponing any action that might benefit the Crown."[28] With respect to the personal profits that the *corregidor* might enjoy as a result of his official decisions, the following observations by Bakewell would seem to be also applicable to what we have recounted regarding Potosí, the Basque miners, and Ortiz de Sotomayor.

> The justice meted out in these situations went hand in hand with the friendship that existed among the parties who were involved . . . The seventeenth-century *corregidores* discovered an activity that was as lucrative for them as it was acceptable to their countrymen; that is the financing of the miners. Often they acted as agents of the silver merchants, professionals from the city of Mexico, who were in the habit of purchasing the miner's silver at a discount in exchange for a loan.[29]

Having examined in some detail the hate and resentment that developed among the various "nationalities" in seventeenth-century colonial society, it is reasonable to wonder whether that Basque cohesiveness that is repeatedly mentioned in Erauso's *Autobiografía* does not just reflect a long-established ethnolinguistic and cultural reality, but also the specific social reality of her time in those particular places where Andalusians,

Extremadurans, and Castilians clashed most violently with Basques. Perhaps many Basques, sensing the growing antipathy toward them, found themselves forced to band together in order to effectively defend themselves and their interests from the attacks of other competing groups who resented their privileged situation.

In my opinion, that is the key that helps us to interpret the underlying meaning of those episodes in which Erauso had sword fights with other Spaniards; for example, the fight with the New Cid. No sooner had the fight begun when all those present sided with the Cid, leaving her to defend herself single-handedly. But she was alone only until the two Basques who happened to be passing by took her side. Vallbona observes that although in the original text of the *Autobiografía* the New Cid's nationality is not mentioned, nor is that of his followers, this detail does appear in a summary of that same episode which is included in the *Segunda Relación*. There we read that "Catalina heard Mass and immediately went to the gambling house; upon entering she saw six men, all of them *Extremadurans and Castilians*, who strutted and stood very tall."[30] In her note, Vallbona quotes a historical source that attributes the hostility between the nationalities to "the excessive power of the Basques, against whom the other four nationalities (Castilians, Andalusians, Extremadurans, and Creoles) conspired; [the Basques] were even hated by the entire population."[31]

In this connection, Vallbona mentions a similar case, that of Don Luis de Valdivielso, who,

> while he was playing ball with some Creoles, and some persons of other nationalities, upbraided a certain Martin de Usúrbil, a Basque, about the game, using some harsh words, which caused Usúrbil to strike Valdivielso with his paddle; he, feeling insulted, took out his dagger, and would have killed [Usúrbil] if the others who were present had not intervened. [Then] they started slashing at each other with their daggers and hitting each other with their paddles, and [in the frácas] many were wounded. [32]

The underlying reason for the quarrel is the strife between the factions. These altercations reflect, on a small scale, a larger social condition characterized by increasing tension between the different national groups.

Aside from the episodes that refer to Ibanez's rebellion and to the fight with the New Cid, in her memoir, Erauso tells of other events that are closely related to this state of affairs. I have already mentioned the episode in which an Indian falsely accused her of attacking a lady, and implicated a Basque barber as well in the crime. By implying that Basques conspired to carry out the act, he played on the antipathy, either concealed or open, which many felt toward them.

A similar case occurred in Cuzco when the *corregidor* Luis de Godoy was murdered. It was later discovered that "a fellow named Carranza" killed him, but as Erauso tells us, "No one knew this at the time, and they lit on me instead. The Sheriff Fernando de Guzmán had me arrested and for five months kept me miserable and uncomfortable, until Almighty God saw to it that the truth came out, and along with it my entire innocence in the matter."[33] It is curious that both Carranza and Erauso were Basques.

Given the resentment felt toward the Basques, it would appear that when a crime was committed, they were automatically thought to be the perpetrators. In this case, however, although they first mistakenly arrested Erauso, it turned out that the guilty party was in fact a Basque.

In conclusion, Catalina de Erauso found herself involved once again in events in which, for good or for bad, her compatriots as a collective group played decisive roles. Previous studies of her life narrative have not taken this very real factor into account. I believe that by giving it the consideration it merits, not only do we obtain a deeper understanding of the social and historical background of her life, we see Erauso herself emerge as an eyewitness, providing a privileged view of seventeenth-century Basque and Spanish historical reality on both sides of the Atlantic.

CHAPTER EIGHT

The Women of Catalina de Erauso's *Autobiografía*

So far we have studied Catalina de Erauso through the prism of her ethnic identity, pointing out how her "rights and obligations" as a member of that collective group define key moments in her life, both in Spain and in the Americas. Now, in the final chapters of this book, I will look at her as an individual, and more specifically at the anomaly that her life represents; that is, the fact that she chose to live as man, disguising her biological identity. This is what has awakened the interest of most researchers in recent years, especially with respect to Erauso's presumed lesbianism. These approaches posited that an analysis of her life might provide valuable insights into the complexities of gender identity, and how it comes to be constructed. In this line of inquiry, what I hope to contribute is a better understanding of the meaning of her life as seen within its historical context. With that end in mind, I will begin by examining the factors that shaped a woman's life in those very spaces that Erauso moved through as she traced out her own path in life: in the Basque Country, in Spain, and in the Americas. To see how these factors are reflected in her own perception of women, I will then address the female types that appear in the memoirs, and note her personal attitude toward them and toward the roles traditionally assigned to them. If we want to understand her sexual identity, we have to consider why she chose to live as a man, because her choice implies a rejection of the role assigned to women in that society. What did it mean to be a woman in sixteenth- and seventeenth-century Spain? Clearly, Erauso took this into account when she made her decision to reject what appeared to be her fate. We will consider the possibilities that might have been open to her, and we will explore the economic and philosophical underpinnings of society that determined the role of women at that time (Chapter 10).

Before addressing those general topics, I will sketch out what a woman's life was like specifically in the Basque Country. Did it differ significantly from women's lives in other parts of Spain? Although the existing research regarding this question is limited, I have tried to provide a partial answer (Chapter 9). Finally, I will address the topics that are clearly sexual in nature: transvestitism, homosexuality, and Erauso's own sexual identity; these are essential in any approach to the social and psychological complexity of her personality. My purpose is to provide a view of Erauso in light of the prevailing values of her time. How did her contemporaries view crossdressing? What opinions did they have about love between women? Taking this perspective will enable us to better understand the meaning of her personal choices, given the world she lived in. In some instances, as we will see, her choices are not as anomalous as one might think. In other instances, however, she is highly iconoclastic, and we have to wonder how—being so radically unconventional and unorthodox—she is able to reconcile this conduct with her unquestioning acceptance of royal and religious authority (Chapter 11).

The Cast of Women in the *Autobiografía*

Who are the women that Erauso mentions in her memoir? What are they like? Since she spent her life disguising the fact that she was a woman, and upon being called a woman was insulted, what can we conclude about the way the female sex is portrayed in the pages of her life story? In general, I would say, the portrayal is not very favorable. I believe one can safely assert that there are few women in the *Autobiografía* for whom Erauso felt true esteem or admiration, or with whom she was able forge a friendship. With men, on the other hand, she establishes several relationships of this type: for example, with her brother; with her employer, Urquiza; and with the Bishop of Guamanga. The theater and the picaresque novel of Spanish Golden Age literature project a similarly unflattering image of women and of the family. The families depicted in the picaresque novel are very much dysfunctional; in them, the mother is never portrayed as a responsible adult.[1] This same absence of responsible adult females is reflected in the *Autobiografía*.

The first female figures to appear in Erauso's story are the nuns of the convent of San Sebastián the Elder, with whom she lived until she was fifteen years old. With the exception of the "big robust" nun, Catalina de Aliri, who beat her, none of the nuns is described individually. In contrast with the abusive nun, the prioress of the convent, Úrsula de Sarauste, who was also Erauso's aunt, treated her niece with tender affection. One day when Erauso was feeling sick, she asked to be excused from matins, and her aunt "touches her hand to [Erauso's] forehead and says to her, 'Go on, go to bed.'"[2] In the text of the *Autobiografía*, the kind of loving kindness displayed by her aunt only appears in those passages in which Erauso refers to her relationship with nuns, although the one she had with her aunt is the one she described with the most feeling.

It would appear that Erauso had a very distant relationship with her mother, about whom we are told nothing except that one day after Erauso returned to Donostia-San Sebastián, in disguise, she attended a mass and found her mother there: "One day I went to hear mass at my old convent, and I saw that when she looked at me she didn't recognize me."[3] Since she was wearing men's clothing, it is not surprising that her mother would not recognize her; and besides, during the eleven years that she lived in the convent, she likely only saw her parents from time to time. While Erauso was employed as a page for Juan de Idiáquez in Valladolid, her father came there in search of her, but he too failed to recognize her. Nevertheless, he clearly felt concern and affection for her. "My father explained how his daughter had run away from the convent, how he had searched high and low for her, and how it was this very thing that had brought him to Valladolid. Don Juan showed his deep concern on account of the grief it had caused my father."[4] But the text of Erauso's memoirs omits any mention of the mother's feelings. This lack of visibility of the mother figure is in keeping with the role assigned to married women in that society.[5]

> As was the case for the mothers of famous people during that period, we know hardly any-thing about Catalina's mother, with the exception of her name. An honorable woman was a woman who had no history, and every woman strived to fulfill that ideal. Besides, they lived out their lives confined to their homes, given over exclusively to domestic activities; therefore, their lives were not interesting enough to merit recording them for posterity.[6]

The first romantic relationship between Erauso and another woman occurred while she was in the employ of the merchant Diego de Solarte. Erauso tells us that she "used to frolic and tease" his wife's two sisters, one of whom had taken a liking to her. Upon being caught by Solarte in the folds of the woman's skirt, Erauso recounts: "Solarte went to his office . . . called for me, asked for the books, took them, fired me, and I left."[7]

It is clear that Erauso charmed the young woman, who wanted to marry her, and she apparently charmed the other sister as well, although to a lesser degree. But it was not the young woman's place to choose a husband for herself, it was her father's, as head of the family. When the moralists of that epoch condemned the practice of allowing young women to choose their own husbands, they were defending a society based on social classes. If these women were to marry on their own volition, there was no guarantee that they would marry someone of their own class.[8] Evidently, as a suitor to his sister-in-law, Erauso does not please Solarte, "who was a wealthy merchant and . . . the chief consul in Lima."[9] These two young women represented both naiveté and powerlessness with respect to a decision that determined their future. At the same time, it is evident that the young woman was acting behind her brother-in-law's back, and, in fact, urged Erauso to go to Potosí, get rich, and come back to marry her. Although she wanted to observe the established social norms, she wanted to tailor them to fit her own wishes.

To continue with Erauso's love interests, there were several women with whom she flirted, and two whom she presumably promised to marry. The mother of one of those two—unlike Erauso's own mother—took her into her home, showed concern for her well- being, and demonstrated her affection:

> The lady was a half breed, the daughter of a Spaniard and an Indian woman, a widow and a good woman. When she saw how broken and friendless I was, she took pity on me, gave me a decent bed to sleep in, a good meal and told me to rest. The next morning she fed me well, and seeing that I was so entirely destitute she gave me a decent cloth suit and went on treating me handsomely. The lady was well off, with a good deal of livestock and cattle, and it seems that since Spaniards were scarce in those parts, she began to fancy me as a husband for her daughter.[10]

A week later, the lady asked Erauso to stay on and manage the place, and, after a few more days, she told her that it would be all right with her if Erauso married her daughter. Although Erauso describes her as "a girl as black and ugly as the devil himself, quite the opposite of my taste, which has always run to pretty faces," she pretended to go along with the mother and accept the proposal. In the comment made by Erauso, Velasco sees an expression of racist colonial ideology because it expressed her preference for lighter-skinned women.[11] The text of the Trigueros' eighteenth-century manuscript of the *Autobiografía* shows an even more pronounced racial prejudice: "My spouse was black and ugly, quite contrary to my taste, which always ran to pretty faces; and for that reason you can imagine that the four months I was with her felt more like four centuries."[12]

Having agreed to the wedding, Erauso accompanies the mother and daughter to Tucumán where the ceremony was to take place. There, while the reluctant groom uses one pretext and another to put off the marriage, she meets Antonio de Cervantes, the bishop's vicar general: "This gentleman took a fancy to me, gave me gifts and wined me and dined me at his house, until finally he came to the point and told me he had a niece living with him who was just my age, a girl of many charms, not to mention a fine dowry, and he had a mind to see us married."[13] As she did previously, Erauso pretends to be pleased and flattered by the marriage proposal, but in this case, she finds the vicar's daughter more to her liking: "I met her and she seemed good enough." The presents given to the intended groom are even more sumptuous: "a suit of good velvet, twelve shirts, six pairs of Rouen breeches, a collar of fine Dutch linen, a dozen handkerchiefs, and two hundred pesos in a silver dish—all of this a gift, sent simply as a compliment, and having nothing to do with the dowry itself." Caught up simultaneously in two marital tangles, Erauso flees, jilting both of the brides. She saddles up a stolen mule and vanishes. Her last words on the matter are somewhat ironic: "I have never heard exactly what became of the black girl or the little vicaress."

Both of these women were badly used: Erauso deceives them, takes advantage of them, robs them, and then abandons them. All of the gifts she had accepted without hesitation represented advance payment on her high worth as a husband. She understands this perfectly, and gets all she can from it. Erauso must view these women, avidly seeking a good marriage catch, with considerable irony. It is noteworthy that in neither case does she acknowledge that she has deceived them by disguising her sexual identity, that the marriage would be impossible, and that those who propose it do not even suspect the truth. She views her deception rather as that of a rogue who uses and abuses others whenever he has the chance to do it; that is, she portrays herself as a man who deceives women, and not as a woman who is forced to deceive them because she must conceal her true sexual identity.

What conclusion can be drawn from this episode? Erauso deceived women, took advantage of their hospitality, and like a real *pícaro* or rogue, got as much as she could out of the situation. The mother, on the other hand, is portrayed as an innocent, good woman who simply wanted to find a fine match for her daughter, about whom we are told nothing, except that she was ugly and obeyed her mother's wishes. The lady's keen desire to marry the "black" girl to Erauso reflects the social reality of New Spain in the seventeenth century, in which any association with a member of the upper class could provide the stepping-stone for moving up socially, even when the union might not be a legitimate one. That the Europeans found these mixed relationships to be incomprehensible is demonstrated by the following comments made at the end of the eighteenth century by a Spanish observer:

> To a much greater degree here than in Spain, there are many families in these parts, who regardless of how distinguished their lineage may be, cannot escape the fact that they have numerous black and mulatto relatives who belong to the rabble. I have seen some [gentlemen] employing their wives' brothers and cousins as coachmen, as black or mulatto footmen; and they make use of their sisters (black, mulatto or of some race) for work in their kitchens or in some other domestic service.[14]

These "free" relationships continued to exist and to be socially accepted, even when, at the end of the sixteenth century, the percentage of women of European descent in upper-class American colonial society becomes more proportional to the number of men. By marrying her daughter to a Spaniard, the *mestiza* lady aspired to move one step up in society.

Another factor that we should keep in mind is the small number of Spanish soldiers in the relatively unexplored territories through which Erauso moved. As she indicated, "We were well received because there were so few of us in Chile." The scarcity of Spanish soldiers throws additional light on the warm reception offered to Erauso by the *mestiza*.[15]

The woman who seems to be most in charge of her own destiny in the *Autobiografía* is Urquiza's mistress. Beatriz de Cárdenas is portrayed as a woman who knew how to get as much material benefit as she could from her liaison with this rich merchant. When Urquiza left Erauso in charge of his shop, in a ledger he wrote the names of the persons whom she could trust to take goods on credit. And he particularly wanted Erauso to know that "this applied to my lady doña Beatriz de Cárdenas, whom he held in perfect confidence and high regard." Cárdenas did what she was wont to do: she began taking out goods and "went on taking so much and for so long, that I began to have my doubts and—without letting her know what I was up to—I wrote to my master in Trujillo, telling him in detail about the whole affair." The latter responded, assuring Erauso that it was perfectly all right, and that "as far as this woman's penchant was concerned, if she asked me for the entire shop, I should give it to her."[16] Though Cárdenas had no legal rights in her relationship to Urquiza, she reaped its economic benefits.

Some time later, Erauso got into a serious scrape with the law because of her brawl with Reyes, during which she cut his face. As a way for her to get out of the mess, it occurred to Urquiza that since Cárdenas's niece happened to be married to Reyes, if Erauso were to marry Cárdenas "everything would calm down." This marriage of convenience would allow Urquiza, as Erauso observes, "to hold on to both of us—me for business and her for pleasure. And they must have worked the whole thing out between

...yo, con un mal golpe en una pierna, maté al cacique que la llevaba,
se la quité...

"I had taken a bad blow to the leg, but I killed the chief who was carrying the flag, pulled it from his body, spurred my horse on, trampling, killing and slaughtering more men than there are numbers." *Lieutenant Nun: Memoir of a Basque Transvestite in the New World*. Michele Stepto and Gabriel Stepto, 20. Drawing by P. Tillac.

...él acudió con las manos a la herida; su amigo sacó la espada
y vino a mi...

"I approached him from behind and said, 'Ah, Señor Reyes.' He turned and asked, 'What do you want?' I said, 'This is the face you were thinking of cutting up,' and gave him a slash worth ten stitches." *Lieutenant Nun: Memoir of a Basque Transvestite in the New World*. Michele Stepto and Gabriel Stepto, 12. Drawing by P. Tillac.

them."[17] Cárdenas does not behave like a victim who is forced to accept such an arrangement; on the contrary she attempts—willingly and using every means possible—to seduce Erauso, who tells us that she would sneak out of the church where she had taken refuge and go to Cárdenas's house. "There she would caress me and implore me to spend the night with her . . . Finally one night she declared that come hell or high water, I was going to sleep with her—pushing and pleading with me so much that I had to smack her and slip out of there."[18] Finding herself the object of Cárdenas's aggressive sexual advances, Erauso had to escape as best she could. Had she not done so, Cárdenas would soon have discovered her secret. She tells her master Urquiza that "the marriage just wasn't going to happen, that there was no way in the world [she] would have anything to do with it." Her master, however, insists, promising her "mountains of gold, and reminding [her] of the lady's beauty and talents." But Erauso holds her ground.

Cárdenas was a sensual woman, but she was also clever and pragmatic. Here is a woman who was sexually aggressive, strong, and determined; as I observed before, she was in charge of her life. We are not in the presence of a victimized woman, but one who actively conspired with her lover to arrange a relationship that was morally questionable but nevertheless advantageous. She is the most astute and independent female figure in the entire text of Erauso's memoirs; yet according to the prevailing moral code of that time she was marginalized. She typifies the kinds of individuals who had to carve out their own places in those new social spaces created by the colonial society of the New World.

The next female to appear in the text is Doña Catarina de Chaves, a widow and a prominent lady of La Plata. Erauso had gone there to work for a miner, Francisco de Aganumen, but because of some unpleasantness with another Basque, she had to leave her new master's home and find another place to stay. Erauso recounts that she "had struck up a friendship with one of Catarina's servants, and it was thanks to him that she promised to take me in."[19] We have previously referred to the events that led to this particular episode. One day, when Doña Catarina de Chaves and Doña Francisca de Marmolejo (another prominent lady) were in church, going through the Stations of the Cross, they argued about who was entitled to sit in the first pew. In the consequent squabble, Marmolejo struck Chaves with one of her shoes, and a great uproar ensued. Chaves returned to her home followed by a flock of relatives, and there "the matter was hotly debated." The other lady remained in church with her own group of backers, not daring to leave until her husband arrived, accompanied by the *corregidor* and two deputies. As they were making their way down the street, the sound of swordplay was heard, and the *corregidor* and the deputies ran to see the cause of the uproar. At this moment, an Indian ran by, "and as he passed the lady Doña Francisca de Marmolejo, he slashed her face from side to side with a knife or a razor, and kept on running." Erauso was blamed for this crime, and was about to be tortured when a note arrived from Catarina de Chaves, exonerating her. "The justice opened it, and read it and then just stood there a while looking at me. At last he said, 'Take the lad down.'"[20]

What can be said about these two women? Of course, the incident between them shows us that violence was rampant in colonial society; it also reveals the importance assigned to where people sit in the church. Preferential seating in churches was codified; it is even recorded in the official documents of that time. In a history of the province of Gipuzkoa, it is pointed out that "only the *parientes mayores*, with the exception of the councilmen, are entitled to preferential pews," and this applied when said *parientes*, or heads of the clans, were patrons of the parish churches, "because only to them has the province granted the right to sit in preferential pews in the churches, although the local authorities have allowed this privilege to be abused, favoring certain families and individuals who do not qualify for such patronage rights."[21] The pew in which one sat became a clear symbol of social status and recognition in a given community.

The episode I have just summarized brings to mind the altercation between Erauso and "a certain Reyes," provoked by their nasty verbal exchange in the theater. On that occasion a face was slashed, and that incident led to even more serious encounters later. The women we see in these episodes are proud, violent, and vengeful; they settle their quarrels in ways that do not differ much from the way men settle theirs. Women, as much as men, displayed pride, revenge, and violence in their relationships with each other. If we are to judge by Erauso's autobiography, that kind of behavior was the *modus operandi* of the time.

Erauso's contacts with other women are also worth noting. After leaving La Plata, she headed for the city of Cochabamba, where she had to settle some business affairs between her master, Juan López de Arguijo, and Pedro de Chavarría, who was married to Maria Dávalos, a woman who played a key role in Erauso's next adventure. Several days after concluding her business with Chavarría, as Erauso was leaving Cochabamba, she happened to pass in front of his house, and hearing some squabbling, she tells us:

"I stopped to see what the story was, and at this very moment doña María Dávalos stuck her head out of the window and cried, 'Take me with you, Señor Capitán—my husband is trying to kill me!'—And with this she jumped out of the window." Two friars came up at this point and asked Erauso to help the lady escape, because "her husband found her with don Antonio Calderón, the bishop's nephew, and he killed him—now he has doña María locked up and has a mind to kill her too." After saying this, "they hoisted her up on the mule's behind," and Erauso rode off with her.[22] They rode for many hours until they reached the city of La Plata. There in the Augustine convent, as Erauso was handing María Dávalos over to her mother, the angry husband—who had been pursuing them all the way—appeared and without asking any questions, attacked Erauso, whom he suspected of being Dávalos's lover. Both were seriously wounded in the sword fight that ensued. Months later, after Erauso and Chavarría had recovered from their wounds, the marital rift between the merchant and his wife was resolved by the bishop and some other dignitaries. They arranged for them both to take holy vows, "she right where she was, and he wherever he liked." But Chavarría was not satisfied; he wanted to prosecute Erauso for having helped his wife to escape. How did she get out of this scrape?

My master Juan de Urquijo came forward and told the archbishop don Alonso de Peralta, and the president and other dignitaries how I had become involved in the affair, innocently, altogether by chance and without malice, despite what the gentleman said, and how I had no choice but to help the woman in question, who had thrown herself at me fleeing bloody murder, and how I had delivered her up to her mother as she had begged me to do. When all of this was attested to and confirmed, they were satisfied and the case ended.[23]

What we know about María Dávalos is that she was discovered *in flagrante delicto*, deceiving her husband in her own house. Again, as in the case of Beatriz Cárdenas, the text portrays a woman of doubtful moral character, and one who was astute enough to save her own life. Erauso did not pass judgment on her; rather, she seems to have felt sorry for her, and when she realized that the lady's life was threatened, she chose to help her. When Dávalos found herself in a tight spot, she was quick-witted and clever. Another facet of the female reality that is displayed here is Dávalos's fear of her husband. Not satisfied by having killed her lover in order to wipe out the stain on his honor, he also demanded that his wife pay with her life.

Later on, once Erauso revealed her true sexual identity in her confession to the bishop, he decided she should go to the convent of Santa Clara of Guamanga. There, she tells us, "I kissed the abbess's hand, embraced and was embraced in return by each of the nuns."[24] With respect to her departure from the convent five months later, she wrote, "the nuns were beside themselves when they took leave of me."[25] From there she went to the Convent of the Most Holy Trinity in Lima, where she lived for more than two years. Again, she notes that as she left, "the sisters bade [her] a sad farewell."[26] Although Erauso offered no details about her relationship to the nuns, we are left with the impression that they professed true affection for her. Before embarking on her return trip to Spain, she traveled once more to Guamanga to say goodbye to the sisters of Santa Clara: "They held me up there for eight days, during which we enjoyed each other's company and exchanged many gifts, and finally, when it was time to go, many tears."[27] They expressed a clear fondness for Erauso and are depicted as warm, loving figures.

The last reference to females in the *Autobiografía* involves two women in Naples. As Erauso (who had again taken to wearing men's clothing) was strolling about the wharves, she heard the titter of two women who "were making conversation with two bucks, and looking at me." They had recognized Erauso, and seeing her dressed as man, were amused. One of them asked, "*Señora* Catalina, where are you going all by your lonesome?" "My dear harlots"—Erauso replied—"I have come to deliver one hundred strokes to your pretty little necks and a hundred gashes with this blade to the fool who would defend your honor." Erauso concluded her memoirs with this sentence: "The women fell dead silent and then they hurried off."[28]

Feeling insulted when they addressed her as "*señora*," Erauso launched a verbal attack on them, expressing her disdain for women who were nothing more than sexual objects. A more violent version of this same episode is found in one of the manuscripts of the *Autobiografía* recently discovered by Pedro Rubio Merino in Seville's Archivo Capitular.

In that variation, Erauso did not just threaten the two prostitutes, she attacked their male companions physically. "I pulled out my sword and my dagger, and went toward them with a beating of sword swipes and they escaped me by running away. Turning to the two women, I gave them many slaps and kicks and I was tempted to cut their faces."[29] In Stephanie Merrim's opinion, these two "public" women can be regarded as Erauso's antithetical doubles. They, too, were transgressive, marginalized figures, but unlike Erauso they subordinated themselves to men's desires. "The hell with you," she said in essence to this kind of woman, and perhaps to women in general.[30]

As stated at the beginning of this chapter, the images of women as they appear in the *Autobiografía* are not very flattering. I question Vallbona's assertion that "not once does Catalina complain about being a woman, because she knows that she has won the respect of brave men, and has achieved a degree of fame that many men would like for themselves."[31] In my opinion, her indirect rejection of her own biological identity is what lay at the heart of the new male identity she constructed for herself. It is as a man, not as a woman, that she won the "respect of brave men" throughout her life. Given this fact, the respect she had earned while pretending to be a man could—in her own eyes—hardly make her feel proud of being a woman. As we saw in the aforementioned episode with the two Neapolitan women, Erauso was insulted when they called her "*señora.*"

The female world from which Erauso distanced herself was comprised of different groups of women. With the exception of the nun who beat her, as a group the nuns are depicted as affectionate and friendly, although they are not very well-defined, which would lead us to believe that Erauso's emotional involvement with them was limited. The next group, composed of the women Erauso deceived, can be broken down into two categories: the two she promised to marry and the one with whom she clearly had an erotic relationship. These were women whose parents wanted to marry them off to Erauso; they were much more passive and had little control over their own lives. Not only did Erauso deceive them, she also deceived their parents or guardians.

The women who were most in charge of their fates were also the most sexually active women, although their sexual conduct clearly placed them socially beyond the bounds of conventional morality. In this group we have Beatriz Cárdenas, Urquiza's mistress; María Dávalos, the married woman caught *in flagrante* with her lover; and finally the two Neapolitan prostitutes who appear in the last episode of the memoirs. All these women, who have something of the *pícara* or female rogue in them, personify the resilience and the cunning that helped them survive in any situation no matter how desperate or unusual it may have been. Each of them was immoral, and as characters in the narrative, sexuality was their most pronounced dimension: Cárdenas harassed Erauso sexually; Dávalos deceived her husband in her own home; and the Neapolitan women mocked Erauso even as they were flirting with two men. And yet, the text of the memoirs passes no judgment on either Cárdenas or Dávalos. Erauso feared Cárdenas's sexual aggressiveness, but she respected her and even seems to have admired her. It was also Erauso who rescued María Dávalos when she was about to be murdered by her husband. Not only did she transport the lady to the convent, she was also forced to engage in a fight with the outraged husband. Just as the new Latin American colonial society had created a space in which our protagonist—who is clearly an anomaly—was able to thrive, it also made it possible for these unconventional women to find a place in that society. Nevertheless, Erauso's insult to the Neapolitan women ("harlots") reveals that when women do exercise sexual freedom beyond the limits recognized by conventional society, this conduct could be conveniently turned against them and used as an excuse for questioning their sense of honor.

What is missing in the text of the memoir are close, affectionate relationships with women, comparable to the ones Erauso establishes with her brother, with her most beloved masters, or with the Bishop of Guamanga himself. Erauso was a friend to her friends, but she was not a friend to the ladies. In their presence, sexual tension seems to have tinged any relationship she might have had with them. When it comes to women, she seemed unable to perceive them as whole persons; she only noticed certain features of their personalities. Nor did she express deep affection or admiration for any of them. The women who are found in the pages of the *Autobiografía* appear only as caricatures of certain female stereotypes that Erauso chose to foreground. In no instance do her relationships with them reach the same degree of emotional involvement that we observe in her relationships with men. This lack of empathy not just for feminine values, but also for the female role models that appear in the memoir, demonstrates, in my judgment, that Erauso wanted to distance herself from the roles she would have been expected to play as woman. She crossed this distance by constructing a male identity that permitted her to explore the paths she deliberately chose to follow.

CHAPTER NINE

The Basque Woman in the Early Modern Age

In this chapter I will be drawing on some sources that provide a broad view of the role of women and the place assigned to them in Basque society during Catalina de Erauso's time. My purpose in doing so is to examine the female role models that Erauso, as a member of the Basque ethnic group, could have had, and consider how the roles then available to her might have affected her decision to live her life as a man. In short, I want to explore the ethnic tradition into which she was born. We know that women's lives were not uniformly the same in all the territories of the Spanish Crown. With respect to this, I have already noted some differences between Spain and the Americas, and I will give more attention to them in Chapter 11. The same can be said about differences between the various regional groups within Spain. Although research about Basque women in the Early Modern Age is only in its beginning stages, it is already yielding some specific details that will be helpful in reading Erauso's *Autobiografía*. The topics I have chosen to address may not be directly connected to her life, but they enable us to better understand the complex realities that shaped a woman's life in Erauso's native land. Those realities will also serve as necessary point of reference when we later examine female sexuality within the larger context of Spanish society.

The Indies Run as Seen from the Other Side: The Women Who Were Left Behind

In his study describing life in the Oiartzun valley during the centuries of Atlantic emigration, Juan Javier Pescador addresses the fate of women who stayed behind when the heads of households emigrated to the Americas. What he details for the Oiartzun valley can be taken as representative of the situation in the Basque Country in general, as the conditions and traditions described were very much the same in all the Basque territory.

While the lives of many of the men who emigrated have been carefully documented by historians, we know little or nothing about what happened to the women and children they left behind. What we know is that many of these women had to assume all the economic, domestic, and legal responsibilities connected to the *baserri* or the family home, as well as managing the family finances and belongings. The increased responsibilities did not, however, always result in an improvement of a woman's status.[1] Often, just the opposite happened; that is, males' migration to the New World created problems for women. Pescador tells the story of Luis Pérez de Eraso, a Basque who migrated to Mexico, leaving his wife and his two sisters behind in the village of Oiartzun. As he had been designated as the sole heir, in his absence the sisters had to assume responsibility for the *baserri,* although that legacy would never belong to them. One of his sisters, María Pérez, married but was widowed and left with a daughter. The other sister had been unable to marry because she did not have a dowry. Both had to take charge of the economic affairs of the family: farming the land, raising animals, participating in the collective tasks, and caring for any family belongings. They were destined to a life of unremitting work for the sake of the family farmstead, without any hope of improving their own lot as individuals.[2]

Emigration to the Americas was viewed as a solution to a family's precarious financial situation. In Luis Pérez de Eraso's case, it proved to be a successful solution. At his death he had redeemed family debts and amassed a small fortune, but it is doubtful that the women in his family (his wife and his sisters) benefited from his success. He never sent for his abandoned wife. In Mexico he entered into a consensual union with another woman, herself a widow with several children, and lived with her until his death. He named his second wife and her children as the main heirs of his estate, favoring them over his sisters and nieces in Oiartzun.[3] His death should have signified the end of his sisters' economic hardships; instead they were forced to deal with the enormous problems involved in retrieving, from Spain, a fortune made in the Americas. After ten years of litigation, the Pérez de Eraso sisters succeeded in getting the inheritance to which they were entitled, but it was greatly diminished by the judicial costs involved, and by the loss of funds due to poor management by those parties in the Americas who had been charged with executing his will.[4]

Both Luis Pérez de Eraso's trip to the Indies and his sisters' self sacrifice were strategies aimed at preserving the family homestead. While each stuck to the role assigned to them, the women were compensated very differently. As Pescador points out, the Eraso sisters got a taste of "the Indies' dark side." First, there were the sacrifices made by the family to finance his initial trip; then, the grim dedication to preserving the family legacy, the renunciation of a dowry in favor of the conservation of the family estate, and finally, the sisters' subordination to the new household their brother had created with his new wife and children in the Americas. As recompense for the sacrifices they had made, these women received too little too late. This family's case was hardly extraordinary. One way or another, countless women in the Oiartzun valley had to link their economic fortunes to the luck of the male relatives who emigrated. Even if they were successful, the women were still dependent on the generosity of those absent males, and may have had to wait indefinitely to receive their inheritance or whatever remained of it.[5]

For Basque women, one positive aspect of the Indies run was the establishment of public endowments for the marriageable females in their families. These dowries, offered by well-established male relatives in the Indies, came to replace the dotal obligations of the main heir, or head of the family homestead, for the women still living under the family roof. And although not every woman had "an uncle in America," nor could every émigré afford to endow his female relatives in Oiartzun, the social expectation in regard to such practices on both sides of the Atlantic created new permanent ties between the absent males and the local women.[6]

Women and the Legitimacy of Children

Pescador addresses another topic that directly affected a woman's life in the village of Oiartzun: the high incidence of children born out of wedlock. At the end of the sixteenth century, 21 percent of baptized infants in the valley were *hijos naturales,* or illegitimate children. Three factors contributed to this high rate of illegitimacy: the respectable social status of bastard children, the lack of ecclesiastical control over family formation, and the persistence of the medieval belief that premarital sexual relations did not constitute sin. Illegitimacy was thus the result of varied circumstances. Principal explanations include the Basque practice of a couple living together before marriage, of marrying after the birth of the first child, and of the fathering of children by local priests. The "natural children" of parents who later legitimized their unions enjoyed the same privileges and rights as those born after the marriage ceremony had taken place. Certain demographic and migratory patterns that became especially relevant during the eighteenth century also contributed to the large number of illegitimate births.[7]

The morality sanctioned by the Council of Trent did not easily replace the marriage customs of the Gipuzkoan rural population. The priests themselves did not observe the dispositions for the ecclesiastical hierarchy, in part due to the fact that only parish priests who had been baptized in the parish could perform marriages and other sacraments. The number of candidates who could meet these requirements was small and in many cases young men with no vocation for the priesthood were ordained, and later "rented" out their positions to non-tenured clergy for a payment. This state of affairs gave rise to great laxity in the performance of ecclesiastical duties; for example, priests did not bother to investigate the birth circumstances of each child they baptized. On two occasions, in 1634 and in 1645, the diocese sent inspectors to Oiartzun in an attempt to exercise greater control on the parishes in the valley, but apparently these measures were ineffective. With respect to keeping records of the births of illegitimate children, the quality of the parish registers hardly improved.[8]

Before 1700, religious marriage ceremony had very little importance in the Basque Country. Only infrequently did ecclesiastical marriage coincide with the start of conjugal life. More relevant factors were the agreement between the engaged couple's families in the civil marriage settlement, and the birth of the first child. In a system dominated by the indivisible inheritance principle, it was important to demonstrate fertility prior to the formal marriage. In addition, as we said, the medieval belief persisted that premarital sex did not constitute sin.[9]

Here we find a striking contrast with women's status in other European countries during the Renaissance. The increasing concern of the nobility regarding the legitimacy of their offspring resulted in greater control over female sexuality. Illegitimate children lost all their rights; this is turn jeopardized the continuation of the family name and the privileges inherent in titles of nobility. This was not the case in the Basque Country, where illegitimate children were not denied their rightful place in the family. There, during the sixteenth and seventeenth centuries, illegitimate children enjoyed the same rights and privileges as their legitimate counterparts. As noted previously, the parish priests did not bother to investigate the birth status of the infants they were baptizing, and if the church did not give much importance to this fact, we must suppose that neither did the rest of the population. This state of affairs can be better understood if we consider that during that period there was an economic boom fueled by a subsistence economy in which the heads of household used their families as productive units in agriculture and industry. In these kinship networks, the illegitimate children had a place as servants and workers in foundries, woods, and ventures in the Indies.[10]

Illegitimate children enjoyed a number of privileges. They usually received their father's name and his legal recognition; they could inherit a portion of both maternal and paternal legacies; some might even be raised in their father's principal home, regardless of their mother's place of residence. Local institutions did not discriminate against illegitimate children, many of whom held positions in the army, the church, and the government.[11] Wills often mentioned both legitimate and illegitimate heirs; fathers bestowed their names on them and saw to it that they would have enough money for their education and maintenance. Sometimes they were even favored over the legitimate heirs, and, not infrequently, the illegitimate son inherited the entire *baserri*, or family homestead. In general, according to Basque custom, all illegitimate children received the father's last name and were recognized by him. If the father and mother were not living together, a sum was negotiated with the mother for their maintenance.[12]

This Oiartzun custom of making little distinction between children born out of wedlock and illegitimate children born as a consequence of an adulterous relationship represents a fundamental difference with Castilian law and Roman law in general, not to mention ecclesiastical dispositions. Children born out of adulterous relationships with local priests were looked upon as "natural children," not as "bastards" or "sacrilegious." Pescador mentions the priest Juan López de Zuaznabar, who in 1624 admitted in his will that he had fathered seven offspring with three different women. All bore his name and were recognized as his "natural children."[13] The truth is that between 1550 and 1670, very few families in the Oiartzun valley did *not* have an illegitimate son as the head of the household. In some parishes, as much as 30 percent of all births were illegitimate. Illegitimacy rates did not decline until the eighteenth century, and even then, they still exceeded the averages for Western Europe. This decline can be traced to the economic crisis, and to the joint efforts of the church and the Spanish Bourbon state to reform customs regarding marriage.[14]

Sexuality and Marriage in the Basque Territories

To better understand a Basque woman's situation with respect to sexual relations and the formation of a family, I will be drawing heavily on Renato Barahona's *Sex Crimes, Honor and the Law in Early Modern Spain: Vizcaya 1528–1735* (2003). In the lawsuits cited by the author, women repeatedly accused men of having seduced them by promising marriage only to be abandoned later.

The charge of *estupro* (rape), employed in the lawsuits, was synonymous with defloration, or the loss of virginity, which was presented as a theft or a loss to the woman.[15] In all of the plaintiffs' accounts, the situation is identical: sexual relations were initiated only after the male pledged marriage; once the offer was accepted, sexual intercourse took place.[16] After a man made this promise and the union was consummated through the loss of the woman's virginity, his responsibility and obligation to the woman was radically transformed; it was no longer the same relationship it had been in the previous courtship.[17] After accepting promises of marriage, some couples became formally or informally engaged. The betrothals were important intermediate steps in the matrimonial process: they could take place in public or in private, alone or with witnesses present, often without any official religious representation. After this ceremony the couple could start living openly as man and wife.[18]

Perhaps even more important than the couple's own understanding of their relationship is how that relationship was regarded by the community. Often it was mistaken for matrimony. In some cases, in spite of the absence of an official representative of the church, the union was considered valid.[19] That was the case, as Barahona tells us, of María Ibáñez de Manchuola and Martín de Asteburuaga. After pursuing her for two months,

> saying he would marry her according to the dictates of the Holy Mother Roman Church . . . and promising her that he would lead a good life with her, he gave her his hand, saying that he was marrying the declarer, and so, under this assurance, and because the said María Ibañez de Manchuela, [her mother] consented to it . . . believing that the said Martín would marry [her] . . . about eight months ago . . . in a bed in the house where her mother lived and lives . . . he corrupted her and took her virginity and cleanliness, having carnal access with her, and since that time also many and various times . . . they have slept together in one bed.[20]

In this case, because Martín expressed his marriage vows in the present tense, an act that was followed by sexual consummation, the marriage could be declared valid by the church. It appears that with respect to oral marriage vows, there was doubt and ambiguity about what constituted a legally binding marriage. The couple could never be sure whether the church would regard their union as legitimate, but what is important to understand is that as long as the promise of matrimony was sustained, no laws or rules of common behavior were considered to have been broken. Premarital sexual relations could continue with the understanding that the parties would eventually formalize their relationship through marriage. Only when these promises were broken did legal action ensue.

Documents reveal that during the sixteen and seventeenth centuries, repeated pastoral visits were made to Erauso's native Donostia-San Sebastián for the purpose of uprooting the sexual misconduct that took place after couples became engaged but were not formally married.[21] In Durango (Bizkaia), for example, there is the case of Martín de Barañao and Catalina de Eguilior, caught *in flagrante* one night in 1614 by a constable and his party who "had been alerted to the existence of a cohabiting couple."[22] They were apprehended and jailed. Eguilior asserted that "she had been found in her house with her husband, who had promised and given his word that he would marry her and do so legitimately as the church ordered."[23] Her defense was that she was married, albeit informally, to her husband, and, apparently, the relationship was openly known. In the village of Amorebieta (Bizkaia), in 1544, we find yet another case: that of Juan Ochoa de Asteiza and Mari López de Amecharri, who were charged by the authorities with cohabitation and the execution of marriage without ecclesiastical dispensation. According to some witnesses, the couple had married in public, linking hands and pledging to receive one another as partner, but apparently not in an official ceremony. When their case reached the courts because of their consanguinity, the couple declared that at the time of their "marriage" they were ignorant of being relatives, and the husband also insisted that she was his wife and that they had been married for four years.[24] These two cases illustrate how widespread the practice of cohabitation was in the Basque territories in these centuries, and how the definition of marriage was quite different from what it was in other parts of the Crown.

A woman who was deserted by her fiancé suffered serious social consequences: loss of social standing, decline in marriage prospects, and a decrease in the dowry amount commanded. The terms used to describe a woman who fell into this category reflect her loss of social status; she was referred to as *burlada* (deceived), *infamada* (disgraced), *disfamada* (defamed or slandered), *deshonrada* (dishonored), *desacreditada* (discredited), and *engañada* (tricked). As a result, she was open to public scorn, insults, and ridicule. With the loss of her reputation, she lost the social capital for negotiating her future.[25] Her compensation was either a promise of marriage, or a monetary settlement that would enable her to marry more or less within the social class she was born into. Married men whose situations prevented them from marrying appear to have used these kinds of offers. The monetary settlement could be used as a dowry for a woman who, without it, could not have hoped to marry. When the liaison had produced children, a sum was demanded for their upbringing.[26]

What is also noteworthy about all these cases of litigation cited by Barahona (cases that refer to the Basque territories) is that the damage to women's reputations did not extend to their families; it affected only the woman. In this sense, Basque families of that era seem to be quite unlike the families of Castile or those of other Iberian and Mediterranean countries in general, where a family's honor was adversely affected by a daughter's dishonor. The truth is that the damage done to a woman's reputation was due more to the failed marriage plans than to promiscuity or loss of virginity.[27] Unlike the dishonored women in Spanish Golden Age plays, who sought revenge against their victimizers, Basque women found more practical and less violent ways to redeem their honor.[28] Those lawsuits that were successful redressed lost sexual honor and reputation to a considerable extent, allowing women to regain their public status in society.

In fact, sometimes the parents only pretended to be unaware that their daughters had initiated sexual relations with their fiancés, in acts that occurred under their very roof. Provided that the relationship ended in formal matrimony, it was not considered illicit. This differs considerably from what was expected of women according to the standard of morality issued by the Council of Trent. In 1599, Fray Juan de la Cerda exhorted parents to watch over their daughters "like dragons," and teach them that obedience and modesty were essential to feminine purity. Fray Juan's advice reflects the widespread belief in Spain during the Counterreformation that chastity was a woman's most important virtue, and that it also was the most vulnerable feminine quality.[29] This mindset differs considerably from the one that characterized the relationships we have described.

A pastoral visitation made at the end of the seventeenth century to the Basque Country recorded and disapproved of these matrimonial agreements. The priests were constantly instructed to make the parishioners understand that an oral agreement was not the equivalent of matrimony unless a clergyman was present. It seems apparent that in this territory such a practice persisted until a very late date. More than a century had passed since the Council of Trent, and yet the new moral standard does not appear to have gained acceptance in the general public. The three most important rules established by The Council of Trent with regard to marriage are the following: its sacramental nature, its indissolubility, and the intervention of the church in its regulation.[30] The Tridentine disposition declared a marriage to be invalid if it was not performed "before a priest and two or three witnesses."[31] In the local customs that prevail throughout the Basque Country, these three requirements were repeatedly ignored. Starting in 1700, this state of affairs changed as the economic climate changed, and the church and state began to impose stricter control over the Basque Country.

As can be seen in the state of affairs that I briefly described, not only was the Basque Country far from adhering to the Tridentine ideal, it also diverged considerably from sixteenth- and seventeenth-century Castilian law. This law was very harsh on men who married women without obtaining the permission of the woman's parents. The punishment for this crime was exile and the loss of property, not just for the man but also for the witnesses of the marriage. The woman could also be disinherited by her parents. Lawsuits in the Basque territories, however, do not refer to the application of these laws. As late as the eighteenth century, the Bourbon monarch Carlos III was forced to enact a law regarding the rights of parents with respect to their children "because of the frequency with which persons of different social classes enter into marriage contracts without the permission of their parents."[32]

Unlike the ambiguity surrounding premarital sexual relations, cohabitation, on the other hand, was clearly regarded as a sin in the Basque Country. Although the Bizkaian *fueros* did not explicitly define cohabitation, it was understood to be a sexual relationship of some duration between a single woman and a cleric or a married man. It was considered to be a transgression against God, royal justice, the community, and morals. The victims of this kind of transgression were not specific individuals; the victims were society and the social order, since it involved the betrayal of religious vows and the disregard of the family as an institution.[33] Some Bizkaian lawsuits in which accusations of cohabitation were made seemed to have been the result of royal or ecclesiastical visitations that urged the local authorities to take action against such misconduct in their jurisdictions. It served the government's interest to combat "public sins," thereby increasing its regulation of public life and the preservation of social order, both at the national and local level. This form of misconduct was most commonly attacked by Bizkaian authorities between 1550 and 1630. After that, and perhaps sparked by the Tridentine measures, there was a decline in cohabitation cases in Bizkaia.[34] Cohabitation seemed to occur largely among people of the lower class, who could not marry because of poverty. Not having the means for a dowry, many women could not aspire to a formal marriage. The penalties for cohabitation were not unduly harsh; in general they were a mixture of fines or banishment. Customarily it was the female who was banished.[35]

Women's Participation in Civic Life

An examination of the legal documents from this period offers indirect access to understanding the role of Basque women in the society of that time. Barahona provides details that allow us to see women playing unusual roles. Women took part in the revolts that occurred in Bilbao during the1630s, caused by the imposition of a tax on salt that Bizkaians refused to pay. One of the important facets of the Salt Tax Revolt was the active participation of women in the street demonstrations, many of them the wives of artisans. Barahona recounts that during the repression of these revolts, one of the movement's leaders, Diego de Charta, escaped the authorities thanks to the intervention of some women, who carried him on their shoulders. "He escaped, running off in the direction of a hill named Zabalbide, and some women who were standing at a fountain carried him uphill to safety on their shoulders."[36] Also mentioned in this context are Bilbao's female porters, known for their strength and stamina in loading and unloading ships in the busy port. These episodes reveal that some women were involved in activities outside the scope of the activities traditionally associated with women, such as jobs that required physical strength, or active participation in the political life of the community.

What is clear is that we should not assume that the repressive and intimidating standards of conduct always determined women's conduct. As far as everyday life was concerned, the rules were more relaxed. For example, a woman's ability to engage in certain activities, or to manage her own house and control the family finances, was closely linked to her age, her civil status, and her social class. Women of the nobility were allowed to manage their inherited estates, and often they became the administrators of the household when the husbands were absent, away at war, or too busy with the government positions they held. Women of the lower class who did not have to be concerned with matters affecting their lineage enjoyed greater liberty of action. In the Basque Country, marriage did not seem to limit a woman's ability to engage in business:

> Eibar [Gipuzkoa] provides a significant example: in 1620 there were 235 heads of household, 106 of which were women; in addition there were four absent men, whose wives paid for them. Of these 106 women, fifteen are widows, two are maidens, and one is a lay sister. The rest of them, whom we can assume to be married, dedicate themselves to diverse occupations; among them we find two millers, a hospital administrator and an innkeeper. There is no mention of poverty; there is even a widow who pays 32 reales for herself, her daughter, and her daughter's husband. While the juridical norms differed for nobles and the common folk, at times practical reality created a distance between them, and at other times, it put them on an equal footing.[37]

Is the state of affairs in Eibar representative of the Basque Country in the Early Modern Age? We do not have similar studies regarding other Basque towns, and we lack studies that compare Basque towns to others in the Spanish realm. This is an aspect of society that must be researched in order to fully understand the world in which women lived in this or any other period. Needless to say, all these Basque women who acted outside the conventional boundaries were links in a chain to which Catalina de Erauso was firmly connected.

CHAPTER TEN

Women's Roles in Spain and the Americas

Examining Erauso's decision to live as a man requires a look into the choices she rejected and for what reasons. The previous chapter offered an initial approach to this question by outlining some aspects of Basque women's lives in the Early Modern Era. Now we will look at the roles assigned to women in the wider spaces of Spain and the Americas. By enlarging our focus this way, we will encompass the entire geographical area through which Erauso moved. This perspective will take into account what we know about Erauso from the standpoint of the kind of life she could have been expected to lead as a woman in the Basque Country, in Spain, or in the Americas during that period, had she chosen to do so. She could have had various reasons for transforming herself into a man; doubtlessly, one of them might have been her desire to escape from the fate that would certainly have awaited her as a woman.

Antecedents: The Middle Ages and the Renaissance

The view of women in Erauso's time, that is, during the Early Modern Age, was shaped by the great economic, social, and political changes that took place during the Renaissance. In her often-quoted article "Did Women Have a Renaissance?" Joan Kelly-Gadol wonders whether the events that transformed the feudal world into a humanistic world had any effect on women. She concludes that there was no renaissance for women during the Renaissance. I will review those points in her essay that are most relevant to understanding the spheres of female activity in the society of that period. By the time that Erauso made her entrance on the world's stage, those spheres had become well defined.

Kelly-Gadol observes that as family and political life were restructured in the transition from medieval society to the early modern state, Renaissance women suffered new constraints. The nobility and the bourgeoisie established chastity as the female norm, and restructured the relations of the sexes to one of female dependency and male domination.[1] In contrast to the latitude afforded to her by medieval literature, an analysis of courtly Renaissance literature reveals a new repression of the noblewoman's affective experience. In the relation of sexes, the Renaissance noblewoman held a position that was not only inferior to that of the male nobleman, but also inferior to her medieval pre-decessor.[2] In medieval courtly love, there was essential freedom in the relation between lovers. Courtly love, with vassalage as its structural model, allowed ideas of homage and mutuality to become incorporated in the concepts that governed heterosexual relations. For the aristocratic woman, the implications were liberating. On one hand the poets of courtly love separated the idea of love from marriage; on the other, they tied it to sex. By opting for a free and reciprocal heterosexual relationship outside marriage, the poets and the theorists of courtly love ignored the demand of patriarchal society for female chastity, in the sense of the woman's bondage to the marital bed. The reciprocal nature of passion-ate love required women to participate in adulterous sexual love. It is not surprising that the ideal lady in medieval courtly literature, the one who appeared in novels of chivalry or in poetry, fascinated women in later centuries.

Regardless of their social class or educational level, Spanish women of sixteenth and seventeenth centuries saw in her an image they wanted to emulate.[3] Courtly love was bound to Christianity because it cultivated deep and intense states of feeling. *Passion*, in Christian Europe, acquired a positive, spiritual meaning that classical ethics and classical erotic feeling had denied to it.[4] As a study regarding the iconography of Jesus as a mother reveals, "feminine" traits such as gentleness and compassion were at times assigned to men, even in the construction of a male deity. Medieval interest in the theme of God's motherhood, and the iconography of Jesus as mother, can be explained in part by the incorporation of feminine qualities in the construction of the male religiosity at a time when these attributes were socially and politically valuable in the development of new religious communities. Because sexual boundaries were quite fluid in the Middle Ages, many medieval authors found it easy to attribute characteristics stereotyped as "male" or "female" to persons of the opposite sex.[5]

With respect to the ideology of courtly love, Kelly-Gadol asks, what were the social conditions that fostered these conventions rather than the more common ones of chastity and female dependence?[6] During the Middle Ages, the system of feudalism permitted inheritance and administration of property by women. Women also exercised power during the absence of their warrior husbands. It was not unusual to find women as land-owners and managers of great estates, particularly during the period of the Crusades. In order to maintain his fief, the husband required his wife's support and even her inheri-tance. Given this, the husband was likely to tolerate his wife's "diversions" if she pur-sued them discreetly. For a feudal nobleman, it was more important to be sure about the security of his tenure than the legitimacy of his children.[7] Both Boccaccio's *Decameron* and Chaucer's *Canterbury Tales* clearly reflect greater mobility and sexual freedom for Euro-pean women during the medieval period. This changes dramatically when we approach the politics and culture that shaped the lady of the Renaissance. When the literature and the values of courtly love made their way to Italy, they were modified and purged of all sexual content. Dante and Castiglione, who transmitted the literary tradition of courtly love, redefined medieval notions of love and nobility. The idealized Renaissance lady that emerged in their works was removed from the equal position she had held in courtly literature, and was relegated to an inferior position, not only with respect to men but with respect to her medieval predecessor. A Renaissance lady's education directs her toward the social and cultural functions of the court. She commissions works of art, and gives gifts for literary works that are dedicated to her. But the court is her husband's, and her role in it is far removed from the position of social equality and even superiority granted to her by the medieval courtly literature. The few women who are admitted to court see themselves relegated to a passive marginal role: they are allowed to dance, but they do not participate in the conversations. When they do speak it is only in order to "moderate" the discussions directed by men. Not only does the noblewoman lose her social influence, she loses her own voice. She becomes a decorative moderator and a patron of the arts, whose role is to draw to her the artists and literati who lend distinction to her husband's court.[8]

Renaissance humanism represented an advance for women's education. It brought Latin literacy and classical learning to the daughters as well as to the sons of the nobility, but at the same time it contributed to a decline in noblewomen's influence over courtly society. Now both brothers and sisters are placed under male cultural authority. The girl of the medieval aristocracy had been brought up in the court of an illustrious lady. Now it is a male tutor who shapes her outlook. As humanists, male tutors suppressed romance and chivalry in order to further classical culture with all its patriarchal and misogynous bias.[9]

During the Renaissance, the lover (who in the Middle Ages appeared as a troubadour or a knight) gave way to a poet scholar. As sex vanished from the poetry, so did the woman, as well as the mutuality and interaction among lovers. Dante's Beatrice personifies this disappearance. In his poems, "he neither conjures her up nor seeks to melt with her. She remains shadowy and remote, for the focus of his poetry has shifted entirely to the subjective pole of love. It is the inner life, *his* inner life that Dante objectifies."[10] In his poems, the disappearance of the social world of the medieval court is what lies beneath the disappearance of sex and of the woman's body. In the poems of Dante and Petrarch, the woman does not respond sexually to her lover. The feelings she arouses in him are transformed into spiritual love, and become a narcissistic experience for the poet. The love of a lady in this kind of union is a step toward love of universal beauty.[11]

In this new ideology, spiritualized love *supplemented* men's sexual experience (both within and outside marriage), while it *defined* extramarital experience for the lady. Chastity had become the convention of Renaissance courts. The dominant institutions of Italian society would not support the adulterous sexuality of courtly love. Women, suffering from a loss of power in these institutions, could not make them responsive to their needs.[12]

Since cultural and political power was held by men, the norm of female chastity came to express the concerns of Renaissance noblemen as they moved into a new status as a hereditary-dependent class. In this changed situation, legitimacy became a significant factor. While the monarchs of Europe were consolidating and centralizing their states, they were at the same time protecting the privileges of the nobility and suppressing feudal power. The nobility began to be stabilized; new laws began to limit and regulate membership in a hereditary aristocratic class, prompting concern with legitimacy and purity of blood. The demand for female chastity doubtlessly addressed this concern.[13]

With respect to the family, the Italian humanists defined a bourgeois code of sexual roles that placed the male in the public sphere and secluded the female in the home. It was a code that required social skills of him, and chastity and maternity of her. The relative sexual and social equality enjoyed by women in the past was left behind.

Mariló Vigil sums up the social importance of virginity and feminine chastity as it concerned the family. The father's honor as well as that of the entire family was dependent on the wife's fidelity and the daughters' virginity. This applied in all the social classes. Marriage contracts signed by peasants and tradesmen mentioned family honor, which was based on the virginity of the intended bride. In Spanish Golden Age literature, and particularly in the plays dealing with honor, a stain on one's honor can only be removed by a bloody revenge, in which the daughter dies at the hand of her father, or the wife dies at the hands of her husband.[14] As was pointed out in the previous chapter, the Basque Country was very different with respect to such matters. A woman's virginity was not a virtue in and of itself, nor did premarital sex and the loss of virginity represent a dishonor for the family.

In his well-known study of Spanish Baroque culture, *La cultura del barroco* (1975), José Antonio Maravall notes that the concept of conjugal honor represents an attempt to "exercise physical control of family succession, both as it applies to the psychological and moral makeup of the progeny, and the patrimonial system of inheritance."[15] But the concept of honor does not just involve paternity and private property; what was in play was "an entire regime that organizes and transmits social power; should that regime be weakened through a relaxation of the rules, women, by using the lure of their sexual attraction, might be able to seize control of society."[16] Such a seizure of social power had to be avoided at any cost.

In short, as the modern European state emerged and began to organize society, a new division between public and private life made itself felt. While the nobility in general suffered a loss of power, the noblewoman suffered an even deeper and wider loss: she lost the possibility of exercising independent power that had been granted to her in feudal society; and was subordinated to the interests of her husband and family.[17]

Humanism, which had offered society a more liberating view of life, had just the opposite effect on women. The existing tensions caused an explosion of misogyny and a proliferation of moral theories whose intent was to subordinate women. Those humanists, the thinkers who most clearly expressed a bourgeois view of the world, were the same ones who firmly insisted that women be restricted to performing domestic roles. During the entire Early Modern Age and, above all, following the Council of Trent, the ideological discourse that was transmitted—in literature as well as in the persecution of witches— represented a real attack on women, who were seen as sexual temptresses and the potential bearers of sin.[18] This was the state of affairs inherited by the sixteenth and seventeenth centuries.

Women in the Sixteenth and Seventeenth Centuries: What Fate Did Erauso Reject?

Leaving aside for the moment the issues of transvestism and Erauso's sexuality, we must consider the life choices that were available to her in the Spain of her time. In other words, from what fate was she escaping? An examination of her life story would be incomplete without considering hypothetically what would have been her fate, *de facto*—a fate on which she turned her back.

During this period a woman's social position was determined by her role in the family. Let us then consider what choices were open to Catalina de Erauso. One choice, the one that had been made for her and for her sisters, was life in the convent.

> At all levels of the aristocracy (high, middle, low), entering the convent was the favored solution for daughters whose parents could not provide a dowry that would enable them to marry in their social class. Either because of economic difficulties, or because there were several sisters and the parents could only afford to marry off one of them, or because they did not want to encumber too much of the estate to be inherited by the oldest son . . . as the economic situation became more difficult and the number of dowries needed increased, the placement of daughters became a worrisome problem, especially for the middle class and lower aristocracy.[19]

In general, the dowry needed to enter the convent was smaller than the one required in arranging good marriages for young women. With this choice, the family was thus able to save money, increasing the fortune to be inherited by the male children or the amount of the dowry for the sister that would marry; or it would at least increase the wealth, whether little or great, at the disposal of the oldest son. The lower classes, however, generally could not afford the dowry needed to enter the convent; and so, for these poor women, there were even fewer life paths.[20] A woman in a convent enjoyed a social status that was superior to that of an unmarried woman, and was, for all intents and purposes, comparable to that of a married woman. For three of Erauso's sisters—Mari Juan, Isabel, and Jacinta—the convent became their destiny. Only one of the five Erauso sisters, Mariana, would eventually marry.

The large increase in the number of women living in the cloister during the Early Modern Age is related to the post-Tridentine proliferation of new religious orders and foundations in Catholic Europe. For many different groups of women, and for varying reasons, religious life appeared as a viable alternative to marriage. Some had a religious calling; others wanted to avoid secular marriage, cultivate their intellect, or find companionship in their lonely widowhoods.[21] Throughout the Early Modern Age, convents were the centers of instruction par excellence for women; even as late as the nineteenth century they housed the largest number of women receiving a formal education. Later, from the sixteenth century on, convents created schools exclusively for women. Those who came to them were women with few economic means from the middle classes, and daughters of noblemen and widowers. The novices received formal instruction and learned to read Latin, since it was expected that they would choose a religious life.[22] Outside the convents, only a small number of upper-class women learned to read and write, and they were usually taught by private tutors in their homes. Evidence of how important convents were in the intellectual and cultural lives of women can be seen in the variety of literature that was produced during this period. That literature reflects a high level of education that encompassed both secular and religious subjects. Many of these convent writings are only now coming to light in numerous research studies that give us new insights regarding the cultural atmosphere that characterized these institutions. "Living in environments that validated their intellectual and spiritual capacities, female religious often infused their texts with a sense of confidence and investment in women's endeavors."[23] Lisa Vollendorf points out that literacy among women of varying class and ethnic background begs fundamental questions about women's access to formal and informal education. Since there has been little access to primary texts, research in this area is often limited to guesswork. The classification of a person's educational level might be based, for example, on whether that person could sign her name on legal documents. These gauges of literacy have limited validity.[24] To a degree, the recent research regarding convent writing during the Early Modern Age can compensate for our lack of documentation regarding the level of education attained by women in these religious institutions. The convent wall functioned as both a barrier and a link between the religious communities and the outside world. The nuns' convents, far from being divorced from the wider world, represented spaces from which a woman (having no other alternative) was supposed to exercise political, ideological, and religious influence. Santa Teresa can serve as an example: "As her tireless search for financial backing suggests, religious women were connected to the outside world through economic necessity, educational background, personal experience, political savoir faire and family ties."[25] These connections are also reflected in the texts written within the convent walls. One of those writers, the nun Valentina Pinelo (born in the 1500s) advocated raising girls in convents because there they received a superior education, unlike the external world where "the boys have teachers and the girls have nursemaids." In her writings she highlights the superior access to education that girls have in convents, where they learn to read, write, "speak with measured words," and "act with proper self-discipline."[26]

Social class obviously affected educational opportunities, and while it is possible to speak of an improvement (relatively speaking) in the level of education for the upper and middle classes during the Early Modern Age, most of the peasantry was illiterate. Literacy rates improved as a consequence of the proliferation of convents and religious foundations and the widespread printing of books. In the sixteenth and seventeenth centuries, estimates fixed men's literacy at 40 percent and women's at 25 percent.

Although literacy varied by social class and urban or rural living, most studies indicate that women's literacy lagged behind men's.[27] In colonial America, the situation was even worse. There was an enormous mass of illiterates, predominantly women, including those who belonged to the upper social sectors. In general, not even the women of the nobility knew how to read.[28]

What other life paths were open to Erauso? Having rejected a religious life, what kind of life could she have expected as a *doncella,* or maiden, in the Spain of her time? Vigil examines in detail the ideal figure of the maiden as it is reflected in the writings of the moralists of the Baroque period; she is depicted as an obedient, humble, modest, discrete, shy, and withdrawn young woman. In her we find an entire compendium of characteristics that excludes agency; a woman is seen as a patient and passive subject to whom things happen. From the sixteenth through the seventeenth centuries, there was no variation in this stereotyped model of ideal womanhood. Her passivity extended even to her speech: maidens were to speak little, and, preferably, to live in solitude and seclusion. When a maiden ventured out, she was required, of course, to be accompanied by her mother or a *dueña* (female chaperone); she had to maintain a certain composure, that was described by the humanist Juan Luis Vives in the following way: "Her step should be neither too quick, nor too slow; and if she should come across a group of people, she should demonstrate good upbringing in her expression and manner." Moreover, "she should not look at men to see if they are looking at her."[29] Nor ought she be allowed to lean out of her window in order to look at or speak to young men who are passing in the street. In other words, she was made to submit to confinement, keep silent, and obey an authority that solely represented the interests of her father, and later, her husband. To this inventory of proscribed behaviors yet another admonition was added: she was to suppress her somewhat culpable and innate sensuality, because it might have awakened sinful desires in innocent men who could not be responsible for their actions.

The image of this ideal, demure, shy woman, who lives shut away from society, appears in Spanish Golden Age literature, particularly in the novels of Cervantes. He, as well as Luis Vives and other more tolerant Humanist writers, believed that women who did not behave properly did so out of ignorance, not evil; therefore, it was thought that it was preferable to give women a good Christian education and allow them some degree of freedom.[30] Other Spanish Golden Age writers, like Fray Luis de León, were opposed to educating women and they based their arguments on what was hypothetically thought to be the "natural" intellectual inferiority of the female.[31] We should not imagine that the idealized image we find in literature is a true portrayal of the young women of that period; rather it embodies an ideal standard of conduct to which all unmarried young women were supposed to aspire. Antonio de Guevara, a sixteenth-century didactic writer, points out that women do not respond well to threats, and that it is preferable to use persuasion to induce them to behave in the desired manner. Some ecclesiastical moralists seemed to admit that there was some truth in that. Juan de Soto, for example, recognized that keeping women locked away is futile because "if she is not her own keeper, it would be like trying to stem the tide."[32] It would be difficult indeed to imagine Catalina de Erauso having to comply with such restrictions of conduct.

During this period, society's idealization of chastity and motherhood placed single women at risk. Because of the absence of male protective figures in their lives, unmarried or single women, widows, and abandoned wives were exposed to disapprobation and scrutiny.[33] Women who did not marry found themselves marginalized by society, and often faced financial hardship: "Forbidden from running businesses or seeking legal recourse, they lacked the legitimacy afforded women in traditional family units."[34] Nevertheless, we find single women of all social classes positioning themselves as educators, leaders, and reformers, not to mention those who became prostitutes, healers, sorceresses, seamstresses, and street sellers. Some even managed small businesses, convents, and schools.

Let us now suppose that Erauso had chosen the third option: marriage. According to the Christian view of marital authority that prevailed during the sixteenth and seventeenth centuries, married women should obey their husbands, who should be amiable, gentle, and affectionate with them. The married woman's role was to be her husband's helpmate in all the household affairs and in the Christian upbringing of their children. Since both social and financial power was exercised by the man, every woman was dependent on her husband's good will for her subsistence. The kind of education given to women not only prevented them from being able to function in any but the domestic sphere, it also placed them in a position of cultural and psychological dependency with respect to their husbands.[35] Numerous moral treatises devoted to the conduct of married women appeared during these centuries; among the most important are Fray Luis de León's *La perfecta casada* (The Perfect Wife, 1583), Antonio Herrera de Salcedo's *El espejo de la perfecta casada* (The Perfect Wife's Mirror, 1637); as well as moral treatises that applied to women in general: Juan Luis Vives' *De Institutione Feminae Christiana* (Instruction of a Christian Woman, 1528), Juan de la Cerda's *Vida política de todos los estados de las mujeres* (Good Conduct for Women of All Classes, 1599), and Juan de Espinosa's *Diálogo en laude de las mujeres* (Dialogue in Praise of Women, 1580).

Influential ecclesiastical leaders advocated strict rules that restricted a woman's orbit: she should live sheltered from the world and devote herself to domestic activities and to reading devout books and pedagogical treatises.[36] Once she was married, a woman's worldly contacts ceased, and her social life was reduced to visiting the ill and attending religious ceremonies and festivities. In the countryside, they were allowed to participate in farming tasks. We should also bear in mind that sixteenth- and seventeenth-century Spanish society was obsessed with *limpieza de sangre* or purity of blood; that is, an untainted Christian lineage. Yet even the *cristianas viejas* (women who could trace their lineage), as well as the *conversas* ("those who had been 'converted'"), were forced to live in a world of isolation and minimal freedom.[37]

The story of a thirty-four-year-old woman, Bernarda Manuela, who was prosecuted in 1650 by the Inquisition for practicing Judaism, tells us a great deal about marital relationships during that time. In her deposition she described her experience as a married woman in Seville; she testified that she went out only to go to church or to visit the family, and that her husband followed her and "did not allow her to communicate with anybody." Manuela also stated that for six months while she lived in the Triana neighborhood of Seville, in a remote spot near the river, she talked to only one person outside her family.[38] While we cannot say that her situation is representative of that of other women, it appears that this degree of isolation was not unusual during that time. The memorial that Manuela wrote in her own defense provides a valuable document about normal gender expectations. In it, the defendant emphasized her religious and domestic obedience and her chastity; she portrayed a life of dedication to her husband and children, in activities totally restricted to her home.[39]

Although this image of the "ideal woman" was given to women as a model, that did not necessarily mean they patterned themselves after it. As time went on, and particularly during the seventeenth century, women became "more talkative; more given to appearing at their windows; more fond of wandering about in the streets, and paying visits to friends; more fond of *fiestas* and less fond of staying at home, where their duties are neglected."[40] Social class was also a determining factor in the gender expectations prescribed by the moralists. Keeping women confined to their homes continued to be the rule for those classes in which the honor code was all-important; that is, the urban middle and upper classes: "It is clear that for the female servants and for the teeming female proletarian class of that period, this rule didn't apply. Nor did it apply for young rural women."[41] Nevertheless, it is not clear that rural women enjoyed a greater degree of freedom than city women. Social control was probably more rigorous in the countryside, even though there it was not necessary to keep women confined to their homes. From the literary perspective, the scanty presence of popular ballads about warrior women in Spain seems to confirm that lower-class women suffered from the same lack of freedom as did upper-class women. In his *Romancero general*, a ballad collection, Agustín Durán provides only four seventeenth-century examples based on that theme, and these clearly echo other European models.[42] Although in general single women seemed to be at a disadvantage, we should not lose sight of the fact that there were individual women who managed to carve out their own places in society. Lisa Vollendorf reports, for example, that in port cities like Seville, some women whose husbands left for the Americas found business opportunities. She also notes that aristocratic women exercised control over social and political affairs. While their numbers were few, the very existence of this group of women may be explained in part because during that period Spanish women enjoyed better legal protection than many of their contemporaries in western Europe.[43]

In conclusion, what can we say about the life that Erauso would have had had she lived as a woman? One fact is clear: had she not ceased being Catalina by transforming herself into Antonio, her story would have ended in that chestnut grove where she told us that she cut off her hair and fashioned a man's suit out of her nun's habit. Had she not disguised her sex, her fate would have been cast: she would have been picked up and returned to the convent or to her home, or she would have been forced to join the ranks of a marginalized female underclass, far removed from the principles of honor and respectability to which her birth entitled her. As we noted previously, a woman who traveled alone risked being robbed or sexually attacked; in fact, it was taken for granted that the woman who traveled alone was a prostitute.

It seems clear, then, that had Erauso continued her life as a woman, her adventures would never have taken place. When she escaped from the convent and decided to conceal her sexual identity, she did so because she had no choice. Abandoning the convent was tantamount to rejecting a nun's life. On the other hand, the secular life of a young maiden would have meant being confined in a family home that she could barely remember, since she had left it when she was only four years old. She chose, instead, to follow the paths chosen by her relatives and countrymen: to leave, to travel, to work, to see the world, even go to the Americas; and once there, who could tell? But to do this was incompatible with being a woman. One of the two choices must be renounced. Erauso renounced being a woman and embraced the male gender: this would be her safe-conduct for a life of independent choices and numerous possibilities.

New Spaces for Women in Seventeenth–Century America

From the very first moment when Europeans set foot in the Americas, the New World inspired people to write letters and reports describing the exotic and marvelous novelties they found. These writings satisfied the insatiable desire for news that had been generated by the discovery of the new lands. But if in the period of discovery and conquest it was the description of the flora, the fauna, and the customs of the indigenous people that inspired wonder, in the seventeenth century what captured the attention of the public were the chronicles detailing the improbable lives of the colonists, lives packed full of scandal and of hardships that would have been unimaginable in their native lands. The timeless popular taste for scandal linked up with the Baroque penchant for the abnormal, the contradictory, the strange, and the "monstrous."[44]

The colonial society of New Spain offered both the limitations and the opportunities that are characteristic of a society in flux. As Kathleen Ann Myers points out, an analysis of the narrative construction of the *Autobiografía* "helps us better understand how Catalina's life reflected Spain's encounter with the Americas—how the ad hoc nature of life in a new colony or on the frontier often pushed literary, historical and societal conventions to new limits."[45] While colonial society was based on a firm hierarchical structure, it offered opportunities for social mobility at the same time. In addition, given a diverse population that did not fit into the old European schemes of social organization, allowances had to be made for those who lived at the margins of society.[46] While singleness, illegitimate relations, and abandonment were the exception rather than the rule in the Spain of that period, they were commonplace in the New World. Historians believe that almost 40 percent of Spanish American couples living together in the seventeenth century were not officially married.[47] We should remember, however, (as we noted when we examined the conditions of a Basque woman's life in Chapter 9) that in the rural areas of the Basque Country there was also a proliferation of illegitimate children during this same time period. Therefore, it is possible that these situations were more common than one might be led to believe.

These new realities in which a woman could not depend on a man's support enlarged the spheres of economic activity available to her. Often she found herself in a situation where she was forced to find the means to support herself and her family. In Latin America, women were in charge of estates engaged in agriculture or cattle raising or, like Erauso, working as storekeepers and wholesaler suppliers. But there were also women working in the more humble occupations: farm workers, teachers, embroiderers, weavers, actresses, and healers.[48] Life in the new territories created conditions that often allowed women to take over for husbands who had died; or, as a few documented cases have revealed, to work alongside their lovers as nurses and soldiers, since wives were often absent. Still other historical sources mention women who made their mark in the New World as colonizers, governors, explorers, and soldiers.[49]

The Creole family to whom the celebrated Mexican writer Sor Juana Inés de la Cruz was born is emblematic of the mobility that characterized the society of New Spain. Her Creole mother, Isabel Ramírez, established an informal union with a Basque captain, Pedro Manuel de Asbaje; she bore him three children out of wedlock, one of whom was Sor Juana. It is possible that theirs was a consensual relationship, one that could not be formalized until the male ceased being a government bureaucrat, since marriages to local women were forbidden to Spanish-born men serving the Crown. Some of these consensual unions resulted in marriage, others in abandonment. Abandonment was what happened to Sor Juana, her mother, and her sisters. Later, the mother established another union with an already married neighboring farmer; a son and two daughters were born of that union. With these six children, all born out of wedlock, she lived a life of economic independence by managing the estate she had inherited, and by farming and raising livestock. One of her daughters, abandoned shortly after her marriage, formed a new union with a man with whom she had four children out of wedlock. Still another daughter gave birth to a girl out of wedlock, who was taken to the convent so that Sor Juana could raise her. This family's situation demonstrates the difficulties that Creole women were likely to experience; they frequently had to deal with abandonment, illegitimate children, and unions not formalized by marriage.[50]

To guarantee its own survival, colonial society had to make allowances for these situations. Although social ideals and rules were still maintained,

> for society to function, it was necessary to allow some leniency in their compliance . . . This explains the ease with which women were permitted to engage in economic activities in which it had not been foreseen that they might have to participate, or the frequency with which illegitimate birth is overlooked in religious matters, or in arranging an advantageous marriage, or in acquiring prestigious social positions. In all these instances, channels

are opened to allow women who find themselves in those "improper" situations to regain social status, and to become "unblemished" members of society.[51]

Erauso herself experienced something like this when she returned to Latin America. In spite of the fact that her sexual disguise was widely known, she regained her full standing as a member of society and was able to work as a mule driver until her death.

The high frequency of illegitimate relationships between men of the higher social classes and women of mixed "caste" did not affect the traditional importance attached to a woman's virtue as it related to family honor. For a woman, the ideal was to become a wife and mother, or a nun, to be jealously guarded in her husband's home or in a convent. That was the goal to which women seeking social prestige aspired. It was not that the traditional norms of behavior had been altered, but rather that generalized practices had broadened the margins of social acceptance. In any case, the leniency that we have been describing has clear limits, and one might say that it ended at that point where the foundations of the social structure were questioned or threatened. When these informal relationships affected the social institutional order, a conflict emerged: for example, when a *mulata* ex-slave inherited the land and wealth of a respectable Creole family, or when a man rejected marriage to a "decent" Creole woman, choosing instead to form a relationship with a woman of a much lower social class.[52]

In short, as Duby and Perrot observe:

> Since its beginnings in the sixteenth century, the society of New Spain develops and organizes itself primarily according to rules in which more laxity is allowed in the enforcement of social codes of behavior. Viewed from this perspective, the process followed in Spain itself is just the opposite. As was the case in all of Europe, after the successive reforms a tightening occurs in the enforcement of social regulations, reflected above all in the application and interpretation of Tridentine policies concerning marriage, celibacy and the control of family life . . . This gives rise to . . . an increased questioning of women's responsibility and trustworthiness. It is what Claire Guilhem has defined as the "devaluation of the feminine word." In its development, therefore, the society of New Spain takes a direction which is very different from the one followed in the [Iberian] peninsula and in Europe in general.[53]

How were women in the Americas affected by the fact that the Spanish Crown was trying to establish its rules in a land that was thousands of miles away? In this context, Myers mentions a detail that is highly relevant: that most of Erauso's adventures took place in the non-urban areas of Peru, and that "even after receiving papal permission to remain in male garb, she chose to return to America, and what is more, to a new viceroyalty and to a career that did not require permanent residency in a city." Not only was it easier for her to live a heterodox life in the Americas; once there, she preferred to live in territories far from the administrative, moral, and social machinery of the cities, that are connected more closely to Madrid and to the Crown in general.[54]

In conclusion, Erauso encountered a less rigid social code in this new American context, one that allowed those persons normally excluded from the traditional social order to carve out a place for themselves. In the Americas new possibilities opened up, possibilities that—conflictive though they may be—do not totally marginalize a heterodox person. How could Erauso have not found herself more comfortable in the atmosphere of freedom that characterized the New World? And how could she not fail to leave Spain as soon as she could return to the Americas? The existence of a less rigid code of conduct, allowing wide margins within which people could live their lives with greater freedom of action, explained the spatial freedom Erauso discovered during her footloose life in the Americas. And it also explains why she would no longer want to return to Spain.

House where Catalina de Erauso may have died (Ayacucho, Peru).
Painting by Francisco de Zabala. Delphi Museum, New York.

CHAPTER ELEVEN

From Catalina to Antonio: Sex and Gender in Catalina de Erauso's *Autobiografía*

Having considered some important aspects of women's social and economic realities during the Early Modern Age, and the role that would have been assigned to Erauso in that society, I will now conclude my study by focusing my attention on the role that she created for herself, a role directly related to sex ideology and the construction of gender. First, I will briefly address the attitudes toward cross-dressing throughout the ages. Most studies regarding Erauso's transvestism have linked it solely to her problematic sexual identity. My own approach to the question is to place it within the broader discourse of European attitudes toward the phenomenon, a discourse that allows us to view this phenomenon in terms of its motivations, its consequences, and its socioeconomic realities. To fully appreciate the significance of Erauso's individual case, we must profile it specifically against the background of sixteenth- and seventeenth-century European cross-dressing. This will let us see more clearly not only how she fit into the tradition, but also—and more importantly—how she deviated from it. While we do not know how many tales regarding disguised women circulated in Erauso's native Donostia-San Sebastián, I think it likely that she was acquainted with the theme, either in accounts based on real cases, or in fictitious narratives transmitted through the oral storytelling tradition. The awareness of this tradition must have figured in her decision to disguise herself as a man just after leaving the convent. Stories about "manly women" were well-liked by the masses, as demonstrated by the enormous popularity that Erauso's own story later enjoyed. I will also address the legal condemnation of cross-dressing, and in view of that condemnation, explore the reasons why it was tolerated in Erauso's case.

Recent research studies have addressed the question of Erauso's homosexuality. While some episodes of the *Autobiografía* contain intimations of it, it is in a broadside, the *Tercera Relación* (Third Account)[1] that she is clearly depicted as having fallen in love with another woman, even offering to enter a convent with her. Nevertheless, in any discussion of sex and gender with respect to Erauso, I believe that the central issue is not whether she was attracted to women or not, but rather how she defined herself sexually as an individual. Was Erauso a man or a woman? We know that she was born a female, and we have no reason to believe that her anomaly might be based on physiological reasons. We should remember that when she confessed to the Bishop of Guamanga, revealing her secret, she offered to submit to a physical examination. The "matrons" who examined her declared her to be a virgin, adding no additional information that might lead us to believe that they discovered any physical peculiarity. Does this mean that she was a woman? In the following pages, I will argue that she was a woman only physically. Hers is a case in which sex and gender are totally divorced; that is, in her we find an individual who was biologically a woman, but psychologically a man. Erauso's transvestism is total and definitive; far from being a disguise, a man's attire becomes her own skin. What was most significant in Erauso's life is that she became a man; that she was born a woman was simply an accident of nature.

The text of the *Autobiografía* contains evidence that suggests Erauso's homosexuality; in my opinion, she was in fact homosexual. Nevertheless, before providing support for my interpretation through a close examination of the text, I think an appropriate starting point would be to provide a definition of homosexuality as it was understood during her time. During that period, human sexuality was entirely phallocentric; sexual desire and love were feelings that women could experience only with men. The only possible sexual love was heterosexual, and the only sexual act consisted in penetration. So completely was the phallus identified with the sexual act that many women who fell in love with other women could not identify their feelings; they believed that if they felt sexually attracted to other women it was because they really were men and not women. In these cases, we witness a total confusion of gender identity.

Finally, in our discussion of homosexuality, we will examine those episodes that suggest erotic relationships between Erauso and other women. In the absence of conclusive proof, we will speculate about this possibility, and outline what the social attitudes toward these kinds of relationships would have been during her time. A consideration of all these historical, cultural, and social factors will provide a coherent framework for interpreting Erauso's life choices and their significance in the world in which she lived.

Clothes Make the Man: Female Transvestism in Sixteenth- and Seventeenth-Century Europe

The position taken by the Christian church with respect to cross-dressing was based on the biblical text in Deuteronomy (22:5): "There is not to be a man's item on a woman, a man is not to clothe himself in the garment of a woman, for an abomination of YHWH your God is anyone doing these!" Nevertheless, during most of its history, Christianity was not particularly hostile to women who donned men's attire, showing a tolerance that can be explained in the light of medieval notions regarding women's inferiority to men. According to these, woman is both inferior and subordinate to man because she represents the less rational part of the soul, while man represents its more rational part. In view of this, when a woman dresses as a man—and especially if she remains a virgin—she repudiates her own sexuality and in so doing becomes a better and more rational being; she is elevated. On the other hand, should a man dress as a woman, he loses his superior status and becomes less rational; in other words, he is demeaned.[2]

Fourth-century ecclesiastical texts like those of Saint Jerome and Saint Ambrose urge women to live like men and attain a higher spiritual level, provided, of course, that their acts do not represent a threat to men. A Catholic hagiographic tradition that dates back to the fifth century includes the life stories of numerous transvestite women, including Margaret of Antioch, Eugenia of Alexandria, and Joan of Arc. Their biographies, which were given the seal of approval by the church, were enormously popular.[3] It was the desire to imitate the male Christ and preserve one's virginity—thus attaining greater virtue—that led these women to assume masculine dress in service, as one critic puts it, to an ideal of androgynous perfection. Calderón de la Barca's play, *El José de las mujeres* (The Women's Joseph) demonstrated that the tradition of female transvestite saints had not disappeared from view in seventeenth-century Spain.[4]

However, acceptable female transvestism had its limits. When a woman usurped a man's role, there were consequences. Joan of Arc offers an example. During her trial (1412), her transvestism was adduced as one of the most important reasons for condemning and executing her. That a woman might dress as a man out of religious motives (following the model of Christ) was permissible, but that she should compete with men in traditional male activities such as weapons and warfare was not. During that time, a woman who did so, and did it well, would normally wind up being accused of witchcraft.

According to Stephanie Merrim, the fact that even in the face of criticism Pope Urban VIII defended Erauso suggests that her life held some religious value. In this context, the tradition of female transvestite saints comes to mind. In her *Pedimento* (Petition), her *Autobiografía,* and several of her *certificaciones,* she emphasizes her virginity, and "the rectitude and rare purity in which she has lived and lives."[5] These arguments, used in her self-defense, possess enormous religious resonance. Her virginity, verified by the church and by the king, was what protected her from civil and ecclesiastical punishment.[6] Although she had passed for a man, because she was a virgin she had not challenged the social order. It is her virginity, together with the association of masculinity and virtue that underlies Erauso's defense.[7]

The European tradition of transvestism also needs to be addressed. Leaving aside the studies that deal with the literary representations of the phenomenon, we will draw mainly on the research done by Rudolph M. Dekker and Lotte C. Van de Pol, that provides information about the everyday lives of real women. Using newspapers, chronicles, medical treatises, collections of anecdotes, and travel reports as their source material, they investigated the cases of 119 women living as men in the Netherlands between 1550 and 1830. Through an examination of multiple aspects of cross-dressing, they offer a comprehensive view of a phenomenon that was more common during that period than might be expected. Since they include findings regarding cases of transvestism, not only in Holland, but also in Denmark, France, England, Italy, and Spain, it is clear that the tradition of cross-dressing had a scope that encompassed all of Europe.[8] In Spain and in the New World, we find cases of women who fought or dressed as men; for example, in chronicle narratives Inés Suárez and María de Estrada are both described as valiant soldiers during the Conquest of the Americas. News items published in Toledo (1538) mention the transvestite soldier Juliana de Cobos, who, like Erauso, was rewarded by the king of Spain for her military service.[9]

The theme of the *mujer varonil* (the manly woman) passes rapidly to literature and can be found in many plays, prints, and operas, as well as in popular songs, novels, memoirs, and fictionalized biographies.[10] In seventeenth-century Spanish drama, the female disguised as a man was an enormously popular stock character, appearing in the plays of Calderón de la Barca, Tirso de Molina, and Lope de Vega—in short, in the entire repertory of every distinguished dramatist. The "manly woman" is the antithesis of the traditional heroine; her conduct is totally at odds with the expected mores of feminine behavior.[11] Lope de Vega used this type in 113 of his plays, and in his *Arte nuevo de hacer comedias* (The New Art of Writing Plays) he acknowledges that women disguised as men figure among the public's favorite characters. The "manly woman" appears in Spanish drama much more than she does in the plays of any other European country, where her presence is relatively minimal.[12] That this figure had a popular appeal that crossed all boundaries is demonstrated by the many translations that circulated throughout Europe; for example, once the manuscript of Erauso's autobiography was "rediscovered" in the eighteenth century, it was translated into many languages. Also underlining the popularity of this theme is the existence of numerous versions of the ballad "La doncella guerrera" (The Warrior Maiden), widely known throughout the Spanish peninsula.[13] In and of itself, the repeated appearance of this figure in diverse literary genres is both proof and means by which the tradition of female cross-dressing was transmitted.

Although only Dekker and Van de Pol have attempted a systematic study of the phenomenon with respect to Holland, their study is not exhaustive. They admit that their findings regarding the 119 known cases probably represent only the tip of the iceberg. What appears to be irrefutable is that these cases were not incidental, but were part of a tradition of cross-dressing of which these women were well aware.[14] In their study, one of the variations they examine is how long women were able to maintain their masculine identity. One-quarter of these Dutch women were discovered within a few days or even hours; another quarter were able to sustain their role for between a month and six months. The remaining half lived longer than six months as a man, and some of them for more than ten years. Occasionally, women who were unmasked more than once, and then sentenced, later resumed their lives as men.[15] This would be the small group of female cross-dressers into which Catalina de Erauso would fit.

The duration of the disguise was often determined by the reasons for assuming it. During the sixteenth and seventeenth centuries, it was socially acceptable for a woman to don a man's attire; for example, when she traveled—above all if she were alone or accompanied by another woman. The female who journeyed alone ran a high risk of being robbed, sexually attacked, or physically injured. Many women who sought greater freedom of movement must have chosen to attempt to pass for men. This would have been especially true during an era when it was thought that garments unquestionably told one's sex, and there was no need to scrutinize any other physical features to determine gender.[16]

A quick look at the sexual crimes committed in Bizkaia during the sixteenth and seventeenth centuries clearly reveals that women faced substantial dangers when they found themselves in remote or uninhabited places. In the documents that record litigations arising from sexual attacks, it is constantly alleged that these occurred "in barren and deserted places."[17]

It is understandable, therefore, that it was not only acceptable but also recommended that in the interest of their own physical protection women disguise themselves as men for a short time. Transvestism was also acceptable on other occasions: during carnival festivities, during riots, or for erotic play. Sometimes this temporary cross-dressing could turn out to be the beginning of a longer transformation than the one originally intended. It is not difficult to imagine that some of these women, having tasted the new freedom available to them while in male disguise, decided to prolong the deceit or practice it more frequently.[18] The soldier Diego Duque de Estrada, for example, recounts in his autobiography how his lover would travel in male garb for safety but then became so attached to the disguise that she chose to continue living dressed as a man for extended periods.[19]

As we reflect on the lives of women who decided to live disguised as men for extended periods of time, the first question that arises is, what was the reason that drove them to it? Why did all these women transform themselves into men? In some cases we learn about their lives by their own depositions when they are prosecuted for cross-dressing. One must bear in mind that to a certain degree, the stories they tell are dictated primarily by the desire to present motives that are socially acceptable, or justifiable in a court of law, or acceptable to the women themselves.

While the reasons given are very diverse, there are underlying patterns. In general, women mention three kinds of personal motives: romantic, patriotic, and economic. The romantic ones are understandable in view of the following facts. A substantial number of the men who went to the Indies never returned. As a rule the ships did not carry women aboard; therefore, for those women who did not want to be parted from their lovers or husbands, their best chance was to don men's garb and sign up on ships bound for the New World as a soldier or a sailor. As a result, there was a group of women who journeyed to the New World in male disguise, either to be reunited with their lovers or to follow their husbands. I mention the professions soldier and sailor because these were the most frequently mentioned in the study regarding Holland; the situation was probably similar in other countries, but we have no comparable studies. Once in the New World, women found opportunities that were far more promising than the ones they left behind. On the one hand, the shortage of white females in the colonial population increased their likelihood of marrying; on the other, because social norms were much more permissive in the new continent, a spotless past was not a requisite for marriage. In addition, a white woman, regardless of how unsavory her past might have been, was still considered greatly superior to any of the native women.[20]

The defense of the homeland was another legitimate reason given by women who chose to become soldiers. It appears that during periods of war the numbers of women dressed as men increased. The social and economic dislocation and the demand for soldiers and sailors doubtlessly reinforced the decision to resort to cross-dressing. A recurrent motif in the tales about female soldiers is their appearance in the court, along with a royal recompense for their service. Probably motivated by patriotism and loyalty to the king, these women had disguised themselves as men, and they had fought valiantly on the battlefield. An appropriate gesture was in order: a pardon and a reward. The king was quite aware of the propagandistic value attached to the fact that even women were inspired to fight under his banner, and granting a reward was used as a way of promoting the Crown. It would be a mistake, however, to assume that all these women were well-received. Novels and plays aside, in the customary characterization of cross-dressing, it was the sensational or comical aspects that prevailed.[21]

Whatever deep reasons impelled Catalina de Erauso to dress as a man, she knew how to make the most of the social values of her era, and so she stated publicly that her motives were patriotic and religious. In her *Pedimento* (Petition) she explains: "The Lieutenant doña Catalina de Erauso . . . says that of the last nineteen years, she has spent fifteen in the service of Your Majesty in the wars of the kingdom of Chile and the Indians of Peru, having traveled to these parts in a man's garb *owing to her particular inclination to take up arms in the defense of the Catholic faith and in service to your Majesty.*"[22]

But if in fact these women did have romantic and patriotic motives, these pale in comparison to the economic motives that must have driven them. Most of the 119 Dutch women studied by Dekker and Van de Pol came from the lower social classes; they were impoverished, orphans, or found themselves in a family situation from which they wanted to escape. This was not the case for Catalina de Erauso. Her family belonged to the nobility, and although her parents no longer enjoyed the prosperity the family once had during her grandfather Miguel de Erauso's time, they were wealthy; they owned land and ships and had a history of commercial success.

Generally speaking, the primary reason for women's cross-dressing in pre-industrial Europe was poverty. A man could always become a soldier or a sailor and was thereby assured of housing and food; a woman did not have that recourse. Faced with total destitution, the female alternative was to become a prostitute, but this involved less security and more contempt from society. Prostitution was considered as marginal as begging and vagrancy, and was defined and prosecuted as a crime.[23] The absence of prostitutes in the group of Dutch women who disguised themselves as men seems to indicate that those who chose to do so in an economically difficult situation did it in part because they rejected prostitution as a viable alternative. These women preferred to "become men," to follow an active, asexual, and masculine life, all the while preserving their sexual honor. In the European tradition of female cross-dressing, adopting a man's role was associated with maintaining virginity.[24] Most of the women studied by Dekker and Van de Pol were unmarried, and a male disguise allowed them to remain virgins, or at least avoid marriage. When, for example, in a case cited by the two researchers, the judges asked Catharina Lincken if she did not know that cross-dressing was forbidden, she answered that she thought this applied to married women only, not to maidens.[25]

Although these transvestite women had not formulated an ideology to express their convictions, they clearly saw their roles as females to be dull and limiting. Only by presenting themselves as men could they claim the same privileges enjoyed by males in their own social class. Transvestism must have been a temptation, or at least a fantasy, for many adventurous young women who understood that they could expect little freedom or latitude in their lives.[26]

Catalina de Erauso's Transvestism: Why Was She Not Punished for It?

If, as we have seen, transvestism was forbidden both by canon and civil law, we cannot fail to wonder why Erauso was never punished for donning men's attire. The answer is complex; in her particular situation a variety of reasons come into play. First, we have already mentioned the importance of her virginity, verified by the church authorities. This quality, which implies asexuality, was considered by society to be admirable and virtuous.[27] In addition, despite the fact that Erauso departed from the social norms, she demonstrated respect for and submission to both ecclesiastical and military institutional authorities; therefore her transgression neither challenged nor threatened the status quo.[28]

During an era when the feminine tradition of cross-dressing was linked to the preservation of virginity, it was conceivable that a woman could live dressed as a man. The example that comes to mind is Joan of Arc, called "the maiden of Orleans"; had she not been a virgin she would surely have met her end much sooner. The title of "maiden" was her safe-conduct, allowing her to play a role that—if only for a short time—would normally fall far beyond a woman's reach.

When Erauso revealed herself to the bishop, the first thing that was done—even before he could believe her story or form an opinion about her—was to verify her virginity.

> The [bishop] invited me to have breakfast with him and continued his lecture, letting me know in the end that mine was the most astonishing case of its kind he had heard in all his life.
>
> "So . . . ," he concluded, "is it true?"
>
> "Yes, *señor*," I answered.
>
> "I am sure you will understand if I tell you that your strange tale raises some doubts."
>
> "*Señor*—" I said, "it is the truth, and if it will remove your doubts, let other women examine me—I will submit to such a test."

"I am glad to hear you say this," he replied. "I will arrange it."

And then I left, as it was his hour to receive visitors. At midday I ate and rested a little, and toward four in the afternoon two old women came in and looked me over and satisfied themselves, declaring afterward before the bishop that they had examined me and found me to be a woman and were ready to swear it under oath if necessary—and what's more they had found me to be an intact virgin, as on the day I came into the world. This piece of news touched His Eminence. He dismissed the women and sent for me, along with the chaplain, and in his presence he lovingly embraced me.

"Daughter," he said, "my doubt is gone. *I believe you now, and I shall believe, from this day forward whatever you may choose to tell me*—I esteem you as one of the more remarkable people in this world, and promise to help you in whatever you do, and to aid you in your new life in the service of God."[29]

As this passage of the memoir demonstrates, until he confirmed that she was virgin, the bishop did not think he had sufficient information to find her account credible. Her virginity suggested a kind of asexuality, or a rejection of sexuality, that, in the eyes of society, placed her on a pedestal. Had she not been a virgin, Erauso would have been classified as belonging to that group of women (prostitutes, vagabonds, and adventuresses) who had lost their sexual honor. Although the facts of her biography remained unchanged, she would never have achieved the recognition and the support accorded her by the church and the state, and her figure would have faded into the blur of anonymity.

Another factor that must be taken into account is the androcentric perspective that prevailed in the seventeenth century. In her desire to pass as a man, Erauso was attempting to transcend her lowly female condition and accede to the superior realm of masculinity. Her transgression was magnanimously forgiven because it was interpreted as a commendable effort in itself. By desperately seeking to become something better, she crossed over into the male social orbit, and her image was considerably enhanced. The use of the adjective *varonil* (manly) as a standard of excellence became widespread during the seventeenth century. Women who departed from the norm in an admirable or positive way were thought to be "*varoniles*," or manly; those who did so in a reprehensible way were just wicked women.[30]

To understand the notion of the "manly woman," the gender ideology of that era must be considered. That a woman could acquire the "manliness" of the "*mujer varonil*" so easily—sometimes simply by changing her appearance—"synchronizes with the scientific model of the times which placed males and females on a single biological continuum rather than viewing them as incommensurable opposites."[31] Up to the eighteenth century this so-called "one sex model" prevailed, "where two genders correspond to but one sex, where the boundaries between male and female are of degree and not of kind."[32] Medical treatises of the time postulated that a woman could turn into a man through a burst of heat, causing her interior male-like genitals to be expelled. Although there was a lack of agreement on this theory, it offered an explanation for cases of hermaphroditism.[33] The body was seen as something less fixed, more mutable, and thus made the transformation from one sex to another appear to be plausible. If the body of a woman was a natural transvestite, containing male organs within it, was not transvestism only a natural social extension of "the myth of mobility" intrinsic to this sliding scale?[34]

The case of Elena de Céspedes (1545?–88) is well-known: when she was seventeen years old, she discovered that she had a penis, and as a result decided to have an affair with a merchant's wife, began to dress as a man, and later became a soldier. Years later, living under the name "Eleno" she made plans to marry and applied for a marriage license. Due to her lack of facial hair, she was assumed to be a eunuch, and the authorities required her to submit to a physical examination before giving permission for the marriage. After passing the examination, she was granted the license and she married. Nonetheless, she continued to be accused of impersonating a man, was arrested and ended up in court. During the trial, Céspedes admitted to being a hermaphrodite, and in a second examination, the same officials who had previously affirmed that she had a penis but no vagina, now testified to just the opposite. Given the discrepancy between the two examinations, it was determined that she was involved in demonic activities; she was punished by the Inquisition, receiving two hundred lashes and a ten-year sentence in a public hospital. "In the end, unable to explain the sexual ambiguities of the case, the courts attributed the unacceptable mutations to magic and the devil. These sixteenth-century documents reveal the flexible and unstable nature of sex assignment as well as the differing attitudes toward homoerotic flirtation that does not involve genital contact."[35]

Erauso's supposed homosexuality was of no great concern to the church or the state, because in her case she had not experienced penetration nor had any known genital contact. As her case demonstrates, the presence of a phallus was and is essential to masculinity. Not possessing one and being unmarried, Erauso fell into a category that was subversive, but could be tolerated. Her appropriation of the male gender expressed itself above all in the occupations she chose and the lifestyle she adopted, characterized by a degree of freedom and mobility she would never have enjoyed as a woman. But she never officially assumed a man's role; for example, she never entered into a publicly acknowledged relationship with a woman.

Another ramification of the "one sex model" for transvestism is the importance of clothing in producing the transformation from one sex to another. Since both sexes possess the same reproductive organs (albeit in different places), gender is "theatricalized" or staged; the "transformative power of clothing" is absolute, in plays as well as in real life. With the exchange of a few social markers, a woman on stage could convert her gender identity. In Erauso's case, this definitive change takes place when she uses her nun's habit to fashion a man's outfit.[36]

There is no doubt that Erauso's transvestism also receives preferential treatment because of her exemplary military record. In the *Pedimento* (Petition) she presents seeking reward for her services, she explains that for fifteen years she had been known *only* as a man, and she points out that witnesses have also borne testimony to her "manly deeds." As we know, the king, Philip IV, accedes to her petition. The positive image of a woman who has dressed as a man to serve the Crown and the church was apparently more compelling than the transgressive nature of her cross-dressing.[37] The Council of Indies recommended that the king grant her the reward, but they advised him to disallow her request to be permitted to continue dressing as a man: "With respect to the change in clothing, it appears that it would be better for her to go back to dressing as a woman."[38] Only later will she succeed in getting that dispensation from the Pope.

We know that the real Erauso became a celebrity in her own time, and later, because of the enormous popularity of Montalbán's play in the theaters of Madrid, she was transformed into a legend. Erauso was not unaware of the appeal of her tale, as is evident by some phrases that appear at the end of her *Pedimento*: for example, "[Erauso] begs that your Majesty be pleased to order that her services and long wanderings and valiant deeds be awarded, thereby showing his greatness; rewarding her for the worthiness of her deeds *and for the singularity and prodigiousness of her life story*."[39] In Merrim's view, these words clearly reveal Erauso's awareness of the sensational and entertaining nature of her autobiography, that in and of itself merited as much recognition as her service to the Crown. Such a self-promotion of the bizarre aspects of her life should be interpreted in the context of the Baroque penchant for everything that was contradictory and astonishing. During the seventeenth century, monsters were displayed in the theater, in the public square, and in paintings; they incited not pity, but the curiosity and wonder of the spectator. By departing from the social norms so radically, there is something "monstrous" about the phenomenon of Erauso. It places her squarely within the esthetic of the Baroque, thus making her very appealing to a public that was attuned to that sensibility. In Erauso the contradictions of male/female, saint/sinner, law-abiding citizen/criminal, Basque/Spaniard, and nun/transvestite are all subsumed. When she claimed a reward for "the singularity and the prodigiousness" of her life story, she was capitalizing on the prevailing esthetic of the surprising and the wondrous for her own gain.[40] Erauso pursued fame because she knew that her "anomaly" could be converted into "notoriety." We know that she sat for two portraits with famous artists, that she wrote several appeals to the Crown, and recounted her story to strangers as well as to friends. In her *Autobiografía*, she herself appears telling her own tale on four separate occasions. She also related her anecdotes to rather famous people, like Pedro del Valle, who recalled that she spoke to him about various incidents in her life.

All this confirms, in Merrim's view, Erauso's predilection for self-disclosure. She traded in on her anomaly, and in so doing, Merrim concludes, became a cultural icon. The church, the state, and the public opened their doors to her; she found an escape valve from the rigidity of a regulated society. By achieving fame, she entered that social space characterized by permissiveness and flexibility, a space reserved for the prodigious and the unusual.[41] In conclusion, Erauso found redemption through her image as a female virgin who exalted masculine values, who loved her country and her king, and was fundamentally anomalous and extraordinary.

Next, I will explore the possibility that Erauso was homosexual. With that purpose, I will begin by analyzing the attitudes toward romantic relationships between women throughout history, and in particular, during the era that concerns us.

Love between Women in the Seventeenth Century

In examining this topic, it is useful to begin by taking a look at the ideas regarding sex in general during that era, and then focus specifically on the relationships between women in Erauso's time. Then I will consider the legal prosecution of homosexuality; we will see why women received much lighter sentences than men.

As we discuss homosexual love and its significance in our heroine's life, we must start by understanding the religious and philosophical social space in which notions of love and sex were formulated. It is a social space dominated by Christian doctrine and its negative attitude toward sex. This attitude did not originate with Christianity, but was inherited from the Persians and other civilizations of the ancient Near East, all of which were restrictive and hostile to all forms of sex not leading to procreation. With the Persians, restrictive sexual life became correlated with sexual morality and salvation. From the beginnings of western European thought, religion, sexual pleasure, and reproduction were closely associated in a complex relationship of interdependence.[42] Christianity incorporated some attitudes that derive from Judaism during a period of its history characterized by great sexual repression. At that time, man was conceived as a difficult creature, born with evil tendencies, his greatest weakness being the desire for sexual pleasures.[43]

If we review the early Christian attitudes toward sex, we find that the church fathers tolerated sexual relations only within marriage, and solely for the purpose of procreation. They preferred celibacy and virginity. By declaring that sexual intercourse was justifiable only for procreation, they were condemning any other kind of sexual act that did not lead to reproduction. Even when pregnancy was the result, sex was not something to be enjoyed. In the early Middle Ages, the attitudes of Western Christianity toward certain forms of sexuality became institutionalized; any form of sexual behavior that did not lead to procreation was regarded as deviant and unnatural; heterosexual, homosexual, and auto-sexual relationships all fell within this category.[44]

During the Early Modern Age, in both Catholic and Protestant countries, the state began to intervene more directly in matters of faith and morality that previously had been within the reserve of the church. With the Council of Trent (1545–64), Catholicism reaffirmed the traditional view of virginity: it was the perfect state, and matrimony was only a remedy for concupiscence. The Virgin was frequently portrayed during the Middle Ages either as pregnant or in the act of breastfeeding; in the Early Modern Age these images—which constituted an entire iconography—became rare and finally disappeared. Anything related to sexuality was considered "socially shameful and disgraceful, becoming a taboo, losing the spontaneity associated with it in previous centuries."[45]

Early sixteenth-century Spain had already witnessed the Catholic reformation and the resurgence of the clergy; therefore the celebration of this ecumenical council was a fervently desired event. Spanish bishops, writers of treatises, and canons played a central role in the Council of Trent, contributing ideas that had already been successfully implemented in the peninsular dioceses. Theologians such as Tomás Sanchez, Francisco de Toledo, Pedro Ledesma, and Luis López were constantly cited as authorities until well into the eighteenth century.[46] As part of carrying out the reform of the clergy required by the Council, Pope Pius V promulgated the *Horrendum* bull requiring the punishment of sodomite priests.[47] Soon after the Council of Trent, Philip II of Spain introduced this papal bull in his kingdom, without applying the restrictions to which, as a monarch, he was entitled. He also published a royal decree that required all Christian monarchs not only to obey, protect, and follow the decrees and commandments of the Holy Mother Church themselves, but to see that their own kingdoms, states, and powers also obey, protect, and follow them as well. The precepts worked out by the church fathers of Trent were spread throughout all the territories of the Spanish Crown.[48]

With respect to the regulation of sexual matters, one of the consequences of the new Tridentine world view was the criminalization of what were previously considered "sins against nature." In the sixteenth century, Charles V proclaimed that if a man lies with a beast, or if two men or two women lie together, both should be burned at the stake. Philip II revalidated this decree in 1598. Nevertheless, in spite of what the letter of the law dictated, the consequences were very different depending on whether those convicted were men or women. In Western Europe sexual relationships between women were met with less hostility, legally or otherwise, than homosexual relationships between men or bestiality. Unlike the women who were accused of a "crime" of this kind, when men were involved, they were sentenced to death, although the sentence was seldom carried out. Vallbona cites the case of a man who in 1530 fought in the conquest of New Spain, "dressed as a woman, [because] from his childhood they had taught him to dress that way, and to make his living from this infamous traffic; the general ordered that he be burned alive"; and this despite the fact that he had distinguished himself as the most valiant soldier in a hard-fought battle.[49] This fate, that was not common for men, would be exceptional in women's cases. To more completely understand the attitudes of this period, it is important to review the ideology regarding sex and women that explains this state of affairs.

Are Sexual Relationships between Women Possible?

In early writings of Hebrew scholars it was assumed that female sexuality was satisfied through a conjugal relationship, and only occasionally were alternative forms of sexual expression mentioned. Since the view of sexuality was centered on men, and on penetration, it was assumed that women could do little on their own. Thus, although lesbianism was some times equated with prostitution, there were few prohibitions against female association, and homosexual relationships between women were generally ignored or dismissed. Gregorio López, a sixteenth-century jurist, referred to it as the *Peccatum mutum,* "the silent sin." Crimes that cannot be named have no name; therefore they leave few traces in historical records.[50]

In her study of a lesbian nun in Renaissance Italy, Judith Brown finds that the subject of lesbian sexuality is neglected in the law, the theology, and the literature of that era, suggesting an almost active willingness to disbelieve. The scarcity of documents citing the love of women for one another is surprising when we compare it to the frequency with which male homosexuality is mentioned, especially after the thirteenth century, when references to it appear in civil and canon law, in penitentials and confessional manuals, in popular sermons, and in literature. Brown discovered that in a period of fifteen hundred years, there were only a dozen or so scattered references to female homosexuality.[51]

The contradictory notions Western Europeans had regarding female sexuality made it impossible to discuss female homosexuality openly. As Judith Brown observes, "Silence bred confusion and confusion bred fear. On these foundations Western society built an impenetrable barrier that has lasted for nearly two thousand years."[52] When it is thought that sexual relations are impossible without a penis, women who love other women find themselves lacking a cultural vocabulary that can express their feelings. Often this produces great confusion with respect to gender identity: the thought is, if I am a woman, but I love another woman, then in reality I must be a man, regardless of what my anatomy is telling me. This kind of logic, that may or may not seem absurd to us today, turns up in studies of contemporary adolescents.

In a study of children and adolescents who suffer from gender disorder, Kenneth Zucker and others describe several cases of adolescents who expressed the wish to have a sex change. As an awareness of their same-sex erotic feelings emerged—that is, as they became aware of their homosexuality—that desire became intensified. One of these male adolescents, who grew up in a Spanish-speaking working-class family, explained that he did not want to be "gay" because a homosexual identity was viewed with disdain in his country of origin. He added that if on the other hand he could be a female, then he would be "normal"; his attraction to males would then be considered heterosexual. In still another case, the sister and mother of a girl who wanted to undergo a sex change operation said they preferred that she have it so that her sexual attraction to females would be seen as "normal" and would not defy "God's will."[53] In the examples we have cited, it would appear that an increasing awareness of their own homoerotic feelings was the factor that intensified the inner struggles of these adolescents with respect to their gender identity. While this is not the same as the gender confusion of the past centuries to which we alluded, it does demonstrate the enormous problems experienced by an individual who needs to make those very real feelings fit into the social and sexual mores of a world that makes no allowance for such feelings.

Amorous relationships between women take center stage in the writings of Early Modern Age Spanish authors like María de Zayas (1590–?) and Mariana de Carvajal (1619–?). Both provide in-depth portrayals of female friendships and sexuality, "allowing us to glean an understanding of the fluid boundaries of female friendship and desire."[54] Fictional scenes of same-sex attraction can also be found in works such as Jorge de Montemayor's *La Diana*, Fernando de Rojas's *La Celestina*, and Ludovico Ariosto's *Orlando Furioso*, among others.[55] These literary representations clearly provide a challenge to the social restrictions on gender and sexuality that governed women's lives, although, as Vollendorf points out, we cannot know with certainty the extent to which female homoeroticism was "intelligible" to early modern readers. In Zaya's *Amar sólo para vencer* (Love for the Sake of Conquest), the absence of any strong reaction to female homoeroticism by the characters involved suggests that "they do not (and perhaps cannot) see the homoeroticism . . . as anything more than a non-threatening extension of female friendship."[56] Here we see what we previously alluded to: on one hand, the ambiguity surrounding intimate female relationships; on the other, the return to the heterosexual model when a relationship is finally perceived as erotic. The characters "cannot fully accept that a woman could love another woman, and so they keep looking for a male body to resolve their doubt."[57] In Zaya's novel, Estafanía does in fact turn out to be Esteban. As Velasco points out, "This neoplatonic expression of same-sex love attempts to define romantic relationships between women as chaste and therefore morally superior to the physically based heterosexual love."[58] Estefanía joins other women in discussing the spiritual advantages of love between women. The defense of this same-sex love is based on its spiritual and chaste nature, distancing it from corporeal lust for the loved one. Velasco notes that, during the early Early Modern Period, examples of female homoeroticism are found not only in literature and theater, but also in legal proceedings, medical treatises, pornographic pictures, songs, and anecdotes.

As noted previously, sexual relationships between women were generally not taken seriously during Catalina de Erauso's times; rather they were seen as a way of enhancing sex with a man. Without doubt, this is the notion that underlies the lack of attention given to female homosexuality, which is virtually ignored. The poet Edmund Waller describes how men of the Renaissance and the Baroque would regard two young women who appeared to be taken with each other: they would present nothing more than "a tantalizing double vision of beauty." The love they ostensibly feel is only a sham, nothing more than a trick used to manipulate men.[59] Waller implies that these romantic friendships are charming to observe but have little substance and would not exist at all if women did not want to use them as a tool with which to tease their male lovers.[60] Brantôme expresses a similar attitude when he describes female lovemaking between women in the French court in the seventeenth century. In his view, women "imitate men," and the attraction they feel for each other was not to be taken seriously; in fact, his descriptions of these amorous scenes were often laughable. In any case, these unions were considered less sinful than extramarital heterosexual relations. Brantôme found Sapphic love even more acceptable in the case of young girls still virgins, and widows; it was an innocent way for women to satisfy their sexual needs. Seen in this light, same-sex acts appeared to be a way of protecting women from what might be more dangerous relationships with men. The situation was not very different in Italy; a sixteenth-century author, Agnolo Firenzuola, agreed with Brantôme that sexual relations between women could have only one purpose: "to enhance and glorify real sex; that is, sex with a man."[61]

Finally, an additional reason for not condemning female same-sex unions was the notion that since women were by nature inferior to men, when they fell in love with other women they were in fact trying to emulate men, and thus attained a more perfect state of being. This is clearly related to what we have observed regarding the permissive attitude sometimes taken by society toward female cross-dressing.

The Social Response

The attitude of society toward a woman who was involved in a same-sex relationship depended on whether or not she was able to continue maintaining other aspects of her role as a woman. While these romantic friendships did not necessarily imply a sexual relationship, the records left by women regarding their attachments suggest that they had a sensual interest in the beloved. Perhaps it was assumed that what appeared to be sensuality was an overflow of the spiritual, and the importance of the spiritual would keep eroticism in check.[62]

In a society that marked such great distances between male and female roles, great latitude was given to the affection that women could openly display for each other; even when they were discovered in a sexual relationship, the punishment was lighter than that which was applied to two males in similar circumstances. It was expected that women would have intimate friendships, and it is easy to imagine that sometimes these would cross the line that separated the sensual from the sexual. With respect to early modern Europe, Dekker and Van de Pol state that even when there was clear proof of a physical relationship between two women, they were rarely sentenced to death, in sharp contrast to the fate of male homosexuals who were executed for sodomy.[63]

Lesbian relationships were accepted, at least in more libertine circles, as long as they did not represent a challenge to the role that women were supposed to play in society. When a woman renounced other aspects of her role, such as wearing conventional garments, she aroused societal anxiety and was rejected, because this implied that a woman ceased being feminine—that is, "ruled," and the man ceased being masculine—that is, "ruling." It has been shown that in most cases of punishment for lesbianism, the accused was a transvestite.[64] If a woman wore men's clothing, it was assumed that she behaved like a man sexually; therefore, she was violating male property rights over women's bodies. What two women dressed as women do together was not alarming, but was viewed as entertainment when men were not available; it was even seen favorably when viewed as training for the real heterosexual sex act. On the other hand, if one of the women was dressed as a man, it was then seen as a usurpation of a male's prerogative, and if a dildo was used, it aroused even more societal anxiety. These women represented a double challenge to society: first, by having sex with other women; and second, when they impersonated men, they claimed for themselves all the privileges usually reserved for men—self-sufficiency, freedom to wander, and varied occupations. When the sex act was accompanied by the usurpation of roles, it was judged to warrant harsh punishment.[65] As Lillian Faderman observes, what was really threatening to sixteenth- and seventeenth-century Spanish society was not the existence of sexual relations between women, but the fact that these women impersonated men and rejected their female roles. Although these women's lives might have been seen as acceptable, and at times even praiseworthy, had lesbianism become the norm it would have had serious consequences for the privileged lives of men. The claim of male prerogative combined with the commission of certain sexual acts, especially if they involved the use of a phallic substitute, seems to have been necessary to provoke extreme social condemnation.

All this clearly reveals, among other things, the enormous importance attached to clothing during this period. Clothing acted as a signifier that could be interpreted; it was an indication of wealth and social class, distinctions that assumed extraordinary importance in a society in which those distinctions were being erased or blurred by changing conditions. The code regulating dress stipulated what kind of clothing could be worn, not only with respect to gender but with respect to social class and occupation. In the eyes of his contemporaries, a sailor wearing trousers, smoking a pipe, his hair short and tousled, could only be a man. This state of affairs obviously benefited individuals who, like Erauso, tried to pass for persons of the opposite sex. Numerous treatises published during the Baroque period dealt with sumptuary matters, establishing rules regarding the appropriate clothing to be worn by people, according to the social class to which they belonged.[66] In such a socially stratified society, class and gender determined the individual's dress. A treatise written by Fray Hernando de Talavera at the close of the fifteenth century criticizes both men and women for zealously desiring new fashions in clothes that "depart from what is normal, and strive to discover a thousand ways to do so." He adds that women are guiltier than men of these excesses; and that the parents or the husbands who consent to such extremes are equally guilty. His moral treatise was very influential during the sixteenth and seventeenth centuries. Fray Tomás de Trujillo, the author of still another well-known sixteenth-century treatise, argues that clothing should be a precise symbolic system that expresses social stratification; therefore, he asserts: "I do not think that everyone should dress in identical cloth, tailored identically; rather each person should differentiate himself according to the quality of his person, his social status, and his profession."[67]

Every aspect of clothing and adornment was regulated: their cost, their shape, their size, their fabric, and so forth. New regulations kept replacing the old ones, which were not observed, although they sometimes gave rise to waves of repressive police action. The constables went into the streets, cutting men's hat brims, slashing at women's laces, ribbons, and hooped petticoats, and pulling off their jewelry.[68] Not just at the national level were decrees issued; some cities and towns promulgated their own laws intended to regulate who could wear what in any given situation. Seventeenth-century England witnessed real hysteria when fashions in dress shifted to what was considered masculine for women and feminine for men.[69] If minor shifts in appropriate male and female dress produced such anxiety, we can imagine the horror that transvestites must have caused by their total subversion of clothing and general appearance. In her study regarding female transvestism in sixteenth- and seventeenth-century England, Valerie Staub observes that by appropriating a man's clothing a woman "takes on not just the male gender role but the male physical role, in other words, the phallus."[70] In the seventeenth century, gender membership and roles were in a state of confusion, as reflected by the belief that wearing the clothing of the other sex could alter the sex of the wearer. This can be associated, as we previously observed, with the sexual ideology of the time.[71]

To discuss the social attitude toward homosexuality or "sodomy," we must begin by examining the way that Spanish legislation historically dealt with this sexual conduct. During the early Early Modern Age, Ferdinand and Isabel proclaimed the first *Pragmática* (proclamation or decree) against sodomy in 1497. Although the Catholic Monarchs had used Chapter XXI of *Las Siete Partidas* (the Seven Part Code, or laws compiled by Alfonso X in the thirteenth century) as their point of departure, in their proclamation they made the punishment for those suspected of sodomy much harsher. Although it confirmed the death penalty (as originally prescribed in the *Partida*) for convicted sodomites who were more than twenty-five years old, it was found to be insufficient, and a new penalty was instituted: death by burning. Only fire, the natural purifier of evil, could remedy sodomy, "an unspeakable and abominable crime against nature."[72] The Catholic Monarchs prescribed punishments that made sodomy as grave a crime as heresy and treason; as a result, "the confiscation of wealth and the torture figure prominently in the prosecution of these cases." The proclamation decrees systematic torture of "any man accused of this abominable sin, including the nobility and the clergy." Nevertheless, it appears that those two social classes received privileged treatment during the reign of Ferdinand and Isabel. "The nobility enjoyed special privileges, such as trials conducted in particularly specified ways, and in general they were exempted from torture, except in cases involving sodomy and heresy."[73]

In his 1556 commentary regarding the laws of *Las Siete Partidas,* Gregorio López reflects a hardening of the original position by extending the death penalty not just to men but also to women who engaged in homosexual acts: "Although the law specifies men, women should also be included when one of them commits unnatural acts with another woman, just as when a man engages in unnatural intercourse with a woman . . . and so women are also capable of committing abominable sins that must be punished."[74] While the original legal code written in 1256 did not mention women, López observed that if they committed female sodomy, in order to comply with the decree issued by the Catholic Monarchs, they should also be burned. A comparable legal stance developed in France. Jean Papon, in his 1565 *Compendium of Valuable Decisions of the Supreme Courts of France,* noted that "a woman involved in a lustful act with another woman shall die."[75]

Nevertheless, it appears that in Spain as well as in the rest of Europe, guilty women were spared the death penalty. And while Gregorio López recognized the possibility of female sodomy, he believed that it did not alter "the economy of creation, since intercourse that involved the waste of male semen was impossible between them, unlike sodomy between men; therefore female sodomy did not directly offend the image of God."[76] As a result, his opinion is that women should receive a less harsh punishment, and that the death penalty should be applied only in those cases in which they had employed "*aliquot instrumento virginitas violetur*," that is, a phallic device.[77] Another sixteenth-century moralist, Antonio Gómez, who thought that the death penalty should be mandatory in those cases in which a material instrument was used, refers to two Spanish nuns who were burned at the stake for using "instruments."[78] When a phallic instrument was not involved he believed that a minor punishment was appropriate, for example, some lashes. In Judith Brown's view, these differences of opinion regarding how to deal with lesbian sexuality betray a fundamental ignorance about what women did with each other and how that fit into the established sexual categories and sexual crimes.[79] The reign of Philip II of Spain (1555–98) was even more repressive than that of the Catholic Monarchs. Although he did not increase the penalties for sodomy, he relaxed the evidentiary requirements for prosecution and sentencing in such crimes. For Philip II, "one witness sufficed" to guarantee the conviction of a sodomite. If the respective testimonies of two or three witnesses were found to be inconsistent, even though one of them had participated in the act, the *Pragmática* of 1592 declared that the testimony of just one participant was enough to convict a sodomite.[80]

Scholars who have examined the opprobrium attached to homosexuality during the Early Modern Age have concluded that Spain incurred "what is possibly the most violent history of persecution of male homosexuals in Europe."[81] During the Early Modern Age, the punishment of male sodomites becomes a public spectacle. Contemporaneous documents report the scandal surrounding the accusations, as well as the crowds that come to witness the accused being burned at the stake. In December 1622,

> Five young men were burned at the stake for having committed the abominable crime. The first was Mendocilla, the court jester; the second, a boy servant in the court of the Count of Villamediana; the third, a little mulatto slave; the fourth, another servant of the Count of Villamediana. The last was don Gaspar de Terrazas, a page in the employ of the Duke of Alba. It was an execution widely discussed in the Royal Court.[82]

A similar report appears in 1626. After Diego Gaytán had confessed under torture, "They burned two young boys for the abominable sin, and one of them, who shouted his retraction as they were leading him through the streets to be burned, was among those who accused don Diego Gaytán. It caused great pity in the entire Court."[83] In 1624 the execution of a woman in Seville is reported, although in her case, in addition to sodomy she was also accused of robbery and assassination, and these may have been the factors that determined that the death penalty be carried out.[84] The year 1636 appears to have been especially intense with respect to the repression of male homosexuality; thirty-seven accusations are recorded, which caused a great commotion in Madrid and led to the enactment of a law prohibiting men from wearing their hair long because it made them look effeminate. As we observed earlier, justice was not blind when it passed sentence on the accused; it appears that fame and wealth were significant factors in the punishment of sodomy. "With respect to those who are incarcerated for the abominable sin, the expected severity was not exercised . . . that is, power and money can truly work wonders. We see that the Count of Castillo's page, don Nicolás, is walking free in the streets, and they have released Juan Rana, the famous representative; and none of the incarcerated has been burned at the stake."[85]

This last observation makes it clear that in spite of what the letter of the law decreed, in no way was the death penalty the usual outcome in these cases. Alain Saint-Saëns underlines the importance of social class in the way the punishment was meted out. "In seventeenth-century Spain, noble and privileged people always succeeded in escaping death. Only poor people among the sodomites were condemned to be hanged or burnt at the stake."[86] He then provides numerous testimonies regarding homosexual practices in the courts of Henry IV of Castile, Philip IV of Spain, Henry III of France, and James I of England.[87]

In seventeenth-century Spain, it was believed that the decline of the empire was due to the emasculation of the country; the people had become "soft and effeminate and used to luxury." In 1621, Cristóbal Suárez de Figueroa described the royal court as a "breeding place for young sodomites, for useless and effeminate little courtiers."[88] What these epithets referring to homosexuality really betray was the fact that a new political order had emerged in early Early Modern Age Spain. It was accompanied by "the construction of a new kind of masculinity, urbane and courtly in nature, that attempted to undermine the gender boundaries that had been socially and culturally constructed."[89] When it was forced to deal with the new bureaucratic and administrative needs of the modern state, the Spanish nobility of the late sixteenth and early seventeenth centuries became urbanized and domesticated. While a courtier had to conduct himself in the sophisticated manner befitting a statesman, he had to be careful not to engage in "conduct that might give the impression that he had crossed the line into those areas proscribed and feared"[90] by the guardians of the social order: that is, that he could be accused of being a sodomite.

In this social climate, the theater which regales the senses with dance, music, and festive celebrations, is also accused of making the national character less masculine. Given the fact that transvestism in Spanish Golden Age drama had great appeal for the public, and that women were allowed to appear on the stage, moralist writers of the time complained of a "slow and continuous erosion of the traditional gender roles . . . both on and off the stage."[91]

As we have seen, the social attitude toward female homosexuality seems to be reflected in the fact that as long as such conduct did not involve cross-dressing, nor the use of an instrument that substituted for the phallus, the legal authorities showed little inclination to prosecute or condemn it. Over time, however, the evolving legal tradition revealed increasing harshness in the punishments prescribed. What appears to be consistent is that neither in the church nor in the state did female homosexuality arouse the same fear and anxiety as did male homosexuality. Partly this is because the nature of these female relationships was not understood; in addition, it is because they did not lead to "wasted or spilled semen"; that is, possible fertilization was not prevented by their acts. For these reasons, the law courts ignored most of these cases, and for the most part did not take them seriously. This is precisely the attitude that is reflected in the social reaction to Catalina de Erauso's presumed homosexuality. It was suspected; it was discussed; but it caused no anxiety. Next we will examine those episodes of her memoirs in which the case can be made for her presumed homosexuality.

The Homosexual Erauso

The *Autobiografía* allows a reading that leads us to believe that Catalina de Erauso felt sexually attracted to women.[92] In some episodes, her comments are what bring us to this conclusion; in others her own actions clearly suggest it. That is what Chloe Rutter seems to imply when she asserts that "Erauso's codes of behavior identify him as a man, therefore his desire for women fits into the accepted conventions of male/female relationships."[93] Next I will review in sequential order those episodes of the text that suggest or imply Erauso's amorous relationships with women. Although the topic of her supposed homosexuality has been addressed repeatedly in recent studies, I believe that it is necessary to anchor the discussion more firmly on an analysis of the texts themselves, and in particular through a close reading of the *Autobiografía*, the single text that is undoubtedly most faithful to what we have been able to establish about the facts of her life.

The first woman with whom Erauso was involved was Beatriz de Cárdenas, her master Urquiza's lover. As we previously noted, to resolve Erauso's quarrel with Reyes, Urquiza had proposed that she marry Beatriz, who was one of Reyes' relatives. Erauso tells us that at night she would frequent that lady's home, and there she received many caresses. We know that one night Cárdenas insists that, come hell or high water, Erauso was going to sleep with her. Erauso refuses, manages to put her off, and slips out. But the fact that Erauso did not want to place herself in a situation in which her true sex would be discovered does not mean that she did not enjoy engaging in erotic play, as long as it does not endanger her. In fact, we must assume that this was the case since, as she herself discloses, she would visit the lady's home night after night. She knew that once her true sex was revealed the arrangement proposed by Urquiza would not work out. Moreover, if her secret was discovered, there would be no reason why Cárdenas would agree to being her accomplice, and Erauso would risk losing the friendship and esteem of her great benefactor, Urquiza. For these reasons she rejected the arranged marriage, after which Urquiza offered to send her to Trujillo, setting her up "in the same kind of store and with the same arrangement," an offer that Erauso of course accepted.

The next episode is perhaps the one that most clearly reveals Erauso's sexual attraction to women. She left Trujillo and traveled to Lima, where she presented the letter of recommendation written by her master Urquiza to Diego de Solarte, a wealthy merchant, who received her in a kind and gracious manner. Nevertheless, at the end of nine months she was told "to think about making [her] living elsewhere." Solarte decided to send Erauso away because she had been flirting with his wife's two young sisters, especially with one of them, as we noted in a previous chapter. In this instance, it is obvious that Erauso sought out and enjoyed this kind of contact. She writes, "I had become accustomed to frolicking with them and teasing them—one in particular—who had taken a fancy to me." She initiated these relationships with the two young ladies because she was attracted to them both. It was not her own preference that made her spend more time with one rather than the other, but the fact that one of them seemed to be more receptive to her. The description of the scene in which Erauso and her lover are surprised *in flagrante* is decidedly sensual in tone. Since Erauso had spent nine months in this house, it is probable that the amorous relationship had existed for some time, especially in view of the fact that the young woman was thinking of matrimony. The marriage proposal also makes it clear that the relationship between the two had been emotionally satisfying.

It is difficult to believe, as it is ridiculous to think, as has been suggested, that her only motive was the need to appear to be a man in every aspect of her life and thus not awaken any suspicion about her true identity. Since her relationship with this woman was secretive, whom would she be trying to convince by her actions? In my opinion, she was driven by the sexual desire she felt for these women. That Erauso's conduct was not perceived as dishonest is borne out by the fact that when the young woman's father, Solarte, learned that she had signed on as a soldier, he lamented her decision and offered to return the money that the Crown had allotted her: "When my master found out, he took it very hard. Apparently this was not exactly what he had in mind. He offered to speak to the company officers and get my enlistment annulled and to repay the money that had given me." And so, Solarte probably thought that Erauso had behaved as any other young man would have in her situation, and although he was forced to fire her, he still felt affection for her and attempted to help her.

Erauso's relationship with this young woman provides an example of the distinction that was made between courtship and seduction during this historical period. In his study regarding litigation initiated by women in early modern Spain, Barahona emphasizes the significant differences between the two concepts. Courtship was carried out openly before the community; a man initiated a relationship with a woman and thus showed that he intended to marry her eventually. As I will point out later, this was the kind of relationship that Erauso had with the two women whom she promised to marry. In both instances gifts were exchanged, discussions with the family took place—in short, all the behaviors that customarily led up to the union of two families through matrimony. Seduction, on the other hand, is more secretive and guarded; carried out in private, its goal is to establish a sexual relationship between a man and a woman. Almost always, it began by offering a promise of marriage, which later may or may not have resulted in a legal union between the two lovers. Without doubt, the episode involving Solarte's sister-in-law fits into this second category. There was a sexual relationship (to

Young Basque woman (Maria Lusa de Arizmendi, *Vascos y Trajes*).

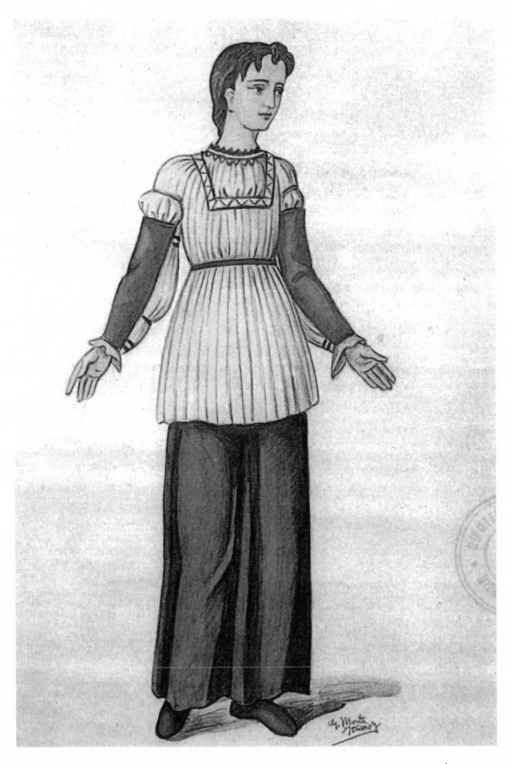

Maiden from Donostia-San Sebastián (Maria Lusa de Arizmendi, *Vascos y Trajes*).

Woman from Hondarribia, Gipuzkoa (María Lusa de Arizmendi, *Vascos y Trajes*).

Young Basque man (María Luisa de Arizmendi, *Vascos y Trajes*).

the degree possible) between them, plans for marriage were discussed, and all of this transpired secretly, hidden from public view. The promise of marriage became the critical link between courtship and seduction. When every other instrument of courtship at his disposal had been exhausted, the male suitor played the last card remaining to him: the promise of marriage. Once a woman lost her virginity, the nature of the couple's relationship was altered; the couple crossed over a threshold into the area of more permanent unions. Plaintiffs' accounts in the lawsuits brought by women were unanimous on this point: the loss of virginity and sexual intercourse occurred *only* after the woman had received pledges of marriage from the man.[94]

In a previous part of my study, when I addressed the topic of Erauso's amorous episodes involving women, I suggested that they might possibly have been later additions superimposed on the original lost text. My thought was that it was difficult to believe that Erauso would voluntarily include such compromising details in her memoir at the same time that she was preparing her *Pedimento,* or Petition to the Crown, a document in which she highlights her heroic acts with the intention of receiving a royal pension. Now, however, I will speculate on the possibility that these episodes really were penned by Erauso herself and that they do recount real events in her life. William A. Douglass points out another motive for their inclusion: to show a more "human" side of the character, as a counterbalance to the more heroic and virtuous side that is so amply developed in the *Autobiografía.* Her character as a whole thus becomes more credible and realistic. There is a second possibility, also suggested by Douglass. Given the tightly-knit relationships that characterized the members of the Basque community, had these episodes been known, someone could have reported them. Therefore, Erauso took precautions, preferring that they hear about them from her own pen. This particular hypothesis would explain why Erauso included episodes describing the two attempted arranged marriages, because in both these instances the families involved, as well as all the other people around her, would have heard about them.[95]

On the other hand, the inclusion of these episodes can also be explained if we remember that Erauso always counted on using her virginity as her trump card. Since she was a proven virgin, these amorous flirtations could be viewed as "harmless"; that is, just the innocent sport of a woman soldier who was thought to be basically asexual. Since she had to be constantly concerned about disguising her true sexual identity, any of these relationships would have very clear physical limitations. In light of these circumstances, the legal and ecclesiastical transgressions implied by her behavior could be considered less serious.

Shortly following this episode, Erauso encountered her brother for the first time. Miguel de Erauso arranged to have her assigned to his own military post, and they spent three years together. During this time she recounts,

> I went with him to the house of the mistress he kept in town, and on other occasions, I went there without him. It wasn't long before he found out, and imagining the worst, he told me that he'd better not catch me at it again. But he spied on me, and when he caught

me there the next time, he waited outside, and when I came out he lit into me with his belt, wounding me in the hand.[96]

Here, just as was the case with Urquiza's mistress, we see Erauso paying visits to her best friend's love interest. In this instance, much more than was true in the episode involving Beatriz de Cárdenas, it is clear that Erauso felt a strong sexual attraction for the woman, and she was willing to challenge her own brother because of it. First she visited her with Miguel, and later without him, obviously wanting to play the leading man in the erotic flirtation. Had she not felt such an attraction, it is hard to imagine that having received a stern warning from her brother, she would risk seeing the woman again.

Next in sequence are the episodes describing the two attempted marriages. With respect to the first, we must emphasize that the fiancée was not the kind of female that Erauso was attracted to: "a girl as black and ugly as the devil himself, quite the opposite of my taste, which has always run to pretty faces." Indirectly, this was a confession that she liked women, especially the good-looking ones. The second fiancée came closer to her idea of feminine beauty: "I met the girl, and she seemed good enough." One cannot help but imagine that during the time she was courting both girls, Erauso must have displayed some affection for them, since neither family seemed to have the slightest suspicion that they were going to be victims of a fraud. And so, even though marriage would not have been viable with either of them, Erauso tells us which one of the two intended brides pleases her and which one doesn't.

Erauso's final erotic relationship with a female involved María Dávalos, the woman who begged her help because her husband had found her in bed with another man. The husband killed the lover, and now wanted to kill her too. After some friars who were on the scene explained the situation to Erauso, urging her to help Dávalos escape, she agreed to take the lady to a convent in La Plata founded by Dávalos's mother, who had taken the veil. What is of particular interest is the denouement of this story. Chavarría, Dávalos's husband, filed a complaint against Erauso because he believed that her true motive in rescuing his wife was not to help her escape, but to have an illicit relationship with her. Prior to the episode involving Dávalos's flight, Erauso had spent two days in the Chavarría household, settling some accounts, and she recounts that she was received very well there. Did something happen during Erauso's stay that caused Chavarría to have doubts about her true intentions regarding his wife? Although Chavarría had no conclusive proof to support his accusation, clearly something led him to believe that.

In the trial that ensued, several witnesses came forward to explain that Erauso "had become involved in the affair innocently, altogether by chance and without malice." Of course we know—in view of episodes we have just summarized—that in her relationships with many of her lovers, Erauso was far from being innocent and without malice. Let us now focus on her own remarks after the case was settled in her favor: "I came out of hiding, settled my affairs, and went quite often to visit my little nun and her mother, and some of the other ladies there, all of whom were invariably pleased by my company and made me many gifts of this, that, and the other thing." It is curious that María

Dávalos—whom, according to the story, Erauso hardly knew—is later referred to as "my little nun," a person whom she visits frequently. As we have been able to observe, whenever Erauso paid visits to ladies, she had either an erotic or an economic motive. In her words there seems to be a veiled insinuation that something similar was also involved in her relationship with María Dávalos

Catalina de Erauso: Male or Female?

I will now consider Erauso's gender identity and its bearing on her decision to live as a man. Thus far, all the personal motives we have adduced as explanations of female transvestism in the Early Modern Age have been "external" in nature: love, patriotic fervor, or simple economic necessity. Nevertheless, there are other reasons of a more psychological or "internal" nature that are directly related to the subject of sexuality. It is essential to draw a clear difference between women who for specific reasons occasionally wanted to impersonate men, and those who decided to try spending the rest of their lives (or until such time as they are discovered) as individuals who belong to the opposite sex.

Earlier I observed that Erauso's transsexuality was not caused by any physical irregularity in her anatomy. In their sources, Dekker and Van de Pol do document one such case, and although they believe that there were probably more of them, it is difficult to get enough information to confirm them. What these women have in common with Erauso, and with other women who transform themselves into men "forever," is that they feel that their genetic sex was a mistake, and so they seek a permanent transformation to a gender identity to which they do not biologically belong. In these cases of transsexuality, the traditional gender dichotomy ceases to have validity; these individuals (men who consider themselves women, or women who consider themselves men) contain two sexual poles within themselves: they feel and act like men or women, but they do not have the corresponding physiological characteristics.

Women who disguise themselves as men because they believe that, psychologically, they *are* men, are totally different from women who dress as men for limited periods of time. In other words, transvestism and transsexualism are two different phenomena. While "dressing" would satisfy the true transvestite (who is content with his/her morphological sex), to the transsexual it is only incidental and no more than a temporary solution. Transsexuals feel that they belong to the other sex; they want to function and be like members of the opposite sex, not just to appear as such.[97] Harry Benjamin defines transvestism as a social problem with a sex and gender implication; in the case of women, it applies to women who are set on the social aspects of men, and seek to emulate them in expressing their masculinity, which means their clothing, adornment, hairstyle, and mannerisms.[98] In transvestism the emotions are always involved, tinged more or less with eroticism, and sexual stimulation. In contrast, what seems to predominate in transsexualism is a low sex drive and gender dissatisfaction.[99]

My own opinion regarding Catalina de Erauso is that she suffered from what today is called "gender dysphoria," an atypical development in the relationship between the sex and the gender of an individual, that in its most extreme manifestation is known as transsexualism. Gender identity describes the psychological identification within an individual's mind as "male" or "female"; that is, the recognition of oneself as fitting into the social categories: "boy/man" or "girl/woman." Sex, on the other hand, is understood to represent the external appearance of the genitalia and the presence of the gonads (testicles or ovaries) that determine the reproductive function. Typically, the elements of sex and gender identity will be consistent with each other and with the underlying chromosomal pattern: XX for a girl, and XY for a boy. But this is not always the case.[100]

In the early investigations of transsexualism and transvestism made during the 1960s, Benjamin divides the principal theorists into two groups: a European school that presupposed a biological cause, and an American school that based its theories on psychological causes. Two possible biological sources of transsexualism are the genetic and the endocrine. The genetic source referred to a disturbed "chromosomal sex"; that is, a disturbance in the function of the sexual chromosomes (X and Y). As for the possible endocrine cause of transsexualism, numerous male transsexuals have been found to have more or less distinct signs of a degree of sexual underdevelopment (hypogonadism). In different transsexual males, investigators discovered large amounts of estrogen in the testes. In recent years, evidence has accumulated that hormone medication during pregnancy can have serious consequences for the newborn. If a mother was given testosterone or progesterone for any length of time during her pregnancy, it is thought that the genetic sex of the child could be affected. Since the fetus is under the influence of the mother's estrogen for a nine month period, it is possible that even when a normal amount of estrogen is present, under certain circumstances it could interfere with the sexual development of the fetus.[101]

Recent studies have shed additional light on the etiology of transsexualism. Current knowledge regarding the biological components of phenomena related to transsexuality or gender dysphoria has validated some of the scientific theories reported by Benjamin forty years ago. According to the Gender Research & Education Society, transsexualism is associated with the neurodevelopment of the brain; it can be traced to a nucleus situated in the hypothalamic area of the brain. In males, the size of this nucleus is twice as large as that in females and its number of neurons is almost double. In studies involving transsexuals it has been observed that this nucleus has characteristics that correspond to those of a person of the opposite sex.[102] The sexual differentiation of the brain begins during fetal development and continues after birth. What is now hypothesized is that hormones have a decisive influence in the development of the nucleus, although the exact mechanism is not known. It is also thought that these hormonal changes take place at critical periods of development of the sexual differentiation of the brain, during which the gender identity is established: initially during the fetal period, later at birth, and also after birth. As had been theorized previously, the factors that could contribute to the development of an altered hormonal environment in the brain during these critical stages might include genetic influences, medication taken by the mother, or stress or trauma to the mother during pregnancy.

Currently it is impossible to identify one single cause of transsexualism; it appears that its causality is complex and multifactoral. In addition to the causes we have mentioned, one must also take into account the social and psychological factors. Even in those cases involving a predisposition for transsexualism, factors in the psychosocial environment can subsequently play a decisive role. However, there is no proof that nurturing, education, and socialization in contradiction to a sexual type can cause such a condition, nor that nurture in consistence with a sexual type can prevent it. It appears that nurturing is only part of the story. Unless there is a constitutional predisposition, psychosocial conditioning in and of itself is not enough.[103]

It may seem anachronistic to apply current scientific concepts that explain sexual behavior to individuals who lived in the sixteenth and seventeenth centuries. And yet, the problem is one of form rather than substance. Evidently, the phenomenon known today as transsexualism is not new. Why should it be? Sex changes were reported as far back as the classical world; in fact, if we consider the recent theories that give more weight to biological than to psychological or cultural factors, it could not have been otherwise. What is novel is to view Erauso from this perspective. In her life story, we see a drama of conflicted gender identity that manifests itself through cross-dressing. Her transvestism is superficial in nature; she was not pretending to be a man, she probably felt that she was a man.

Dekker and Van de Pol report another probable case of transsexuality: that of Maria van Antwerpen, born in Breda in 1719. Faced with a situation of poverty in which she would be forced to become a prostitute in order to survive, she decided to don men's clothing and become a soldier in the Dutch army. She married a woman who was unaware of the deceit, with whom she lived for three years, successfully avoiding sexual contact by feigning moodiness and illness until she was discovered by a member of the family. Years later, in spite of the trial and banishment she suffered as a consequence of the first marriage, she entered into wedlock with another woman. During her second trial in 1769, she was asked by the magistrates whether she was a man or a woman. She answered: "By nature, and character, a man, but in appearance, a woman." Her words express the reality of an individual who feels "trapped in a body of the wrong sex."[104]

Luzmila Camacho Platero wonders whether in fact "it would be possible to classify Catalina as a transsexual; . . . that is, a female who feels like a male, and in her case, a heterosexual male." She rejects this possibility citing the *Tercera Relación,* in which "we are told about the genuine attraction that Catalina/Antonio feels for a woman who wanted to take the veil, for whom she was ready to sacrifice everything: part of the pension she would receive from the Crown, the male status for which she had struggled, and her freedom."[105] Admittedly, an Erauso who would be willing to enter a convent and live as a nun for the rest of her life in order to be near the woman she loved would indeed be agreeing to transform herself into a completely different person. The problem with this interpretation is that the historical authenticity of the *Tercera Relación* is highly questionable, and we cannot allow our conception of Catalina de Erauso to be based on such a document. This *Tercera Relación*, or broadside, was published in Mexico twenty-eight years after the publication of the *Autobiografía*, the *Primera*, and the *Segunda Relación*; and also, after the death of our protagonist.

There are various reasons for questioning its historical truthfulness. First, it is noteworthy that of the almost twenty years that covers this particular version of Erauso's life, the only episode worth recounting is that of her frustrated love relationship. Those episodes of her life that can be corroborated by historical documents are absent, while others are added that cannot be documented at all. Vallbona, referring to a passage in the *Relación* that mentions certain gifts that the pope supposedly offered to Erauso in Rome, observes: "This incident is not mentioned in the *Vida e sucesos*. We should recall that her trip overland and her account of how she was arrested are indeed included in her alleged *Autobiografía*. It is noteworthy that those adventures are passed over in this *Tercera Relación*."[106] Although the text attempts to document the amorous attraction by quoting a letter (purportedly written by Erauso) that refers to the episode, hardly anything is said about the other events that took place during the almost twenty-year period covered in the *Relación*; the principal theme of this text is the story of a forbidden and unrequited love.[107] Its content stands in clear contradiction not only to Erauso's conduct as it is portrayed in other publications, but also to what is known about her historical figure. Since no documents exist that can attest to the veracity of this episode, I do not believe we can base our interpretation of her character on its content.

Now I will briefly mention those aspects of Erauso's life story that have led me to elaborate this view of her personality. Her flight from the convent coincided with the onset of her adolescence. During childhood, symptoms of gender dysphoria were almost impossible to detect. For most individuals the discomfort grows through adolescence and adulthood, when the family and society, ignorant of the underlying gender identity, try to reinforce those social expectations imposed on them in accordance with their physical appearance alone. The discomfort begins to emerge during adolescence when sexual feelings are awakened. That Erauso should escape then can be attributed in part to her inner feelings of discomfort as she realized more clearly just what would be expected of her as she became a young woman. In any case, what we know is that when she left the convent, her first act was to change her sexual identity in the eyes of the world.

She did not just present herself as a man; she was always treated as such by others. Over a fifteen-year period, nothing in her physical appearance or her demeanor betrayed her. After living as a man for long years, the transformation experienced by Erauso went beyond just her clothing and her physical appearance. We should recall that at that time the differences between men and woman were clearly obvious, exhibited by characteristics such as language, gestures, and by an entire code of social behavior. In Erauso, her profanity, her fights, her ability to perform physically demanding tasks—the entire repertoire of male behavior—had to turn into a second skin for her, becoming a natural part of her appearance and personality. The vicissitudes of her life during these years include episodes that show how difficult it must have been to maintain her disguise; for example the long sea voyage from Spain to the Americas, when as we know, lacking all privacy, she was forced to live in close quarters with male passengers. Following this we see her engaging in military combat against the Indians, and in an entire repertoire of the kinds of activities typical of men in colonial America: gambling, sword fights, and womanizing. Her ability to adapt herself to all these male behaviors cannot fail to be astonishing. It is truly revealing that she was able to impersonate a man so convincingly that not a single one of her many companions, in battle and in many other of her adventures, suspected her sexual disguise.

In my view, it is logical to conclude that this performance was so long-lasting and persuasive because in reality it fit her nature; that is, she neither needed to pretend nor to hide who she was. She simply adopted, with relative ease, the attitudes and the conduct then deemed to be masculine. There are, nevertheless, some indications that some individuals perceived a certain femininity, or at least, a lack of masculinity in her physical appearance; that is why some of those who attempted to describe her employ the descriptive terms "eunuch" or "castrated." With their beardless faces and the higher pitch of their voices, many of these women must have looked more like young male adolescents than mature men. Although this characteristic is not mentioned in the *Autobiografía*, it does appear in the letter that Pedro de la Valle, "the pilgrim," writes to his friend Mario Schipano on July 11, 1626. "She fought in many battles in these parts, in different companies, and always gave a good account of herself in the various engagements, so she acquired the reputation of being valiant, and since she had no beard on her face, she was considered to be and called castrated."[108] In a document that reported the news in Seville (dated July 4, 1630), a reference to Erauso appeared that states that she was "thought to be a eunuch."[109] It is very likely that these kinds of insults and epithets are at the bottom of the many fights that she had with countless soldiers and gamblers in the New World.

What is extraordinary, however, is that even when her true sexual identity was known in Spain and the Americas, she continued to be treated and referred to as a man, thus making her male status a public and official matter. It is not just that she considered herself a man, but that everyone else did too. In this connection, it is significant that her neighbors in Donostia-San Sebastián and members of her own family referred to her as "The Lieutenant Antonio de Erauso."

Erauso's self-assignment to the male gender is also clearly apparent when, in most of the text of the *Autobiografía*, she employs masculine forms when she refers to herself, although this is an issue that cannot be totally resolved until the lost original or at least an earlier copy of the manuscript is found. Whatever opinion Erauso may have had about the feminine sex in general, what we do know is that she considered it an insult to be identified as a woman. That is how the text of her memoir ends, with her being recognized by two Neapolitan women as she is walking along the street disguised as a man. Here we see that Erauso considers the laughter of those who seek to unmask her as an insult to her honor, and she reacts violently, just as a man who had been dishonored would react, threatening to kill not just the guilty women but also—so there would be no doubt regarding her manliness and valor—the two gentlemen who were accompanying them.

We know that during that historical period conditions of life on board ships were very hard; that is why very few of the women who tried to pass for men in the navy could maintain their disguise for very long. For women who wanted to conceal their female identity, the best choice was to live a stable civilian life, a life that Erauso, as a matter of fact, always preferred. As we have seen, she signed on as a soldier only when she found herself penniless and without a job; it was her only recourse in a tight situation. While it is true that military life afforded her some good experiences (for example, the encounter and the comradeship with her brother, and the recognition given her when she was awarded the title of lieutenant), it is also true that she abandoned that life quite willingly in order to return to the anonymity of a civilian life as a merchant. Many transvestite women who engaged in civilian jobs were discovered only in extreme circumstances, such as the examination of their bodies after death. Who knows whether Erauso would have been discovered had she pursued a civilian life as a merchant and not become repeatedly involved in all manner of brawls and fights? What has been corroborated is that Erauso, both as a soldier and a merchant, functioned very successfully as a man in the society of her time.

Twenty-two years after having abandoned her birthplace, in 1629, after both her mother and her father had died, she returned to Donostia-San Sebastián. The local citizens who commented on her visit referred to the Lieutenant Alférez Don Antonio de Erauso, not to Catalina. On this trip, she renounced her share of the paternal and maternal estate, signing it over to her sister Mariana in exchange for a sum of money. This is revealed as a consequence of a lawsuit in which the litigant, Ana de Hoa, asks several witnesses to provide testimonies. In 1649, Ana de Hoa, a second cousin to the Erauso sisters and brothers, presented a petition regarding the administration of the estate left by the "Lieutenant D. Antonio de Erauso." In defense of her rights, she mentioned that Catalina's parents had left considerable property and goods, "inherited by the Lieutenant D. Antonio de Erauso, a legitimate son of the aforementioned, [who has been] absent more than fourteen years." Since the Lieutenant Antonio de Erauso had not designated a person to look after his estate, she stated that "if something is not done, my part [of the estate] will be lost." As a relative of the Erausos she was seeking information regarding the lieutenant's absence and this explains why witnesses appeared and provided testimonies about having seen the lieutenant in Donostia-San Sebastián. By 1649, Erauso had again established herself in the Americas, but according to Tellechea's account, several witnesses recalled her visit to Donostia-San Sebastián in 1629. They all declared that the person who returned was a man, the Lieutenant Antonio de Erauso:

> Aguirre, the priest, had been acquainted with the parents, the nuns Mari Juan and Jacinta, and the *lieutenant*; he was aware (as he had heard mentioned) of the fact that *he* was in the Indies, and that he had left San Sebastián 13 or 14 years ago . . . The priest Juan de

Echave . . . made the acquaintance of *Lieutenant D. Antonio de Erauso*, who was well known in this town thirteen or fourteen years ago, before he returned to the Indies . . . Captain Juan Pérez de Aguirre states he knew *Lieutenant D. Antonio de Erauso* both here and in the Indies, where this witness had also lived, and had seen him and spoken to him in the port of Vera Cruz during the year sixteen hundred and thirty-nine, there he left the said *Lieutenant Erauso*, and in the aforesaid year this witness returned to this city, and had heard that he is still in the Indies.[110]

An additional example of Erauso's being identified socially as a male can be found in the statements made by witnesses who testified regarding the assault suffered by her and several other companions as they were traveling through the Piedmont on their way to Rome. The six witnesses who made their statements to a clerk of the royal tribunal call her *Lieutenant Antonio de Herausso*, and never acknowledge that this lieutenant is the famous Catalina de Erauso. The clerks and notaries involved in the trial refer to her with the same name, for example: "I, Baltasar Salgado, a clerk in the service of his Royal Majesty, who resides in his court and province, copied this information from the original, given to me for this purpose by the person known as *Lieutenant Antonio de Herausso*."[111] We should bear in mind that this happened one year after her return to Spain; that is, after her true feminine identity had been revealed to everyone. As Aranzazu Borrachero Mendíbil points out, "Erauso's masculinity is so convincing that [to the reader of her memoirs] the scene in which she again dons the nun's habit seems like an act of violence perpetrated on the character."[112] Many other examples similar to the ones I have noted can be found in documents of the period. They are significant because they confirm the public transformation of Catalina into Antonio, even in the eyes of the law. When identifying her as Antonio, these friends and neighbors sanctioned the male gender role she reassumed after her biological sexual identity had been discovered. This should not be surprising. As we have noted, Erauso requested permission from the king and the pope to continue dressing as a man, and it was granted by both of them.

Once she ceased wearing female clothing she would never voluntarily wear it again. Erauso was requesting that her identity not be stolen from her, that she be allowed to continue being the person she had been since the early years of her youth. Having succeeded in obtaining leave to do so, she disappeared into anonymity, living as an ordinary man. When shortly following her return to Spain she decided to go back to the New World, she turned her back on a celebrity status that had spread across the globe to the Far East. Instead of exploiting the fame she had acquired through the *Relaciones* or broadsides, the *Autobiografía*, and the enormous popularity of Pérez de Montalbán's play, *La Monja Alférez* (1626), she left it all behind. With her pension, and the dispensation to continue living as Antonio, she departed for the Americas never to return again. She rejected a life of iconic fame to resume her life as a man in Latin America, working as an anonymous muleteer and small merchant. Regarding this last segment of her life we have only two reports, and in both of them Catalina disappeared from sight and definitively became Antonio. The first comes from Captain Juan Pérez de Aguirre who testified in Donostia-San Sebastián (1640) during a hearing regarding the Erauso estate.

> In the city of New Veracruz, in the Kingdom of New Spain, in March of 1639, I had asked Captain Domingo de Portu, of San Sebastián, and Captain Francisco de Endara, also of San Sebastián, for news of Miguel, Francisco, Martín, and Domingo de Erauso, and had been told that they were all dead—Francisco in the city of Lima, in his capacity as mayordomo or secretary to the Viceroy; Miguel in Chile; and that he couldn't remember where the others were said to have died, but it was common knowledge that they were all dead, all excepting a brother of theirs called *Don Antonio de Erauso, alias Alférez Monja*, with whom he had spoken at this same time, in the city of Veracruz, and who had confirmed the deaths of the four brothers.[113]

A second document recorded declarations made in Seville by the Capuchin friar Nicolás de Rentería, also a Basque, who stated that in 1645 while he was still a layman he saw and spoke to Erauso in Veracruz. In the year 1645, he served on the galleons of General D. Pedro de Ursua, and in Veracruz

> he saw and spoke several times with [the Lieutenant Nun] Doña Catalina de Erauso (who went there by the name of Antonio de Erauso); that she had a mule pack with which she, along with some slaves carried stuff all over, and that on those mules, and with the help of those slaves, she transported goods to Mexico; that she was the King's subject and known as a person of much courage and skill; that she dressed in a man's clothing and wore a sword and dagger ornamented in silver. She seemed to be about fifty years old, of strong build, somewhat stout, swarthy in complexion, with few hairs on her chin.[114]

In this description of Erauso's physical appearance, the last detail regarding the "few hairs on her chin" suggests that she was considered a "eunuch," as we previously noted. Although the documents available to us contain no observations regarding her psychological transformation, they do, on the other hand, allude to her physical appearance. In a letter written to Mario Schipano mentioned earlier, Pedro de la Valle (who happened to be in Rome while Erauso was there and had invited her to his home) provides a detailed portrait of her.

> Tall and powerfully built, and with a masculine air, she has no more breasts than a girl. She told me she had used some sort of remedy to make them disappear. I believe it was a poultice given her by an Italian—it hurt a great deal, but since it neither harmed nor deformed her, the effect was very much to her liking. Her face is not ugly, but it is very worn with years, she wears her black hair cut like a man's, a little long, as is now the fashion. Her appearance is basically that of a eunuch rather than a woman. She dresses like a man, in the Spanish style. She girds her sword bravely, and holds her chest high, but carries her head a little low and bent over, more like an ungainly soldier than a courtier on his way to flirt with ladies. Only by [looking at] her hand can you tell that she is a woman; though it is strong and sturdy, it is plump and fleshy, and she gesticulates in a somewhat feminine manner.[115]

Here we learn about the remedy used by Erauso to alter her body so that it would more resemble a man's. Can this physical change not be seen as the Baroque equivalent of sex reassignment operations conducted on modern transsexuals? In both instances, the premises are the same: to modify the body so that it better reflects the person's gender; to make sex and gender agree. While it is true that one of Erauso's reasons for doing this was the need to maintain her disguise, her real reason for wanting to change her body was a deeper one: it was the conflict between her sexual identity and her gender identity. Submitting her body to this invasive procedure implies that she early on chose a path of no return with respect to a male identity; her life story would later demonstrate that this was really the true path for Erauso.

Notes

Notes, Chapter One

1. María Estíbaliz Ruíz de Azúa y Martínez de Ezquerecocha, *Vascongadas y América* (Madrid: Editorial MAPFRE, 1992), 220.

2. William A. Douglass, "For the Bookshelf," *Basque Studies Program Newsletter* 54 (1996), 1.

3. Catalina de Erauso, *Historia de la Monja Alférez, Catalina de Erauso, escrita por ella misma*, ed. Angel Esteban (Madrid: Cátedra, Letras Hispánicas, 2002), 77–82.

4. Mary Elizabeth Perry, "La monja alférez: Myth, Gender, and the Manly Woman in a Spanish Renaissance Drama," in *La Chispa '87. Selected Proceedings,* ed. Gilbert Paolini (New Orleans: Tulane University, 1987), 246.

5. Ruiz de Azua, *Vascongadas y América*, 230–31.

6. Kathleen Ann Myers, *Neither Saints nor Sinners: Writing the Lives of Women in Spanish America* (New York: Oxford University Press, 2003), 149.

7. Sherry Velasco, *The Lieutenant Nun: Transgenderism, Lesbian Desire, and Catalina de Erauso* (Austin: University of Texas Press, 2000), 46.

8. Rima R. Vallbona, *Vida i sucesos de la Monja Alférez (Autobiografía atribuida a doña Catalina de Erauso)* (Tempe, Ariz.: Center for Latin American Studies, Arizona State University, 1992), 3.

9. In the prologue to his edition, Ferrer declares: "Persuaded that it was not about an imaginary being, I read it again more carefully, because of the simple language in which it was written, and because of the many historical facts it contains, the consistency of the persons and the times she refers to, I was persuaded that it bore the seal of truth." José María Ferrer, prologue, Catalina de Erauso: *Historia de la monja alférez, doña Catalina de Erauso, contada por ella misma*, ed. José María Ferrer (Paris: Julio Didot, 1829), xxiii.

10. Stephanie Merrim, "Catalina de Erauso: From Anomaly to Icon," in *Coded Encounters: Writing, Gender, and Ethnicity in Colonial Latin America,* eds. Francisco Javier Cevallos-Candau, et al. (Amherst: University of Massachusetts Press, 1994), 179.

11. Three historians wrote about Erauso during her lifetime, but their works were not published until the seventeenth (Pedro Salazar de Mendoza and Gil González Dávila) and the nineteenth centuries (Lope Martínez de Isasti), José Ignacio Tellechea Idígoras, *Doña Catalina de Erauso, la Monja Alférez. IV Centenario de su nacimiento* (San Sebastián: Sociedad Guipuzcoana de Ediciones y Publicaciones, 1992), 147–59.

12. Ibid., 208–9.

13. See also other contemporary editions; for example, that of Luis Iñigo-Madrigal, *Cinco textos, supuestamente autobiográficos, sobre la vida de Catalina de Erauso, conocida como* La Monja Alférez, *acompañados de la relación de los últimos años de su vida en la Nueva España* (Genéve: Université de Genève, 1997).

14. Lisa Vollendorf, *The Lives of Women: A New History of Inquisitorial Spain* (Nashville: Vanderbilt University Press, 2005), 74.

15. Bárbara Mujica, *Women Writers of Early Modern Spain: Sophia's Daughters* (New Haven and London: Yale University Press, 2004), 162. Velasco, *The Lieutenant Nun: Transgenderism, Lesbian Desire, and Catalina de Erauso,* provides a complete review of the character's presence in movies, plays, and comic books. For the most recent edition of Montalbán's play see Luzmila Camacho Platero, *La Monja Alférez de Juan Pérez de Montalbán* (Newark, Del.: Juan de la Cuesta, 2007).

16. Luis de Castresana, *Catalina de Erauso, la monja alférez* (Barcelona: Ediciones Internacionales Universitarias, 1996); Gloria Durán, *Catalina, mi padre* (Mexico, D.F.: Planeta, 1994); Juanita Gallardo, *Confesiones de la Monja Alférez* (Providencia, Santiago, Chile: Seix Barral, 2005); Roberto González Echevarría, *The Oxford Book of Latin American Short Stories* (New York: Oxford University Press, 1997); Ricard Ibáñez, *La monja alférez* (Barcelona: Devir, 2004); Chufo Llorens, *Catalina, la fugitiva de San Benito* (Barcelona: Ediciones B, 2001); Markus Orths, *Catalina* (London: The Toby Press, 2006); Armonía Rodríguez, *De monja a militiar Caterina de Erauso* (Barcelona: La Busca Ediciones, 2003).

17. For example, the anthologies edited by Mujica, *Women Writers of Early Modern Spain* and Nina M. Scott, *Madres del Verbo/Mothers of the Word: Early Spanish-American Women Writers. A Bilingual Anthology* (Albuquerque: University of New Mexico Press, 1999) respectively, or José Manuel Fajardo's biographical collection, *De aventureros y revolucionarios* (Montevideo: Ediciones de la Banda Oriental, 2003). Also new editions or reprints: Milbry Polk and Mary Tiegreen, *Women of Discovery: A Celebration of Intrepid Women Who Explored the World* (New York: Clarkson Potter Publishers, 2001), Vicenta M. Marquéz de la Plata y Ferrándiz, *Mujeres de acción en el Siglo de Oro* (Madrid: Editorial Castalia, 2006); Juan Antonio Mateos, *La monja alférez* (Barcelona: Linkgua, 2006); Myers, *Neither Saints nor Sinners*; Elizabeth Herminia Paredes Calderón, *Algunos aspectos de la tradición palmista. A propósito de ¡A iglesia me llamo!* (Lima: Universidad Ricardo Palma, Editorial Universitaria, 2006).

18. Catalina de Erauso, *Lieutenant Nun: Memoir of a Basque Transvestite in the New World*, trans. and intro. Michele Stepto and Gabriel Stepto, foreword by Marjorie Garber (Boston: Beacon Press, 1996), 5.

19. Ibid., 6.

20. Ibid., 11.

21. Ibid., 12.

22. Ibid.

23. Ibid., 40.

24. Ibid., 64.

25. Pedro Rubio Merino, *La monja alferez: Doña Catalina de Erauso. Dos manuscritos inéditos de su autobiografía conservados en el Archivo de la Santa Iglesia Catedral de Sevilla* (Sevilla: Cabildo Metropolitano de la Catedral de Sevilla, 1995), 86.

26. Ibid.

27. Velasco, *The Lieutenant Nun: Transgenderism, Lesbian Desire, and Catalina de Erauso*, 5.

28. Myers, *Neither Saints nor Sinners*, 145.

29. "His Eminence left the palace with me at his side, and we made our way slowly through a crowd so huge, it was hard to believe there was anyone left at home, or that we would ever get to the church. Finally we came around to the convent gate, for it was impossible to enter at the main doors, as His Eminence had planned. All the nuns were there, bearing lighted candles." Erauso, *Lieutenant Nun: Memoir of a Basque Transvestite in the New World*, 66.

30. Ibid., 74.

31. Ibid., 78.

Notes, Chapter Two

1. José Ramón Zubiaur, "Euskara y castellano en el País Vasco en la época de Iñigo de Loyola," in *El pueblo vasco en el Renacimiento (1491–1521)*, ed. José Luis Orella (Bilbao: Ediciones Mensajero, 1990), 481.

2. Koldo Zuazo, "The Basque Country and the Basque Language: An Overview of the External History of the Basque Language," in *Towards a History of the Basque Language* (Amsterdam: John Benjamins Publishing Company, 1995), 10.

3. Gregorio Monreal, "Annotations Regarding Basque Traditional Political Thought in the Sixteenth Century," in *Basque Politics: A Case Study in Ethnic Nationalism,* ed. William A. Douglass (Reno: Associatied Faculty Press and Basque Studies Program, 1985), 44.

4. José Luis Pinillos, "Sobre el carácter de los vascos," in *Los vascos y América. Ideas, hechos, hombres,* ed. Ignacio Arana Pérez (Madrid: Gela S.A., Espasa-Calpe/Argantonio, 1990), 12.

5. Miguel de Cervantes Saavedra, *Don Quixote*. The Ormsby Transl., eds. Joseph Jones and Kenneth Douglas (New York: Norton, 1981), 680.

6. Cervantes Saavedra, *Don Quixote*, 63.

7. Miguel de Cervantes Saavedra, *Miguel de Cervantes' Interludes/Entremeses*, trans., intro. and notes Randall W. Listermann (Lewiston, NY: Edwin Mellen Press, 1991), 82–83.

8. *Ortografía castellana* (Mexico, 1609), quoted by Juan Antonio Frago Gracia, *Historia del español de América* (Madrid: Gredos, 1999), 101–2.

9. Julio Caro Baroja, *Introducción a la historia social del Pueblo Vasco.* (San Sebastián: Txertoa, 1974), 55.

10. Frago Gracia, *Historia del español de América*, 108–9.

11. Monreal, "Annotations Regarding Basque Traditional Political Thought in the Sixteenth Century," 28.

12. Ibon Sarasola, *Historia social de la literatura vasca* (Barcelona: Akal, 1976), 44.

13. Quoted in Miren Jaione Markaida-Golzarri, "La articulación de la identidad nacional euskérica in textos de los siglos XVI, XVII, y XVIII" (Ph.D. diss., 2001), 137–38 (emphasis added).

14. Note by José María Ferrer in Catalina de Erauso, *Historia de la monja alférez, doña Catalina de Erauso, contada por ella misma*, ed. José María Ferrer (Paris: Julio Didot, 1829), quoted by Rima R. Vallbona, *Vida i sucesos de la Monja Alférez (Autobiografía atribuida a doña Catalina de Erauso)* (Tempe, Ariz.: Center for Latin American Studies, Arizona State University, 1992), 49 (emphasis added).

15. María Teresa Echenique, *Estudios lingüísticos vasco-románicos* (Madrid: Ediciones Istmo, 1997), 80.

16. Ibid., 80–81.

17. Ibid., 81.

18. Luis Michelena, *Textos arcaicos vascos* (San Sebastián: Diputación Foral de Guipúzcoa-Universidad del País Vasco, 1990), 124.

19. Ibid.

20. Koldobika J. Bijuesca, "Propuesta de interpretación del texto vasco de sor Juana Inés de la Cruz en su contexto," in *Los vascos en las regiones de México, Siglos XVI a XX,* ed. Amaya Garritz (México: Universidad Nacional Autónoma de México, 1996), 289.

21. Bijuesca, "Propuesta de interpretación del texto vasco de sor Juana Inés de la Cruz en su contexto," 294.

22. Echenique, *Estudios lingüísticos vasco-románicos*, 76.

23. Zubiaur, "Euskara y castellano en el País Vasco en la época de Iñigo de Loyola," 477.

24. Zubiaur, "Euskara y castellano en el País Vasco en la época de Iñigo de Loyola"; Echenique, *Estudios lingüísticos vasco-románicos*; Michelena, *Textos arcaicos vascos*.

25. Adela Colera, "Situación lingüística de Azpeitia, fines del siglo XV–XVI: La(s) Lengua(s) de Iñigo de Loyola," in *El pueblo vasco en el Renacimiento (1491–1521)*, ed. José Luis Orella (Bilbao: Ediciones Mensajero, 1990), 483–84.

26. Cristina Oses, "La vertiente 'lingüística románica' del País Vasco," in *El pueblo vasco en el Renacimiento (1491–1521)*, ed. Orella, 467.

27. Quoted in Markaida-Golzarri, "La articulación de la identidad nacional euskérica in textos de los siglos XVI, XVII, y XVIII," 136.

28. Frago Gracia, *Historia del español de América*, 109.

29. Echenique, *Estudios lingüísticos vasco-románicos*, 76.

30. Renato Barahona, *Sex Crimes, Honour, and the Law in Early Modern Spain: Vizcaya, 1528–1735* (Toronto: University of Toronto Press, 2003), 55.

31. Ibid.

32. Michelena, *Textos arcaicos vascos*; Zuazo, "The Basque Country and the Basque Language," 9.

33. Zuazo, "The Basque Country and the Basque Language," 10.

34. Ramón Menéndez Pidal, "Introducción al estudio de la lingüística vasca," in *Curso de Lingüística.* (Sociedad de Estudios Vascos, 1921), 18.

35. José Ignacio Tellechea Idígoras, *Doña Catalina de Erauso, la Monja Alférez. IV Centenario de su nacimiento* (San Sebastián: Sociedad Guipuzcoana de Ediciones y Publicaciones, 1992), 196.

36. Cited by Encarnación Juárez, "La mujer militar en la América colonial: el caso de la monja alférez," *Indiana Journal of Hispanic Literatures* 10–11 (1997), 188.

37. Vallbona, *Vida i sucesos de la Monja Alféréz,* 8 (emphasis added).

38. Ibid.

39. Echenique, *Estudios lingüísitcos vasco-románicos*, 534.

40. Personal conversation with Rima R. Vallbona.

41. Vallbona, *Vida i sucesos de la Monja Alferéz,* 38; Catalina de Erauso, *Lieutenant Nun: Memoir of a Basque Transvestite in the New World,* trans. and intro. Michele Stepto and Gabriel Stepto, foreword by Marjorie Garber (Boston: Beacon Press, 1996), 6.

42. Frago Gracia, *Historia del español de América,* 113.

43. Ibid.

44. Ibid., 122.

45. Ibid., 131.

46. Ibid., 132.

47. Juana Alcira Arancibia, *"Vida y sucesos de la Monja Alférez:* Conversaciones de Juana Alcira Arancibia con Rima de Vallbona," in *Nuevos acercamientos a la obra de Rima de Vallbona (Actas del Simposio-homenaje),* ed. Jorge Chen Sham (San José: Editorial de la Universidad de Costa Rica, 2000), 186.

48. Frago Gracia, *Historia del español de América,* 110, 111.

49. For a discussion of the use of masculine and feminine pronouns that refer to Catalina, see Sherry Velasco, *The Lieutenant Nun: Transgenderism, Lesbian Desire, and Catalina de Erauso* (Austin: University of Texas Press, 2000), 6–7.

50. Vallbona, *Vida i sucesos de la Monja Alferéz,* 123 (emphasis added).

51. Ibid., 52.

52. Quoted in ibid., 6 (emphasis added).

53. Kathleen Ann Myers, *Neither Saints nor Sinners: Writing the Lives of Women in Spanish America* (New York: Oxford University Press, 2003), 147, 150.

54. Catalina de Erauso, *Historia de la Monja Alférez, Catalina de Erauso, escrita por ella misma,* ed. Angel Esteban (Madrid: Cátedra, Letras Hispánicas, 2002), 16.

55. Vallbona, *Vida i sucesos de la Monja Alferéz,* 8.

56. Alcira, *"Vida y sucesos de la Monja Alférez:* Conversaciones de Juana Alcira Arancibia con Rima de Vallbona," 186–87.

57. Vallbona, *Vida i sucesos de la Monja Alferéz,* 133.

Notes, Chapter Three

1. Julio Caro Baroja, *Los vascos y el mar* (Donostia-San Sebastián: Txertoa, 1985), 103.

2. Andrés E. Mañaricua, *Historia general del Señorío de Bizcaya, apéndice III. Polémica sobre Vizcaya en el siglo XVII. El Buho Gallego y El Tordo Vizcayno* (Bilbao: La Gran Enciclopedia Vasca, 1976), 68–69.

3. William A. Douglass and Jon Bilbao, *Amerikanuak: Basques in the New World* (Reno: University of Nevada Press, 1975), 68.

4. Luis Navarro García, "La colonia vasca en Andalucía en la Edad Moderna," in *Los vascos y América. Ideas, hechos, hombres,* ed. Ignacio Arana Pérez (Madrid: Gela; Espasa Calpe/Argantonio, 1990), 58.

5. Douglass and Bilbao, *Amerikanuak,* 69–70.

6. José Manuel Azcona Pastor, *Possible Paradises: Basque Emigration to Latin America* (Reno: University of Nevada Press, 2004), 112.

7. Bernardo Estornes Lasa et al. *Enciclopedia General Ilustrada del País Vasco,* vol. 11 (San Sebastián: Auñamendi, 1980), 79.

8. Douglass and Bilbao, *Amerikanuak,* 74.

9. Caro Baroja, *Los vascos y el mar,* 93.

10. Douglass and Bilbao, *Amerikanuak,* 79.

11. Javier Sanchiz Ruiz, "Redes vasco-navarras de poder en el México virreinal: la orden militar de Santiago," in *Los vascos en las regiones de México. Siglos XVI a XX,* ed. Amaya Garritz (México: Universidad Nacional Autónama de México, 1996), 195.

12. Valentín Vázquez de Prada and Juan Bosco Amores, "La emigración de navarros y vascongados al Nuevo Mundo y su repercusión en las comunidades de origen," in *Los vascos y América. Ideas, hechos, hombres*, ed. Ignacio Arana Pérez (Madrid: Gela; Espasa Calpe/Argantonio, 1990), 104.

13. Douglass and Bilbao, *Amerikanuak*, 74.

14. Ibid.

15. Ibid., 75.

16. José Mallea-Olaetxe, "The Private Basque World of Juan Zumárraga, First Bishop of México," *Revista de Historia de América* 114 (1992), 43.

17. Ibid., 44–45.

18. Ibid., 54.

19. Juan Javier Pescador, *The New World Inside a Basque Village: The Oiartzun Valley and Its Atlantic Emigrants, 1550–1800* (Reno: University of Nevada Press, 2004), 22.

20. See Chapter 7.

21. Azcona Pastor, *Possible Paradises: Basque Emigration to Latin America*. 112–13.

22. María Estíbaliz Ruiz de Azúa y Martínez de Ezquerecocha, *Vascongadas y América* (Madrid: Editorial MAPFRE, 1992), 234; Elisa Luque-Alcaide, "Asociacionismo vasco en la Nueva España: modelo étnico-cultural," in *Los vascos en las regiones de México. Siglos XVI a XX*, ed. Amaya Garritz (México: Universidad Nacional Autónoma de México, 1996), 71.

23. Pierre Lhande, *La emigración vasca*, vol. 1, trans. Ignacio Basurko Berroa (San Sebastián: Editorial Auñamendi, 1975), 25.

24. Ibid.

25. Douglass and Bilbao, *Amerikanuak*, 394.

26. Ibid., 374.

27. Caro Baroja, *Los vascos y el mar*, 60.

28. Juan Antonio Frago Gracia, *Historia del español de América* (Madrid: Gredos, 1999), 104–5.

29. Andrés E. Mañaricua, *Historia general del Señorío de Bizcaya, apéndice III. Polémica sobre Vizcaya en el siglo XVII. El Buho Gallego y El Tordo Vizcayno* (Bilbao: La Gran Enciclopedia Vasca, 1976), 141–42.

30. Ibid.

31. Douglass and Bilbao, *Amerikanuak*, 85.

32. Caro Baroja, *Los vascos y el mar*, 24.

Notes, Chapter Four

1. Vicenta M. Márquez de la Plata y Ferrándiz, *Mujeres de acción en el Siglo de Oro* (Madrid: Editorial Castalia, 2006), 24–25.

2. Pierre Lhande, *La emigración vasca*, vol. 1, trans. Ignacio Basurko Berroa (San Sebastián: Editorial Auñamendi, 1975), 27.

3. Julio Caro Baroja, *Introducción a la historia social del Pueblo Vasco* (San Sebastián: Txertoa, 1974); Valentín Vásquez de Prada y Juan Bosco Amores, "La emigración de navarros y vascongados al Nuevo Mundo y su repercusión en las comunidades de origen," in *Los vascos y América. Ideas, hechos, hombres*, ed. Ignacio Arana Pérez (Madrid: Gela S.A., Espasa Calpe/Argantonia, 1990).

4. José Manuel Azcona Pastor, *Possible Paradises: Basque Emigration to Latin America* (Reno: University of Nevada Press, 2004), 141.

5. Julio Caro Baroja, *Los vascos y el mar* (San Sebastián: Txertoa, 1985), 82.

6. Azcona Pastor, *Possible Paradises: Basque Emigration to Latin America*, 141–42.

7. Josefa Arregui Aranburu, "Euskadi-América, mar abierto," in *Los vascos y América. Ideas, hechos, hombres*, ed. Arana Pérez, 38.

8. Azcona Pastor, *Possible Paradises: Basque Emigration to Latin America*, 143–44.

9. Caro Baroja, *Introducción a la historia social del Pueblo Vasco*, 53.

10. Azcona Pastor, *Possible Paradises: Basque Emigration to Latin America*, 23.

11. William A. Douglass and Jon Bilbao, *Amerikanuak: Basques in the New World* (Reno: University of Nevada Press, 1975) 71–72.

12. Azcona Pastor, *Possible Paradises: Basque Emigration to Latin America*, 131.

13. María Estíbaliz Ruiz de Azúa y Martínez de Ezquerechoa, *Vascongadas y América* (Madrid: Editorial MAPFRE, 1992), 219.

14. Julio Caro Baroja, *Ser o no ser vasco* (Madrid: Espasa Calpe, 1998), 140.

15. Azcona Pastor, *Possible Paradises: Basque Emigration to Latin America*, 81.

16. Douglass and Bilbao, *Amerikanuak*, 52.

17. Caro Baroja, *Los vasco y el mar*, 42.

18. Douglass and Bilbao, *Amerikanuak*, 53.

19. Azcona Pastor, *Possible Paradises: Basque Emigration to Latin America*, 82.

20. Douglass and Bilbao, *Amerikanuak*, 53–55 and note.

21. Ibid., 56.

22. Azcona Pastor, *Possible Paradises: Basque Emigration to Latin America*, 20.

23. Caro Baroja, *Introducción a la historia social del Pueblo Vasco*; *Los vascos y el mar*; *Ser o no ser vasco*.

24. Caro Baroja, *Los vascos y el mar*, 80.

25. Ibid., 50.

26. Ibid., 71.

27. Azcona Pastor, *Possible Paradises: Basque Emigration to Latin America*, 22.

28. Caro Baroja, *Introducción a la historia social del Pueblo Vasco*, 78–79.

29. Azcona Pastor, *Possible Paradises: Basque Emigration to Latin America*, 20.

30. Douglass and Bilbao, *Amerikanuak*, 69–70.

31. Luis Navarro García, "La colonia vasca en Andalucía en la Edad Moderna," in *Los vascos y América. Ideas, hechos, hombres*, ed. Arana Pérez, 59.

32. Azcona Pastor, *Possible Paradises: Basque Emigration to Latin America*, 21.

33. Caro Baroja, *Introducción a la historia social del Pueblo Vasco*, 103–4.

34. Azcona Pastor, *Possible Paradises: Basque Emigration to Latin America*, 21.

35. Caro Baroja, *Introducción a la historia social del Pueblo Vasco*, 73–74, 91.

36. Ibid., 92.

37. Ibid., 94.

38. Peter Bakewell, *Silver Mining and Society in Colonial Mexico: Zacatecas, 1546–1700* (Cambridge: Cambridge University Press, 1971), 188.

39. Caro Baroja, *Introducción a la historia social del Pueblo Vasco*, 100.

40. Azcona Pastor, *Possible Paradises: Basque Emigration to Latin America*, 21–22.

41. Ibid., 87–88.

42. Catalina de Erauso, *Lieutenant Nun: Memoir of a Basque Transvestite in the New World,* trans. and intro. Michele Stepto and Gabriel Stepto, foreword by Marjorie Garber (Boston: Beacon Press, 1996), 35.

43. José Ignacio Tellechea Idígoras, *Doña Catalina de Erauso, la Monja Alférez. IV Centenario de su nacimiento* (San Sebastián: Sociedad Guipuzcoana de Ediciones y Publicaciones, 1992), 49 (emphasis added).

44. Ibid., 39.

45. Marjorie Garber, "Foreword" to *Lieutenant Nun: Memoir of a Basque Transvestite in the New World* (Boston: Beacon Press, 1996), xxvii.

46. Tellechea Idígoras, *Doña Catalina de Erauso, la Monja Alférez*, 59.

47. Navarro García, "La colonia vasca en Andalucía en la Edad Moderna," 58–60.

48. Tellechea Idígoras, *Doña Catalina de Erauso, la Monja Alférez*, 41.

49. Caro Baroja, *Los vascos y el mar*, 38.

50. Douglass and Bilbao, *Amerikanuak*, 68.

51. José Angel García de Cortázar, *Vizcaya en el siglo XV. Aspectos económicos y sociales* (Bilbao: Ediciones de la Caja de Ahorros Vizcaína, 1966), 210.

52. Ibid.

53. Andrés E. Mañaricua, *Historia general de Señorío de Bizcaya, apendice III. Polémica sobre Vizcaya en el siglo XVII. El Buho Gallego y El Tordo Vizcayno* (Bilbao: El Gran Enciclopedia Vasca, 1976), 142.

54. Ibid., 68–69.

55. Azcona Pastor, *Possible Paradises: Basque Emigration to Latin America*, 78.

56. Catalina de Erauso, *Lieutenant Nun: Memoir of a Basque Transvestite in the New World*, trans. and intro. Michele Stepto and Gabriel Stepto, foreword by Marjorie Garber (Boston: Beacon Press, 1996), 7.

57. Catalina de Erauso, *Historia de la Monja Alférez, Catalina de Erauso, escrita por ella misma*, ed. Angel Esteban (Madrid: Cátedra, Letras Hispánicas, 2002), 98.

58. We do not know whether this Captain Miguel de Echazarreta is related to Captain Juanes de Echazarreta, a friend and business associate of Erauso's grandfather, Miguel de Erauso.

59. In Ferrer's edition of Erauso's autobiography, this document is appended to the text with the title "Final notes added to the manuscript belonging to Don Cándido María Trigueros." Tellechea Idígoras, in *Doña Catalina de Erauso, la Monja Alférez*, refers to the same text in the Colección Muñoz, found in the Real Academia de la Historia.

60. Lucas Castillo Lara, *La asombrosa historia de doña Catalina de Erauso, la monja alférez, y sus prodigiosas aventuras en Indias (1602–1624)* (Caracas: Planeta Biblioteca Andina, 1992), 39.

61. Erauso, *Historia de la Monja Alférez*, ed. Esteban, 98. Erauso, *Lieutenant Nun: Memoir of a Basque Transvestite in the New World*, 7.

62. Rima R. Vallbona, *Vida i sucesos de la monja Alférez (Autobiografía atribuida a doña Catalina de Erauso)* (Tempe, Ariz.: Center for Latin American Studies, Arizona State University, 1992), 41.

63. Erauso, *Historia de la Monja Alférez*, ed. Esteban, 98. Erauso, *Lieutenant Nun: Memoir of a Basque Transvestite in the New World*, 8.

64. Rima R. Vallbona, "Realidad Histórica y ficción en Vida y Sucesos de la Monja Alférez" (Ph.D. dissertation, Middlebury College, 1981), 55.

65. Ruiz de Azua, *Vascongadas y América*, 215.

66. Azcona Pastor, *Possible Paradises: Basque Emigration to Latin America*, 125.

67. Ibid., 146.

68. Ibid., 124–26.

69. Ibid., 128.

70. Vallbona, *Vida i sucesos de la monja Alférez (Autobiografía atribuida a doña Catalina de Erauso)*, 55.

71. Ibid., 55–56.

72. Douglass and Bilbao, *Amerikanuak*, 71.

73. Erauso, *Lieutenant Nun: Memoir of a Basque Transvestite in the New World*, 8.

74. Azcona Pastor, *Possible Paradises: Basque Emigration to Latin America*, 147.

75. Vicenta M. Márquez de la Plata y Ferrándiz, *Mujeres de acción en el Siglo de Oro* (Madrid: Editorial Castalia, 2006), 34–35.

76. Erauso, *Lieutenant Nun: Memoir of a Basque Transvestite in the New World*, 55–56.

77. Ibid., 57.

78. In the manuscript on which Vallbona bases her critical edition, Lope de Alcedo, who befriends the narrator, is called Lope de Salcedo. Salcedo, we are told, was a relative of Arostegui, which is clearly a Basque surname, as are the names of those who helped Erauso arrange her departure: Carranza and Arzaga (Arnizaga in the Vallbona text).

79. Vallbona, *Vida i sucesos de la monja Alférez*, 219–20; Stepto and Stepto, *Lieutenant Nun*, 71.

80. Azcona Pastor, *Possible Paradises: Basque Emigration to Latin America*, 79.

81. Cited by Vallbona, *Vida i sucesos de la monja Alférez*, 116.

82. Ibid.

83. For Vallbona, the Castilian spelling of this name could be interpreted as a clue that the text of the *Autobiografía* was not written by Catalina de Erauso, inasmuch as Erauso certainly would have recognized the surname and therefore would not have made this error.

84. Tellechea Idígoras, *Doña Catalina de Erauso, la Monja Alférez*, 97.

Notes, Chapter Five

1. Julio Caro Baroja, *Ser o no ser vasco* (Madrid: Espasa Calpe, 1998), 125.

2. Catalina de Erauso, *Lieutenant Nun: Memoir of a Basque Transvestite in the New World,* trans. and intro. Michele Stepto and Gabriel Stepto, foreword by Marjorie Garber (Boston: Beacon Press, 1996), 4.

3. Ibid., 5.

4. Ibid., 6. The translators, Michele Stepto and Gabriel Stepto, refer to don Carlos de Arellano as "a native of Santiago." I believe that what the original text implies is that the gentleman "belongs to the Order of Santiago" (translator's note).

5. José Ramón Zubiaur, "Euskara y castellano en el País Vasco en la época de Iñigo de Loyola," in *El pueblo vasco en el Renacimiento* (1491–1521), ed. José Luis Orella Unzué (Bilbao: Ediciones Mensajero, 1990), 478.

6. Julio Caro Baroja, *Introducción a la historia social del Pueblo Vasco* (San Sebastián: Txertoa, 1974), 56.

7. José Manuel Azcona Pastor, *Possible Paradises: Basque Emigration to Latin America* (Reno: University of Nevada Press, 2004), 67–68.

8. Caro Baroja, *Ser o no ser vasco*, 90.

9. Other famous Basque secretaries of this period who are worthy of mention are Antonio de Eraso and Francisco de Arrieta. Later, the Basques Esteban de Ibarra, Cristóbal de Ipiñarreta, and Antonio de Aróstegui served as secretaries to Philip III.

10. Antonio Juan Frago Gracia, *Historia del español de América* (Madrid: Gredos, 1999), 101.

11. Caro Baroja, *Ser o no ser vasco*, 130.

12. Lucas Castillo Lara, *La asombrosa historia de doña Catalina de Erauso, la Monja Alférez, y sus prodigiosas aventuras en Indias (1602–1624)* (Caracas: Planeta Biblioteca Andina, 1992), 130.

13. Real Academia de la Historia, *Diccionario Histórico-Geográfico del País Vasco*, 2nd ed., vol. 4 (Bilbao: La Gran Enciclopedia Vasca, 1980), 335.

14. Ibid., 335–36.

15. Mariló Vigil, *La vida de las mujeres en los siglos XVI y XVII*, 2nd ed. (Madrid: Siglo Veintiuno de España, 1994), 49.

16. José Ignacio Tellechea Idígoras, *Doña Catalina de Erauso, la Monja Alférez. IV Centenario de su nacimiento* (San Sebastián: Sociedad Guipuzcoana de Ediciones y Publicaciones, 1992), 16.

17. Ibid., 23.

18. Ibid., 27.

19. The ship María San Juan was the property of Joanes de Echazarreta, a close friend of Erauso the Elder.

20. Tellechea Idígoras, *Doña Catalina de Erauso, la Monja Alférez*, 55.

21. Ibid.

22. Ibon Sarasola, *Historia social de la literatura vasca* (Barcelona: Akal, 1976), 35.

23. Erauso, *Historia de la Monja Alférez*, ed. Esteban, 78.

24. Ibid.

25. María Estíbaliz Ruiz de Azúa y Martínez de Ezquerecocha, *Vascongadas y América* (Madrid: Editorial MAPFRE, 1992), 222.

26. Juan Javier Pescador, *The New World Inside a Basque Village: The Oiartzun Valley and Its Atlantic Emigrants, 1550–1800* (Reno: University of Nevada Press, 2004), 10.

27. Rima R. Vallbona, *Vida i sucesos de la Monja Alférez (Autobiografía atribuida a doña Catalina de Erauso)* (Tempe, Ariz.: Center for Latin American Studies, Arizona State University, 1992), 43.

28. Jaime Vicens Vives, ed., *Historia de España y América*, vol. 3 (Barcelona: Vincens Vives, 1957), 525.

29. Ruth El Saffar, "The Fabrication of Self: Oedipal Structures in *El médico de su honra*," in *La Chispa '89. Selected Proceedings,* ed. Gilbert Paolini (New Orleans: Tulane University, 1989), 96–97.

30. Erauso, *Lieutenant Nun: Memoir of a Basque Transvestite in the New World*, 10.

31. Vallbona, *Vida i sucesos de la Monja Alférez*, 45.

32. Erauso, *Lieutenant Nun: Memoir of a Basque Transvestite in the New World*, 10–11.

33. Ibid., 11.

34. Ibid., 13–14.

35. Ibid., 14.

36. Ibid., 15.

37. Ibid., 19.

38. Tellechea Idígoras, *Doña Catalina de Erauso, la Monja Alférez*, 56–57.

39. Erauso, *Lieutenant Nun: Memoir of a Basque Transvestite in the New World*, 19.

40. Ibid., 20.

41. Ibid.

42. Ibid., 20–21.

43. Vallbona, *Vida i sucesos de la Monja Alférez (Autobiografía atribuida a doña Catalina de Erauso)*, 75.

44. Erauso, *Lieutenant Nun: Memoir of a Basque Transvestite in the New World*, 52.

45. Vallbona, *Vida i sucesos de la Monja Alférez*, 97.

46. Ibid.

47. Erauso, *Lieutenant Nun: Memoir of a Basque Transvestite in the New World*, 30.

48. Tellechea Idígoras, *Doña Catalina de Erauso, la Monja Alférez*, 192.

49. Ibid., 193.

50. Erauso, *Lieutenant Nun: Memoir of a Basque Transvestite in the New World*, 39.

51. On this, see two works by Deborah Tannen, "How is Conversation Like Literary Discourse?: The Role of Imagery and Details in Creating Involvement," in *The Linguistics of Literacy*, ed. Pamela Downing, Susan D. Lima, and Michael Noonan (Amsterdam and Philadelphia: John Benjamins, 1992) and *Talking Voices: Repetition, Dialogue and Imagery in Conversational Discourse* (Cambridge: Cambridge University Press, 1989).

52. Erauso, *Lieutenant Nun: Memoir of a Basque Transvestite in the New World*, 34.

53. Castillo Lara, *La asombrosa historia de doña Catalina de Erauso, la Monja Alférez*, 8.

54. Ibid., 155.

55. Peter Bakewell, *Silver Mining and Society in Colonial Mexico: Zacatecas, 1546–1700* (Cambridge: Cambridge University Press, 1971), 23.

56. Ibid., 28.

57. Ibid.

58. Erauso, *Lieutenant Nun: Memoir of a Basque Transvestite in the New World*, 44 (emphasis added).

59. Ibid., 48.

60. Ibid.

61. Vallbona, *Vida i sucesos de la Monja Alférez*, 92.

62. Ibid.

63. Erauso, *Lieutenant Nun: Memoir of a Basque Transvestite in the New World*, 73.

Notes, Chapter Six

1. Beatriz Arizaga, "La vida urbana en el País Vasco en la época bajomedieval," in *El pueblo vasco en el Renacimiento (1491–1521)*, ed. José Luis Orella (Bilbao: Ediciones Mensajero, 1990), 44.

2. Felipe Picatoste, *Estudios sobre la grandeza y decadencia de España*, vol. 3 (Madrid: Librería de la Viuda de Hernando y Ca, 1887), 87–88.

3. Catalina de Erauso, *Lieutenant Nun: Memoir of a Basque Transvestite in the New World*, trans. and intro. Michele Stepto and Gabriel Stepto, foreword by Marjorie Garber (Boston: Beacon Press, 1996), 3, 5.

4. Ibid., 12.

5. Ibid.

6. Ibid., 13.

7. Ibid., 14.

8. Ibid., 15.

9. Ibid.

10. Ibid.

11. Ibid.

12. Ibid., 43 (emphasis added).

13. Ibid., 13.

14. Alberto Crespo, *La Guerra entre Vicuñas y Vascongados, Potosí, 1922–1925* (Lima: s.p.i., 1956), 107.

15. Emphasis added. In their translation of this particular passage, Michele Stepto and Gabriel Stepto omit the phrase "*gracias a la bella industria*" with which the sentence ends in the original text. In his translation, however, Fitzmaurice Kelly assigns the following meaning to the phrase: "thanks to intelligent knavery." We have chosen to include that rendering because we consider it essential for a careful interpretation of the text (translator's note).

16. Erauso, *Historia de la Monja Alférez*, ed. Esteban, 131.

17. Excelentísima Diputación Provincial, *Fueros, franquezas y libertades del M.N. y M.L. Señorío de Vizcaya* (Bilbao: Imprenta Provincial, 1898), 23.

18. Ibid. (emphasis added).

19. Jaime Vicens Vives, ed. *Historia de España y América*, vol. 3 (Barcelona: Vincens Vives, 1957), 528, 530.

20. Xosé Estévez, *Historia de Euskal Herria*, vol. 2 (Tafalla: Txalaparta, 1996), 134.

21. Antonio Beristain, María Angeles Larrea, and Rafael María Mieza., *Fuentes del derecho penal vasco (Siglos XI–XVI)* (Bilbao: La Gran Enciclopedia Vasca, 1980), 2.

22. Julio Caro Baroja, *Ser o no ser vasco* (Madrid: Espasa Calpe, 1998), 90–91; Julio Caro Baroja, *Los vascos y el mar* (San Sebastián: Txertoa, 1985), 142.

23. Caro Baroja, *Ser o no ser vasco*, 92.

24. Lope Martínez de Isasti, *Compendio historial de Guipúzcoa* (Bilbao: La Gran Enciclopedia Vasca, 1972), 36.

25. Ibid., 36.

26. Amalio Marichalar and Cayetano Manrique, *Historia de los fueros de Navarra, Vizcaya, Guipúzkoa y Alava*, 2nd ed. (San Sebastián: Editorial Auñamendi, 1971), 335.

27. Ibid., 335.

28. Ibid.

29. Ibid., 337.

30. Martínez de Isasti, *Compendio historial de Guipúzcoa*, 37–38.

31. Excelentísima Diputación de Guipúzcoa, *Nueva recopilación de los Fueros, Privilegios, buenos usos y costumbres, leyes y órdenes de la M.N. y M.L. Provincia de Guipúzcoa* (San Sebastián: Imprenta de la Provincia, 1919), 18.

32. Marichalar and Manrique, *Historia de los fueros de Navarra, Vizcaya, Guipúzkoa y Alava*, 336.

33. Beristain, Larrea, and Mieza, *Fuentes del derecho penal vasco (Siglos XI–XVI)*, 410.

34. Paz Alonso, "El proceso penal en el fuero de San Sebastián," in Sociedad de Estudios Vascos, *Congreso "El fuero de San Sebastián y su época"* (San Sebastián: Eusko Ikaskuntza, 1982), 398.

35. Alberto Basabe, "Estudio lingüístico del Fuero de San Sebastián," in Sociedad de Estudios Vascos, *Congreso "El fuero de San Sebastián y su época,"* 37, 38, 39.

36. Ibid., 45, 36.

37. Excelentísima Diputación de Guipúzcoa, *Nueva recopilación de los Fueros*, 44–45.

Notes, Chapter Seven

1. Ruth El Saffar, "The Fabrication of Self: Oedipal Structures in *El médico de su honra*," in *La Chispa '89. Selected Proceedings*, ed. Gilbert Paolini (New Orleans: Tulane University: 1989), 166.

2. Julio Caro Baroja, *Ser o no ser vasco* (Madrid: Espasa Calpe: 1998), 91.

3. William A. Douglass and Jon Bilbao, *Amerikanuak: Basques in the New World* (Reno: University of Nevada Press, 1975), 81–82.

4. Ibid., 114.

5. Julio Caro Baroja, *Los vascos y el mar* (San Sebastián: Txertoa, 1985), 145.

6. María Estíbaliz Ruiz de Azúa y Martínez de Ezquerecocha, *Vascongadas y América* (Madrid: Editorial MAPFRE, 1992), 231.

7. Alberto Crespo, *La Guerra entre Vicuñas y Vascongados, Potosí, 1922–1925* (Lima: s.p.i., 1956), prologue, no page no.

8. Ibid.

9. Lucas Castillo Lara, *La asombrosa historia de doña Catalina de Erouso, la Monja Alférez, y sus prodigiosas aventuras en Indias (1602–1624)* (Caracas: Planeta Biblioteca Andina, 1992), 157.

10. Peter Bakewell, *Silver Mining and Society in Colonial Mexico: Zacatecas, 1546–1700* (Cambridge: Cambridge University Press, 1971), 221.

11. Crespo, *La Guerra entre Vicuñas y Vascongados, Potosí, 1922–1925*, 33–34.

12. Ibid., 33.

13. Ibid., 107.

14. Jaime Vicens Vives, ed., *Historia de España y América*, vol. 3 (Barcelona: Vincens Vives, 1957), 518.

15. Ibid.

16. Crespo, *La Guerra entre Vicuñas y Vascongados, Potosí, 1922–1925*, 34–35.

17. Ibid., 32.

18. Ibid., 57.

19. Ibid., 66.

20. Ibid.

21. Ibid., 67.

22. Catalina de Erauso, *Lieutenant Nun: Memoir of a Basque Transvestite in the New World*, trans. and intro. Michele Stepto and Gabriel Stepto, foreword by Marjorie Garber (Boston: Beacon Press, 1996), 31.

23. Rima R. Vallbona, *Vida i sucesos de la Monja Alférez (Autobiografía atribuida a doña Catalina de Erauso)* (Tempe, Ariz.: Center for Latin American Studies, Arizona State University, 1992), 74.

24. Crespo, *La Guerra entre Vicuñas y Vascongados, Potosí, 1922–1925*, 31.

25. Ibid., 33.

26. Ibid., 35.

27. Ibid.

28. Bakewell, *Silver Mining and Society in Colonial Mexico: Zacatecas, 1546–1700*, 129.

29. Ibid., 131–32.

30. Vallbona, *Vida i sucesos de la Monja Alférez (Autobiografía atribuida a doña Catalina de Erauso)*, 168 (emphasis added).

31. Ibid., 101.

32. Ibid., 102.

33. Erauso, *Lieutenant Nun: Memoir of a Basque Transvestite in the New World*, 51.

Notes, Chapter Eight

1. Emilie Bergmann, "The Exclusion of the Feminine in the Cultural Discourse of the Golden Age: Juan Luis Vives and Fray Luis de León," in *Religion, Body and Gender in Early Modern Spain*, ed. Alain Saint-Saëns (San Francisco: Mellen Research University Press, 1991), 125.

2. Catalina de Erauso, *Lieutenant Nun: Memoir of a Basque Transvestite in the New World*, trans. and intro. Michele Stepto and Gabriel Stepto, foreword by Marjorie Garber (Boston: Beacon Press, 1996), 4

3. Ibid., 7.

4. Ibid., 5.

5. Chap. 11 will address the expectations for married women's conduct.

6. Vicenta M. Marquéz de la Plata y Ferrándiz, *Mujeres de acción en el Siglo de Oro* (Madrid: Editorial Castalia, 2006), 22.

7. Erauso, *Lieutenant Nun: Memoir of a Basque Transvestite in the New World*, 17.

8. Mariló Vigil, *La vida de las mujeres en los siglos XVI y XVII*, 2nd ed. (Madrid: Siglo Veintiuno de España, 1994), 80.

9. Erauso, *Lieutenant Nun: Memoir of a Basque Transvestite in the New World*, 16.

10. Ibid., 28.

11. Sherry Velasco, *The Lieutenant Nun: Transgenderism, Lesbian Desire, and Catalina de Erauso* (Austin: University of Texas Press, 2000), 55.

12. Pedro Rubio Merino, *La monja alférez: Doña Catalina de Erauso. Dos manuscritos inéditos de su autobiografía conservados en el Archivo de la Santa Iglesia Catedral de Sevilla* (Sevilla: Cabildo Metropolitano de la Catedral de Sevilla, 1995), 68.

13. Erauso, *Lieutenant Nun: Memoir of a Basque Transvestite in the New World*, 29–30.

14. Georges Duby and Michelle Perrot, *Historia de las mujeres*, vol. 3 (Madrid: Taurus, 2000), 653.

15. Kathleen Ann Myers, *Neither Saints nor Sinners: Writing the Lives of Women in Spanish America* (New York: Oxford University Press, 2003), 161.

16. Erauso, *Lieutenant Nun: Memoir of a Basque Transvestite in the New World*, 11.

17. Ibid., 13.

18. Ibid.

19. Ibid., 35.

20. Ibid., 37.

21. Lope Martínez de Isasti, *Compendio historial de Guipúzcoa* (Bilbao: La Gran Enciclopedia Vasca, 1972), viii–ix.

22. Erauso, *Lieutenant Nun: Memoir of a Basque Transvestite in the New World*, 45.

23. Ibid., 47.

24. Ibid., 67.

25. Ibid., 68.

26. Ibid.

27. Ibid., 69.

28. Ibid., 80.

29. Rubio Merino, *La monja alférez: Doña Catalina de Erauso*, 92; see also Velasco, *The Lieutenant Nun: Transgenderism, Lesbian Desire, and Catalina de Erauso*, 3–4.

30. Stephanie Merrim, *Early Modern Women's Writing and Sor Juana Inés de la Cruz* (Nashville: Vanderbilt University Press, 1999), 8.

31. Rima R. Vallbona, *Vida i sucesos de la Monja Alférez (Autobiografía atribuida a doña Catalina de Erauso)* (Tempe, Ariz.: Center for Latin American Studies, Arizona State University, 1992), 22.

Notes, Chapter Nine

1. Juan Javier Pescador, *The New World Inside a Basque Village: The Oiartzun Valley and Its Atlantic Emigrants, 1550–1800* (Reno: University of Nevada Press, 2004), 49.

2. Ibid., 51.

3. Ibid., 52.

4. Ibid., 50.

5. Ibid., 53.

6. Ibid., 68.

7. Ibid., 69.

8. Ibid.

9. Ibid., 70.

10. Ibid., 71.

11. Ibid.

12. Ibid., 72.

13. Ibid.

14. Ibid., 70–71.

15. Renato Barahona, *Sex Crimes, Honour, and the Law in Early Modern Spain: Vizcaya, 1528–1735* (Toronto: University of Toronto Press: 2003), 18.

16. Ibid., 17.

17. Ibid., 14.

18. Ibid., 19.

19. Ibid., 20.

20. Ibid., 21.

21. Ibid., 107.

22. Ibid.

23. Ibid.

24. Ibid., 109.

25. Ibid., 30–31.

26. Ibid., 22–23.

27. Ibid., 31–33.

28. Ibid., 121.

29. Mary Elizabeth Perry, *Gender and Disorder in Early Modern Seville* (Princeton: Princeton University Press, 1990), 124.

30. Valentina Fernández Vargas and María Victoria López Cordón Cortezo, "Mujer y régimen jurídico en el Antiguo Régimen: una realidad disociada," in *Ordenamiento jurídico y realidad social de las mujeres. Siglos XVI a XX*, ed. Mª Carmen García-Nieto Paris (Madrid: Seminario de Estudios de la Mujer, Universidad Autónama de Madrid, 1984), 26.

31. Ellen G. Friedman, "El estatus jurídico de la mujer castellana durante el Antiguo Régimen," in *Ordenamiento jurídico y realidad social de las mujeres. Siglos XVI a XX*, ed. García-Nieto Paris, 42.

32. Ibid., 44.

33. Barahona, *Sex Crimes, Honour, and the Law in Early Modern Spain*, 96.

34. Ibid., 115.

35. Ibid., 114–17.

36. Ibid., 36–37.

37. Fernández Vargas and López Cordón, "Mujer y régimen jurídico en el Antiguo Régimen," 35.

Notes, Chapter Ten

1. Joan Kelly-Gadol, "Did Women Have a Renaissance?" in *Becoming Visible. Women in European History*, ed. Renate Bridenthal and Claudia Koontz (Boston: Houghton Mifflin Company, 1977), 40.

2. Ibid., 141.

3. Mariló Vigil, *La vida de las mujeres en los siglos XVI y XVII*, 2nd ed. (Madrid: Siglo Veintiuno de España, 1994), 62.

4. Kelly-Gadol, "Did Women Have a Renaissance?" 143.

5. Anne Cruz, "Studying Gender in the Spanish Golden Age," in *Cultural and Historical Grounding for Hispanic and Luso-Brazilian Feminist Literary Criticism*, ed. Hernan Vidal (Minneapolis: Institute for the Study of Ideologies and Literature, 1989), 196.

6. Kelly-Gadol, "Did Women Have a Renaissance?" 144.

7. Ibid., 145–46.

8. Ibid., 150–51.

9. Ibid., 152.

10. Ibid., 153.

11. Ibid., 156.

12. Ibid., 156–57.

13. Ibid., 157.

14. Vigil, *La vida de las mujeres en los siglos XVI y XVII*, 145.

15. Quoted by Vigil, *La vida de las mujeres en los siglos XVI y XVII*, 145.

16. Ibid.

17. Kelly-Gadol, "Did Women Have a Renaissance?" 160–61.

18. Xosé Estévez, *Historia de Euskal Herria,* vol. 2, *Del hierro al roble* (Tafalla: Txalaparta, 1996), 206.

19. Vigil, *La vida de las mujeres en los siglos XVI y XVII*, 208–9.

20. Vicenta M. Márquez de la Plata y Ferrándiz, *Mujeres de acción en el Siglo de Oro* (Madrid: Editorial Castalia, 2006), 23.

21. Lisa Vollendorf, *The Lives of Women: A New History of Inquisitorial Spain* (Nashville: Vanderbilt University Press, 2005), 93–94.

22. Marquéz de la Plata y Ferrándiz, *Mujeres de acción en el Siglo de Oro*, 23.

23. Vollendorf, *The Lives of Women*, 97.

24. Ibid., 170.

25. Ibid., 98.

26. Ibid., 177.

27. Vollendorf, *The Lives of Women*, 4.

28. Márgara Russotto, "Condiciones y preliminares para el resurgimiento y formación de los discursos femeninos en la Colonia (siglos XVI–XVII)," in *Mujeres latinoamericanas: Historia y cultura siglos XVI al XIX,* ed. Luis Campuzano, vol. 1 (La Habana: Casa de Américas; México: Universidad Autónoma Metropolitana Iztapalapa, 1995), 16.

29. Vigil, *La vida de las mujeres en los siglos XVI y XVII*, 21.

30. Ibid., 22–23.

31. Cruz, "Studying Gender in the Spanish Golden Age," 196.

32. Vigil, *La vida de las mujeres en los siglos XVI y XVII*, 23.

33. Vollendorf, *The Lives of Women*, 147.

34. Ibid., 148.

35. Vigil, *La vida de las mujeres en los siglos XVI y XVII*, 104.

36. Georges Duby and Michelle Perrot, *Historia de las mujeres*, vol. 3 (Madrid: Taurus, 2000), 560.

37. Ibid.

38. Vollendorf, *The Lives of Women*, 35.

39. Ibid., 52–53.

40. Vigil, *La vida de las mujeres en los siglos XVI y XVII*, 27.

41. Ibid.

42. Stephanie Merrim, "Catalina de Erauso: From Anomaly to Icon," in *Coded Encounters: Writing, Gender, and Ethnicity in Colonial Latin America*, ed. Francisco Javier Cevallos-Candau, et. al. (Amherst: University of Massachusetts Press, 1994), 186.

43. Vollendorf, *The Lives of Women*, 5.

44. Merrim, "Catalina de Erauso: From Anomaly to Icon," 193–94.

45. Kathleen Ann Myers, *Neither Saints nor Sinners: Writing the Lives of Women in Spanish America* (New York: Oxford University Press, 2003), 149.

46. Duby and Perrot, *Historia de las mujeres*, 649.

47. Myers, *Neither Saints nor Sinners*, 161.

48. Duby and Perrot, *Historia de las mujeres*, 654.

49. Myers, *Neither Saints nor Sinners*, 160.

50. Duby and Perrot, *Historia de las mujeres*, 655.

51. Ibid., 665–66.

52. Ibid., 665.

53. Ibid., 667.

54. Myers, *Neither Saints nor Sinners*, 160.

Notes, Chapter Eleven

1. The complete title is *Última y Tercera Relación, en que se hace verdadera del resto de la vida de la Monja Alférez, sus memorables virtudes, y ejemplar muerte en estos Reinos de la Nueva España* (The last and third account, in which the remainder of the Lieutenant Nun's life is revealed, her memorable virtues, and her exemplary death in these kingdoms of New Spain). The text of this *Relación* offers such fantastic and implausible episodes that it has led one critic to suggest that "its context appears to have been a scheme by publishing houses to spread lies and fictional stories intended to reawaken interest, after her death, in the legend of the Lieutenant Nun." Lucas Castillo Lara, *La asombrosa historia de doña Catalina de Erauso, la Monja Alférez, y sus prodigiosas aventuras en Indias (1602–1624)* (Caracas: Planeta Biblioteca Andina, 1992), 325.

2. Stephanie Merrim, "Catalina de Erauso: From Anomaly to Icon," in *Coded Encounters: Writing, Gender, and Ethnicity in Colonial Latin America,* ed. Francisco Javier Cevallos-Candau, et al. (Amherst: University of Massachusetts Press, 1994), 188.

3. Kathleen Ann Myers, *Neither Saints nor Sinners: Writing the Lives of Women in Spanish America* (New York: Oxford University Press, 2003), 140.

4. Merrim, "Catalina de Erauso: From Anomaly to Icon," 190.

5. Rima R. Vallbona, *Vida i sucesos de la Monja Alférez (Autobiografía atribuida a doña Catalina de Erauso)* (Tempe, Ariz.: Center for Latin American Studies, Arizona State University, 1992), 133.

6. Adrienne L. Martín, "Desnudo de una travesti, o la 'Autobiografía' de Catalina de Erauso," in *Actas Irving '92, Asociación Internacional de Hispanistas II, La mujer y su representación en las literaturas Hispánicas,* ed. Juan Villegas (Irvine: University of California Press, 1994), 36.

7. Merrim, "Catalina de Erauso: From Anomaly to Icon," 189.

8. In addition to the research of Dekker and Van de Pol, see Sherry Velasco, *The Lieutenant Nun: Transgenderism, Lesbian Desire, and Catalina de Erauso* (Austin: University of Texas Press, 2000), 32, who provides a list of the scholars who document the lives of warrior women (including soldiers, sailors, and pirates) in historical as well as fictional sources.

9. Velasco, *The Lieutenant Nun: Transgenderism, Lesbian Desire, and Catalina de Erauso*, 34.

10. Rudolf M. Dekker and Lotte C. Van de Pol, *The Tradition of Female Transvestism in Early Modern Europe* (New York: St. Martin's Press, 1989), 2.

11. Anita K. Stoll, "Lope's *El Anzuelo de Fenisa:* A Woman for All Seasons," in *The Perception of Women in Spanish Theater of the Golden Age,* ed. Anita Stoll and Dawn L. Smith (Lewisburg, Pa.; London: Bucknell University Press; Associated University Press, 1991), 245; Ruth Lundelius, "Paradox and Role Reversal in *La Serrana de la Vera*," in *The Perception of Women in Spanish Theater of the Golden Age,* ed. Stoll and Smith,, 220.

12. Luzmila Camacho Platero, *La Monja Alférez de Juan Pérez de Montalbán* (Newark, Del.: Juan de la Cuesta, 2007), 48.

13. Encarnación Juárez, "La mujer militar en la América colonial: el caso de la monja alférez," *Indiana Journal of Hispanic Literatures* 10–11 (1997), 151.

14. Dekker and Van de Pol, *The Tradition of Female Transvestism in Early Modern Europe*, 3.

15. Ibid., 19.

16. Lillian Faderman, *Surpassing the Love of Men* (London: The Women's Press, 1985), 48.

17. Renato Barahona, *Sex Crimes, Honour, and the Law in Early Modern Spain: Vizcaya, 1528–1735* (Toronto: University of Toronto Press, 2003), 69.

18. Dekker and Van de Pol, *The Tradition of Female Transvestism in Early Modern Europe*, 7–8.

19. Velasco, *The Lieutenant Nun: Transgenderism, Lesbian Desire, and Catalina de Erauso*, 35.

20. Dekker and Van de Pol, *The Tradition of Female Transvestisim in Early Modern Europe*, 27–30.

21. Ibid., 30–32.

22. Catalina de Erauso, petititon presented to the Council of the Indies, cited by Vallbona, *Vida i sucesos de la Monja Alférez (Autobiografía atribuida a doña Catalina de Erauso)*, 131 (emphasis added).

23. Dekker and Van de Pol, *The Tradition of Female Transvestisim in Early Modern Europe*, 32.

24. Ibid., 26.

25. Ibid., 44.

26. Faderman, *Surpassing the Love of Men*, 61.

27. Juárez, "La mujer militar en la América colonial: el caso de la monja alférez," 191.

28. See Catalina de Erauso, *Lieutenant Nun: Memoir of a Basque Transvestite in the New World*, trans. and intro. Michele Stepto and Gabriel Stepto, foreword by Marjorie Garber (Boston: Beacon Press, 1996), 65–66.

29. Perry, cited by Juarez, "Señora Catalina, ¿dónde está el camino? La autobiografía como búsqueda y afirmación de identidad en *Vida i sucesos de la Monja Alférez*," in *La Chispa '95. Selected Proceedings*, ed. Claire J. Paolini (New Orleans: Tulane University, 1995), 191.

30. Merrim, "Catalina de Erauso: From Anomaly to Icon," 188.

31. Stephanie Merrim, *Early Modern Women's Writing and Sor Juana Inés de la Cruz* (Nashville: Vanderbilt University Press, 1999), 13.

32. Ibid., 14.

33. Lisa Vollendorf, *The Lives of Women: A New History of Inquisitorial Spain* (Nashville: Vanderbilt University Press, 2005), 13.

34. Merrim, *Early Modern Women's Writing and Sor Juana Inés de la Cruz*, 15.

35. Velasco, *The Lieutenant Nun: Transgenderism, Lesbian Desire, and Catalina de Erauso*, 23.

36. Merrim, *Early Modern Women's Writing and Sor Juana Inés de la Cruz*, 15.

37. Martín, "Desnudo de una travesti, o la 'Autobiografía' de Catalina de Erauso," 37.

38. Cited in Vallbona, *Vida i sucesos de la Monja Alférez (Autobiografía atribuida a doña Catalina de Erauso)*, 132.

39. Cited in ibid., 133.

40. Merrim, "Catalina de Erauso: From Anomaly to Icon," 192; see also Merrim, *Early Modern Women's Writing and Sor Juana Inés de la Cruz*, 25–29.

41. Merrim, "Catalina de Erauso: From Anomaly to Icon," 196–97.

42. Vern Bullough, *Sexual Variance in Society and History* (New York: Wiley, 1976), 68–69.

43. Ibid., 75.

44. Ibid., 194.

45. Valentina Fernández Vargas and María Victoria López Cordón Cortezo, "Mujer y régimen jurídico en el Antiguo Régimen: una realidad disociada," in *Ordenamiento jurídico y realidad social de las mujeres. Siglos XVI a XX* (Madrid: Seminario de Estudios de la Mujer, Universidad Autónoma de Madrid, 1984), 17.

46. Ibid., 27.

47. Alain Saint Saëns, "Homoerotic Suffering, Pleasure, and Desire in Early Modern Spain," in *Lesbianism and Homosexuality in Early Modern Spain*, ed. María José Delgado and Alain Saint-Saëns (New Orleans: University Press of the South, 2000), 15.

48. Alain Saint-Saëns, *Art and Faith in Tridentine Spain (1545–1690)* (New York: Peter Lang, 1995), 1.

49. Vallbona, *Vida i sucesos de la Monja Alférez*, 52.

50. Judith Brown, *Immodest Acts. The Life of a Lesbian Nun in Renaissance Italy* (New York: Oxford University Press, 1986), 19–20.

51. Ibid., 9.

52. Ibid., 20.

53. Kenneth Zucker, et al., "Gender-Dysphoric Children and Adolescents: A Comparitive Analysis of Demographic Characteristics and Behavioral Problems," *Clinical Child Psychology and Psychiatry* 7 (2002), 408–9.

54. Vollendorf, *The Lives of Women*, 59.

55. Velasco, *The Lieutenant Nun: Transgenderism, Lesbian Desire, and Catalina de Erauso*, 16.

56. Vollendorf, *The Lives of Women*, 64.

57. Ibid.

58. Velasco, *The Lieutenant Nun: Transgenderism, Lesbian Desire, and Catalina de Erauso*, 17.

59. Faderman, *Surpassing the Love of Men*, 72.

60. Ibid.

61. Saint Saëns, "Homoerotic Suffering, Pleasure, and Desire in Early Modern Spain," 25–26.

62. Faderman, *Surpassing the Love of Men*, 73.

63. Dekker and Van de Pol, *The Tradition of Female Transvestisim in Early Modern Europe*, 78.

64. Faderman, *Surpassing the Love of Men*, 47–49,

65. Ibid., 52.

66. Lázaro Lima, "Pablos como travestí: vestimentas, disfraces, encubrimiento y movilidad social en *El Buscón*," *Dactylus* 13 (1994), 62.

67. Mariló Vigil, *La vida de las mujeres en los siglos XVI y XVII*, 2nd ed. (Madrid: Siglo Veintiuno de España, 1994), 183.

68. Ibid., 192.

69. Faderman, *Surpassing the Love of Men*, 48.

70. Cited by Luzmila Camacho Platero, *La Monja Alférez de Juan Pérez de Montalbán*, 50.

71. Saint Saëns, "Homoerotic Suffering, Pleasure, and Desire in Early Modern Spain," 38.

72. Alfonso Pozo Ruiz, at http://www.personal.us.es/alporu/histsevilla/leyes_sodomia.htm.

73. Ibid.

74. Alfonso Pozo Ruiz, "La homosexualidad o sodomía en la Sevilla del XVI," at http://www.personal.us.es/alporu/histsevilla/homosexualidad_sodomia.htm.

75. Saint Saëns, "Homoerotic Suffering, Pleasure, and Desire in Early Modern Spain," 22.

76. Pozo Ruiz, "La homosexualidad o sodomía en la Sevilla del XVI."

77. Ibid.

78. Camacho, *La Monja Alférez de Juan Pérez de Montalbán*, 40.

79. Brown, *Immodest Acts. The Life of a Lesbian Nun in Renaissance Italy*, 15.

80. Camacho, *La Monja Alférez de Juan Pérez de Montalbán*, 40.

81. Merrim, *Early Modern Women's Writing and Sor Juana Inés de la Cruz*, 17.

82. Quoted in Sherry Velasco, *Male Delivery: Reproduction, Effeminacy, and Pregnant Men in Early Modern Spain* (Nashville: Vanderbilt University Press, 2006), 119.

83. Ibid.

84. Ibid.

85. Ibid.

86. Saint Saëns, "Homoerotic Suffering, Pleasure, and Desire in Early Modern Spain," 32–33.

87. Ibid., 32–38.

88. José Cartagena-Calderón, "'Él es tan rara persona'. Sobre cortesanos, lindos, sodomitas y otras masculinidades nefandas en la España de la temprana Edad Moderna," in *Lesbianism and Homosexuality in Early Modern Spain*, ed. María José Delgado and Alain Saint-Saëns (New Orleans: University Press of the South, 2000), 139–40.

89. Ibid., 141.

90. Ibid., 155.

91. Ibid.

92. Velasco, *The Lieutenant Nun: Transgenderism, Lesbian Desire, and Catalina de Erauso*, 14–15, summarizes the discussion regarding the acceptable terminology to be used when describing same-sex passion between women in the early modern period, and refers in particular to the problems involved in the use of the term "lesbianism."

93. Quoted by Velasco, *The Lieutenant Nun: Transgenderism, Lesbian Desire, and Catalina de Erauso*, 69.

94. Barahona, *Sex Crimes, Honour, and the Law in Early Modern Spain: Vizcaya, 1528–1735*, 17.

95. Personal conversation with William A. Douglass.

96. Erauso, *Lieutenant Nun: Memoir of a Basque Transvestite in the New World*, 19.

97. Harry Benjamin, *The Transsexual Phenomenon* (New York: The Julian Press, 1966), 13.

98. Ibid., 27.

99. Ibid., 36.

100. See under "Gender Variance (Dysphoria)" at the Gender Identity & Education Society website, at http://www.gires.org.uk/dysphoria.php (last accessed April 27, 2009).

101. Benjamin, *The Transsexual Phenomenon*, 77.

102. See "Transsexualism: The Inside Story," at the Gender Identity & Education Society website, at http://www.gires.org.uk/dysphoria.php (last accessed April 27, 2009).

103. Ibid.

104. Dekker and Van de Pol, *The Tradition of Female Transvestisim in Early Modern Europe*, 68.

105. Camacho, *La Monja Alférez de Juan Pérez de Montalbán*, 45.

106. Vallbona, *Vida i sucesos de la Monja Alférez*, 171.

107. Myers, *Neither Saints nor Sinners*, 158.

108. Vallbona, *Vida i sucesos de la Monja Alférez*, 127.

109. Bernardo Estornes Lasa et al., *Enciclopedia General Ilustrada del País Vasco,* vol. 11 (San Sebastián: Auñamendi, 1980), 79.

110. José Ignacio Tellechea Idígoras, *Doña Catalina de Erauso, la Monja Alférez. IV Centenario de su nacimiento* (San Sebastián: Sociedad Guipuzcoana de Ediciones y Publicaciones, 1992), 185 (emphasis added).

111. Vallbona, *Vida i sucesos de la Monja Alférez*, 144 (emphasis added).

112. Aranzazu Borrachero Mendíbil, "Catalina de Erasmo ante el partriarcado colonial: un estudio de Vida i sucesos de la Monja Alférez," *Bulletin of Hispanic Studies* 83 (2006), 493.

113. Stepto and Stepto, *Lieutenant Nun: Memoir of a Basque Transvestite in the New World*, xliii.

114. Ibid., xliii–xliv.

115. Tellechea Idígoras, *Doña Catalina de Erauso, la Monja Alférez*, 135.

Bibliography

Alcira Arancibia, Juana. "*Vida y sucesos de la Monja Alférez*: Conversaciones de Juana Alcira Arancibia con Rima de Vallbona." In *Nuevos acercamientos a la obra de Rima de Vallbona (Actas del Simposio-homenaje)*, edited by Jorge Chen Sham. San José: Editorial de la Universidad de Costa Rica, 2000.

Alonso, Paz. "El proceso penal en el fuero de San Sebastián." In Sociedad de Estudios Vascos, *Congreso "El fuero de San Sebastián y su época"*. San Sebastián: Eusko Ikaskuntza, 1982.

Areitio, Darío de. *Los vascos en la historia de España*. Bilbao: Junta de Cultura de Vizcaya, 1959.

Arizaga, Beatriz. "La vida urbana en el País Vasco en la época bajomedieval." In *El pueblo vasco en el Renacimiento (1491–1521)*, edited by José Luis Orella. Bilbao: Ediciones Mensajero, 1990.

Arocena, Fausto. *Guipúzcoa en la historia*. Madrid: Ediciones Minotauro, 1964.

Arregi Aranburu, Josefa. "Euskadi-América, mar abierto." In *Los vascos y América. Ideas, hechos, hombres*, edited by Ignacio Arana Pérez. Madrid: Gela; Espasa Calpe/Argantonio, 1990.

Arrieta Villalobos, Mons. Román. "Notas sobre la presencia vasca en Hispanoamérica y Costa Rica." In *Los vascos y América. Ideas, hechos, hombres*, edited by Ignacio Arana Pérez. Madrid: Gela; Espasa Calpe/Argantonio, 1990.

Arteta, Gema. "El Barroco y sus máscaras: Vida y sucesos de la monja alférez." *Anuario de estudios americanos* 56 (1999): 241–252.

Azaloa, José Miguel. "Descubrimiento, tiempo y sociedad (Una tentativa de aproximación)." In *Los vascos y América. Ideas, hechos, hombres*, edited by Ignacio Arana Pérez. Madrid: Gela; Espasa-Calpe/Argantonio, 1990.

Azcona Pastor, José Manuel. *Possible Paradises: Basque Emigration to Latin America*. Reno: University of Nevada Press, 2004.

Bakewell, Peter. *Silver Mining and Society in Colonial Mexico: Zacatecas, 1546–1700*. Cambridge: Cambridge University Press, 1971.

Barahona, Renato. "Mujeres vascas, sexualidad y ley en la época moderna (siglos XVI y XVII)." In *Historia silenciada de la mujer. La mujer española desde la época medieval hasta la contemporánea*, edited by Alain Saint-Saëns. Madrid: Editorial Complutense, 1996.

———. *Sex Crimes, Honour, and the Law in Early Modern Spain: Vizcaya, 1528–1735*. Toronto: University of Toronto Press, 2003.

Basabe, Alberto. "Estudio lingüístico del Fuero de San Sebastián." In Sociedad de Estudios Vascos, *Congreso "El fuero de San Sebastián y su época."* San Sebastián: Eusko Ikaskuntza, 1982.

Benjamin, Harry. *The Transsexual Phenomenon*. New York: The Julian Press, 1966.

Bergmann, Emilie. "The Exclusion of the Feminine in the Cultural Discourse of the Golden Age: Juan Luis Vives and Fray Luis de León." In *Religion, Body and Gender in Early Modern Spain*, edited by Alain Saint-Saëns.San Francisco: Mellen Research University Press, 1991.

Beristain, Antonio, María Angeles Larrea and Rafael María Mieza. *Fuentes del derecho penal vasco (Siglos XI–XVI)*. Bilbao: La Gran Enciclopedia Vasca, 1980.

Berruezo, José. *Catalina de Erauso, la Monja Alférez*. San Sebastián: Caja de Ahorros Municipal, 1975.

Bijuesca, Koldobika J. "Propuesta de interpretación del texto vasco de sor Juana Inés de la Cruz en su contexto." In *Los vascos en las regiones de México. Siglos XVI a XX*, edited by Amaya Garritz. México: Universidad Nacional Autónoma de México, 1996.

Borrachero Mendíbil, Aranzazu. "Catalina de Erauso ante el patriarcado colonial: un estudio de Vida i sucesos de la Monja Alférez."*Bulletin of Hispanic Studies* 83 (2006): 485–95.

Bravo Villasante, Carmen. *La mujer vestida de hombre en el teatro español*. Madrid: Mayo de Oro, 1988.

Brown, Judith. *Immodest Acts: The Life of a Lesbian Nun in Renaissance Italy*. New York: Oxford University Press, 1986.

Bullen, Margaret. *Basque Gender Studies*. Reno: Center for Basque Studies, University of Nevada, Reno, 2003.

Bullough, Vern L. *Sexual Variance in Society and History*. New York: Wiley, 1976.

Camacho Platero, Luzmila. *La Monja Alférez de Juan Pérez de Montalbán*. Newark, Del.: Juan de la Cuesta, 2007.

Caro Baroja, Julio. *Introducción a la historia social del Pueblo Vasco*. San Sebastián: Txertoa, 1974.

———. *Los vascos y el mar*. San Sebastián: Txertoa, 1985.

———. *Los vascos*. Madrid: Minotauro, 1958.

———. *Ser o no ser vasco*. Madrid: Espasa Calpe, 1998.

Cartagena-Calderón, José. 2000. "'Él es tan rara persona'. Sobre cortesanos, lindos, sodomitas y otras masculinidades nefandas en la España de la temprana Edad Moderna." In *Lesbianism and Homosexuality in Early Modern Spain*, edited by María José Delgado and Alain Saint-Saëns. New Orleans: University Press of the South, 2000.

Castillo Lara, Lucas. *La asombrosa historia de doña Catalina de Erauso, la Monja Alférez, y sus prodigiosas aventuras en Indias (1602–1624)*. Caracas: Planeta Biblioteca Andina, 1992.

Castresana, Luis de. *Catalina de Erauso, la monja alférez*, Barcelona: Ediciones Internacionales Universitarias, 1996.

Cejador y Frauca, Julio. *Historia de la lengua y literatura castellana*. Volume 4. Madrid: Tip. de la "Revista de Arch., Bibliotecas y Museos," 1916.

Cepeda Gómez, Paloma. "La situación jurídica de la mujer en España durante el Antiguo Régimen y Régimen Liberal." In *Ordenamiento jurídico y realidad social de las mujeres, siglos XVI a XX: Actas de las IV Jornadas de investigación interdisciplinaria*, edited by Mª Carmen García-Nieto Paris. Madrid: Seminario de Estudios de la Mujer, Universidad Autónoma de Madrid, 1986.

Cervantes Saavedra, Miguel de. *Don Quijote de la Mancha*. Barcelona: Planeta, 1980.

——. *Don Quixote*. The Ormsby Translation, edited by Joseph Jones and Kenneth Douglas. New York: Norton, 1981.

——. "El vizcaíno fingido" in *Entremeses*. Madrid: Clásicos Castalia, 1970.

——. *Miguel de Cervantes' Interludes/Entremeses*. Translation, Introduction and Notes by Randall W. Listerman. Lewiston, NY: Edwin Mellen Press, 1991.

Colera, Adela. "Situación lingüística de Azpeitia, fines del siglo XV–XVI: La(s) lengua(s) de Iñigo de Loyola." In *El pueblo vasco en el Renacimiento (1491–1521)*, edited by José Luis Orella. Bilbao: Ediciones Mensajero,1990.

Crespo, Alberto. *La Guerra entre Vicuñas y Vascongados, Potosí, 1622–1625*. Lima: s.p.i., 1956.

Cruz, Anne. "Studying Gender in the Spanish Golden Age." In *Cultural and Historical Grounding for Hispanic and Luso-Brazilian Feminist Literary Criticism*, edited by Hernan Vidal. Minneapolis: Institute for the Study of Ideologies and Literature, 1989.

Dekker, Rudolf M. and Lotte C. Van de Pol. *The Tradition of Female Transvestism in Early Modern Europe*. New York: St. Martin's Press, 1989.

Delay, Florence. *Catalina enquête*. Paris: Seuil, 1994.

Douglass, William A. "For the Bookshelf," *Basque Studies Program Newsletter* 54 (1996): 1–2.

Douglass, William A. and Jon Bilbao. *Amerikanuak: Basques in the New World*. Reno: University of Nevada Press, 1975.

Duby, Georges and Michelle Perrot. *Historia de las mujeres*. Volume 3. Madrid: Taurus, 2000.

Durán, Gloria. *Catalina, mi padre*. México, D.F.: Planeta, 2004.

Echenique, María Teresa. *Estudios lingüísticos vasco-románicos*, Madrid: Ediciones Istmo, 1997.

————. *Historia lingüística vasco-románica. Intento de aproximación*. [San Sebastián]: Caja de Ahorros Provincial de Guipúzcoa, 1984.

————. "La koiné castellana." *Lexikon der romanistischen Linguistik II* (1988): 527–36.

El Saffar, Ruth. "The Evolution of Psyche under Empire: Literary Reflections of Spain in the 16th century." In *Cultural and Historical Grounding for Hispanic and Luso-Brazilian Feminist Literary Criticism*, edited by Hernán Vidal. Minneapolis: Institute for the Study of Ideologies and Literature, 1989.

————. "The Fabrication of Self: Oedipal Structures in *El médico de su honra*." In *La Chispa '89. Selected Proceedings*, edited by Gilbert Paolini. New Orleans: Tulane University, 1989.

Erauso, Catalina de. *Historia de la Monja Alférez, Catalina de Erauso, escrita por ella misma*. Edited by Angel Esteban. Madrid: Cátedra; Letras Hispánicas, 2002.

————. *Historia de la monja alférez, doña Catalina de Erauso, contada por ella misma*. Edited by José María Ferrer. Paris: Julio Didot, 1829.

————. *Historia de la monja alférez escrita por ella misma*. Presentation and epilogue by Jesús Munárriz. Madrid: Hiperión, 1986.

————. *Lieutenant Nun: Memoir of a Basque Transvestite in the New World, Catalina de Erauso*. Translated and Introduction by Michele Stepto and Gabriel Stepto. Foreword by Marjorie Garber. Boston: Beacon Press, 1996.

————. *Vida i sucesos de la Monja Alférez (Autobiografía atribuida a doña Catalina de Erauso)*. Edited by Rima R.Vallbona. Tempe, Ariz.: Center for Latin American Studies, Arizona State University, 1992.

Estévez, Xosé. *Historia de Euskal Herria*. Volume 2. *Del hierro al roble*. Tafalla: Txalaparta, 1996.

Estornés Lasa, Bernardo *et al. Enciclopedia General Ilustrada del País Vasco*. Volume 11. San Sebastián: Auñamendi, 1980.

Excelentísima Diputación de Guipúzcoa. *Nueva recopilación de los Fueros, Privilegios, buenos usos y costumbres, leyes y órdenes de la M.N. y M.L. Provincia de Guipúzcoa*. San Sebastián: Imprenta de la Provincia, 1919.

Excelentísima Diputación Provincial. *Fueros, franquezas y libertades del M.N. y M.L. Señorío de Vizcaya*. Bilbao: Imprenta Provincial, 1898.

Faderman, Lillian. *Surpassing the Love of Men*. London: The Women's Press, 1985.

Fajardo, José Manuel. *De aventureros y revolucionarios.* Montevideo: Ediciones de la Banda Oriental, 2003.

Fernández Vargas, Valentina and María Victoria López-Cordón Cortezo. "Mujer y régimen jurídico en el Antiguo Régimen: una realidad disociada." In *Ordenamiento jurídico y realidad social de las mujeres. Siglos XVI a XX*, edited by Mª Carmen García-Nieto Paris. Madrid: Seminario de Estudios de la Mujer, Universidad Autónoma de Madrid, 1984.

Frago Gracia, Juan Antonio. *Historia del español de América.* Madrid: Gredos, 1999.

Friedman, Ellen G. "El estatus jurídico de la mujer castellana durante el Antiguo Régimen." In *Ordenamiento jurídico y realidad social de las mujeres. Siglos XVI a XX*, edited by Mª Carmen García-Nieto Paris. Madrid: Seminario de Estudios de la Mujer, Universidad Autónoma de Madrid, 1984.

Gallardo, Juanita. *Confesiones de la Monja Alférez.* Providencia, Santiago, Chile: Seix Barral, 2005.

Garate, Donald T. *Juan Bautista de Anza: Basque Explorer in the New World.* Reno: University of Nevada Press, 2003.

Gárate, Montserrat. "Prólogo" to José Garmendia Arruebarrena, *Cádiz, los vascos y la carrera de Indias.* San Sebastián: Eusko Ikaskuntza/Sociedad de Estudios Vascos, 1992.

Garber, Marjorie. "Foreword" to Catalina de Erauso, *Lieutenant Nun: Memoir of a Basque Transvestite in the New World.* Translated by Michele Stepto and Gabriel Stepto. Boston: Beacon Press, 1996.

García de Cortázar, José Angel. *Vizcaya en el siglo XV. Aspectos económicos y sociales.* Bilbao: Ediciones de la Caja de Ahorros Vizcaína, 1966.

Garmendia Arruebarrena, José. *Cádiz, los vascos y la carrera de Indias.* San Sebastián: Eusko Ikaskuntza/Sociedad de Estudios Vascos, 1992.

Gender Identity Research and Education Society. "Gender Variance (Dysphoria)." At www.gires.org.uk/dysphoria.php

——. *Transsexualism. The Inside Story.* At http://www.gires.org.uk/assets/inside-story.pdf.

Goetz, Rainer H. "The Problematics of Gender/Genre in *Vida i sucesos de la monja Alférez.*" In *Women in the Discourse of Early Modern Spain*, edited by Joan F. Cammarta. Gainseville: University Press of Florida, 2003.

González Echevarría, Roberto. *The Oxford Book of Latin American Short Stories.* New York: Oxford University Press, 1997.

González Obregón, Luis. "La monja alférez." In *La Novela del México Colonial*, edited by Antonio Castro Leal. Volume 2. México: Aguilar, 1969.

Green, Richard. "Transsexualism: Mythological, Historical, and Cross-Cultural Aspects." In *The Transsexual Phenomenon*, edited by Harry Benjamin. New York: The Julian Press, 1966.

Hualde, José I., Joseba Lakarra and R.L. Trask, eds. _Towards a History of the Basque Language_. Amsterdam: John Benjamins Publishing Company, 1995.

Ibáñez, Ricard. _La monja alférez_. Barcelona: Devir, 2004.

Íñigo-Madrigal, Luis. _Cinco textos, supuestamente autobiográficos, sobre la vida de Catalina de Erauso, conocida como_ La Monja Alférez, _acompañados de la relación de los últimos años de su vida en la Nueva España_. Genève: Université de Genève, 1997.

Isasi Martínez, Carmen. "El ars notariae de los escribanos vizcaínos en el tránsito a la modernidad." In Itziar Turrez _et al._, _Studia Philologica. In Honores Alfonso Irigoien_. Bilbao: Universidad de Deusto, 1998.

Juárez, Encarnación. "La mujer militar en la América colonial: el caso de la monja Alférez." _Indiana Journal of Hispanic Literatures_ 10–11 (1997): 147–64.

———. "Señora Catalina, ¿dónde está el camino? La autobiografía como búsqueda y afirmación de identidad en _Vida i sucesos de la Monja Alférez_." In _La Chispa '95. Selected Proceedings_, edited by Claire J. Paolini. New Orleans: Tulane University, 1995.

Juaristi, Jon. "La gnosis renacentista del euskera." In _Memorial L. Mitxelena Magistri Sacrum_, edited by Josefa A. Lakarra and Iñigo R. Arzalluz. San Sebastián: Diputación Foral de Guipúzcoa, 1991.

Kelly-Gadol, Joan. "Did Women Have a Renaissance?" In _Becoming Visible: Women in European History_, edited by R. Bridenthal et al. Boston: Houghton Mifflin Company, 1977.

Leonard, Irving A. _Baroque Times in Old Mexico_. Ann Arbor: The University of Michigan Press, 1966.

Lhande, Pierre. _La emigración vasca_. 2 volumes. Translated by Ignacio Basurko Berroa. San Sebastián: Editorial Auñamendi, 1975.

Lima, Lázaro. "Pablos como travestí: vestimentas, disfraces, encubrimiento y movilidad social en _El Buscón_," _Dactylus_ 13 (1994): 60–77.

Llorens, Chufo. _Catalina, la fugitiva de San Benito_. Barcelona: Ediciones B, 2001.

Llorente, Juan Antonio. _Noticias históricas de las tres provincias vascongadas_. Volume 2. Madrid: Imprenta Real, 1807.

Lundelius, Ruth. "Paradox and Role Reversal in _La Serrana de la Vera_." In _The Perception of Women in Spanish Theater of the Golden Age_, edited by Anita K. Stoll and Dawn L. Smith. Lewisburg, Pa.; London: Bucknell University Press; Associated University Press, 1991.

Luque Alcaide, Elisa. "Asociacionismo vasco en la Nueva España: modelo étnico-cultural." In _Los vascos en las regiones de México. Siglos XVI a XX_, edited by Amaya Garritz. México: Universidad Nacional Autónoma de México, 1996.

Mallea-Olaetxe, José. "The Private Basque World of Juan Zumárraga, First Bishop of Mexico." _Revista de Historia de América_ 114 (1992): 41–60.

Mañaricúa, Andrés E. *Historia general del Señorío de Bizcaya, apéndice III. Polémica sobre Vizcaya en el siglo XVII. El Buho Gallego y El Tordo Vizcayno*. Bilbao: La Gran Enciclopedia Vasca, 1976.

Marichalar, Antonio and Cayetano Manrique. *Historia de los fueros de Navarra, Vizcaya, Guipúzcoa y Alava*, 2nd edition. San Sebastián: Editorial Auñamendi, 1971.

Markaida-Golzarri, Miren Jaione. "La articulación de la identidad nacional euskérica en textos de los siglos XVI, XVII, y XVIII – The Articulation of Basque National Identity in XVI, XVII, and XVIII Century Texts." Ph.D. Dissertation, University of Cincinnati, 2001.

Márquez de la Plata y Ferrándiz, Vicenta M. *Mujeres de acción en el Siglo de Oro*. Madrid: Editorial Castalia, 2006.

Martín, Adrienne L. "Desnudo de una travesti, o la 'Autobiografía' de Catalina de Erauso." In *Actas Irving '92, Asociación Internacional de Hispanistas II, La mujer y su representación en las literaturas hispánicas*, edited by Juan Villegas. Irvine: University of California Press, 1994.

Martínez de Isasti, Lope. *Compendio historial de Guipúzcoa*. Bilbao: La Gran Enciclopedia Vasca, 1972.

Mateos, Juan Antonio. *La monja alférez*. Barcelona: Linkgua, 2006.

Menéndez Pidal, Ramón. "Introducción al estudio de la lingüística vasca." In *Curso de Lingüística*. San Sebastián: Sociedad de Estudios Vascos, 1921.

Merrim, Stephanie. "Catalina de Erauso: From Anomaly to Icon." In *Coded Encounters: Writing, Gender, and Ethnicity in Colonial Latin America*, edited by Francisco Javier Cevallos-Candau, et al. Amherst: University of Massachusetts Press, 1994.

——. "Catalina de Erauso: Prodigy of the Baroque Age." *Review: Latin American Literature and Arts* 43 (1990): 38–41.

——. *Early Modern Women's Writing and Sor Juana Inés de la Cruz*. Nashville: Vanderbilt University Press, 1999.

Michelena, Luis. *Historia de la lengua vasca*. Madrid: Ediciones Minotauro, 1960.

——. *Sobre el pasado de la lengua vasca*. San Sebastián: Editorial Auñamendi, 1964.

——. *Textos arcaicos vascos*. San Sebastián: Diputación Foral de Guipúzcoa-Universidad del País Vasco, 1990.

Miras, Domingo. *La Monja Alférez*. Edición, introducción y notas de Virtudes Serrano. Murcia: Universidad de Murcia, 1992.

Monreal, Gregorio. "Annotations Regarding Basque Traditional Political Thought in the Sixteenth Century." In *Basque Politics: A Case Study in Ethnic Nationalism*, edited by William A. Douglass. Reno: Associated Faculty Press and Basque Studies Program, 1985.

Mujica, Bárbara. *Women Writers of Early Modern Spain: Sophia's Daughters.* New Haven and London: Yale University Press, 2004.

Munárriz, Jesús. Presentation and Prologue to Catalina de Erauso, *Historia de la monja alférez escrita por ella misma.* Madrid: Hiparión, 1986.

Myers, Kathleen Ann. *Neither Saints nor Sinners: Writing the Lives of Women in Spanish America.* New York: Oxford University Press, 2003.

Navarro García, Luis. "La colonia vasca en Andalucía en la Edad Moderna." In *Los vascos y América. Ideas, hechos, hombres,* edited by Ignacio Arana Pérez. Madrid: Gela; Espasa Calpe/Argantonio, 1990.

Orths, Markus. *Catalina.* London: The Toby Press, 2006.

Oses, Cristina. "La vertiente 'lingüística románica' del País Vasco." In *El pueblo vasco en el Renacimiento (1491–1521),* edited by José Luis Orella. Bilbao: Ediciones Mensajero, 1990.

Paredes Calderón, Elizabeth Herminia. *Algunos aspectos de la tradición palmista. A propósito de ¡A iglesia me llamo!* Lima: Universidad Ricardo Palma, Editorial Universitaria, 2006.

Perry, Mary Elizabeth. *Gender and Disorder in Early Modern Seville.* Princeton: Princeton University Press, 1990.

——. "La monja alférez: Myth, Gender, and the Manly Woman in a Spanish Renaissance Drama." In *La Chispa '87. Selected Proceedings,* edited by Gilbert Paolini. New Orleans: Tulane University, 1987.

——. "Magdalens and Jezebels in Counter-Reformation Spain." In *Culture and Control in Counter-Reformation Spain,* edited by Anne J. Cruz and Mary Elizabeth Perry. Minneapolis: University of Minnesota Press, 1992.

Pescador, Juan Javier. *The New World Inside a Basque Village: The Oiartzun Valley and Its Atlantic Emigrants, 1550–1800.* Reno: University of Nevada Press, 2004.

Pérez Villanueva, Sonia. "Vida y sucesos de la Monja Alférez: Spanish Dictatorship, Basque Identity, and the Political Tug-of-War over a Popular Heroine." *Bulletin of Hispanic Studies* 83 (2006): 337–47.

Picatoste, Felipe. *Estudios sobre la grandeza y decadencia de España.* Volumes 1 and 3. Madrid: Librería de la viuda de Hernando y Cª, 1887.

Pinillos, José Luis. "Sobre el carácter de los vascos." In *Los vascos y América. Ideas, hechos, hombres,* edited by Ignacio Arana Pérez. Madrid: Gela, Espasa-Calpe/Argantonio, 1990.

Polk, Milbry and Mary Tiegreen. *Women of Discovery: A Celebration of Intrepid Women Who Explored the World.* New York: Clarkson Potter Publishers, 2001.

Pozo Ruiz, Alfonso. "La homosexualidad o sodomía en la Sevilla del XVI." *Alma Mater Hispalense* (2005). At http://www.personal.us.es/alporu/histsevilla/homosexualidad_ sodomia.htm.

———. "Leyes sobre sodomía en la Edad Moderna." *Alma Mater Hispalense* (2005). At http://www.personal.us.es/alporu/histsevilla/leyes_sodomia.htm.

Real Academia de la Historia. *Diccionario Histórico-Geográfico del País Vasco*. 2nd edition, Volume 4. Bilbao: La Gran Enciclopedia Vasca, 1980.

Rico-Avello, Carlos. "La enigmática sexualidad de la monja-alférez." *Asclepio: Archivo iberoamericano de historia de la medicina y antropología médica* 32 (1980): 353–60.

Rodríguez, Armonía. *De monja a militar Caterina de Erauso*. Barcelona: La Busca Ediciones, 2003.

Rubio Merino, Pedro. *La monja alférez: Doña Catalina de Erauso. Dos manuscritos inéditos de su autobiografía conservados en el Archivo de la Santa Iglesia Catedral de Sevilla*. Sevilla: Cabildo Metropolitano de la Catedral de Sevilla, 1995.

Ruiz de Azúa y Martínez de Ezquerecocha, María Estíbaliz. *Vascongadas y América*. Madrid: MAPFRE, 1992.

Russotto, Márgara. "Condiciones y preliminares para el resurgimiento y formación de los discursos femeninos en la Colonia (siglos XVI–XVIII)." In *Mujeres latinoamericanas: Historia y cultura siglos XVI al XIX*, edited by Luis Campuzano. Volume 1. La Habana: Casa de las Américas; México: Universidad Autónoma Metropolitana Iztapalapa, 1995.

Saint-Saëns, Alain. *Art and Faith in Tridentine Spain (1545–1690)*. New York: Peter Lang, 1995.

———. "Homoerotic Suffering, Pleasure, and Desire in Early Modern Spain." In *Lesbianism and Homosexuality in Early Modern Spain*, edited by María José Delgado and Alain Saint-Saëns. New Orleans: University Press of the South, 2000.

Sanchiz Ruiz, Javier. "Redes vasco-navarras de poder en el México virreinal. La orden militar de Santiago." In *Los vascos en las regiones de México. Siglos XVI a XX*, edited by Amaya Garritz. México: Universidad Nacional Autónoma de México, 1996.

Sarasola, Ibon. *Historia social de la literatura vasca*. Barcelona: Akal, 1976.

Scott, Nina M. ed. *Madres del Verbo/ Mothers of the Word: Early Spanish-American Women Writers, A Bilingual Anthology*. Albuquerque: University of New Mexico Press, 1999.

Smith, Paul J. "Writing Women in Golden Age Spain: Saint Teresa and María de Zayas." *Modern Language Notes* 102 (1987): 220–240.

Stepto, Michele and Gabriel Stepto. "Introduction." In Catalina de Erauso, *Lieutenant Nun: Memoir of a Basque Transvestite in the New World*. Translated by Michele Stepto and Gabriel Stepto. Foreword by Marjorie Garber. Boston: Beacon Press, 1996.

Stoll, Anita K. "Lope's *El Anzuelo de Fenisa*: A Woman for All Seasons." In *The Perception of Women in Spanish Theater of the Golden Age*, edited by Anita K. Stoll and Dawn L. Smith. Lewisburg, Pa.; London: Bucknell University Press; Associated University Press, 1991.

Stroud, Matthew."'¿Y sois hombre o sois mujer?': Sex and Gender in Tirso's Don Gil de las calzas verdes." In *The Perception of Women in Spanish Theater of the Golden Age*, edited by Anita K.Stoll and Dawn L. Smith. Lewisburg, Pa.; London: Bucknell University Press; Associated University Press, 1991.

Taddeo, Sara A. "'Mentís, que no soy mujer mientras empuño este acero'. Verdad, Engaño, and Valor in *La monja alférez*." In *Proceedings of 1992 Symposium on Golden Age Drama*. El Paso: University of Texas, 1993.

Tannen, Deborah. "How Is Conversation Like Literary Discourse?: The Role of Imagery and Details in Creating Involvement." In *The Linguistics of Literacy*, edited by Pamela Downing, Susan D. Lima, and Michael Noonan. Amsterdam and Philadelphia: John Benjamins, 1992.

———. *Talking Voices: Repetition, Dialogue and Imagery in Conversational Discourse*. Cambridge: Cambridge University Press, 1989.

Tellechea Idígoras, José Ignacio. *Doña Catalina de Erauso, la Monja Alférez. IV Centenario de su nacimiento*. San Sebastián: Sociedad Guipuzcoana de Ediciones y Publicaciones, 1992.

Trask, R.L. *History of Basque*. London and New York: Routledge, 1997.

Vallbona, Rima R. "Realidad histórica y ficción en Vida y Sucesos de la Monja Alférez." Ph.D. diss., Middlebury College, 1981.

———. *Vida i sucesos de la Monja Alférez (Autobiografía atribuida a doña Catalina de Erauso)*. Tempe, Ariz.: Center for Latin American Studies, Arizona State University, 1992.

Vázquez de Prada, Valentín and Juan Bosco Amores. "La emigración de navarros y vascongados al Nuevo Mundo y su repercusión en las comunidades de origen." In *Los vascos y América. Ideas, hechos, hombres*, edited by Ignacio Arana Pérez. Madrid: Gela; Espasa Calpe/Argantonio, 1990.

Velasco, Sherry. *Male Delivery: Reproduction, Effeminacy, and Pregnant Men in Early Modern Spain*. Nashville: Vanderbilt University Press, 2006.

———. *The Lieutenant Nun: Transgenderism, Lesbian Desire, and Catalina de Erauso*. Austin: University of Texas Press, 2000.

Vicens Vives, Jaime, ed. *Historia de España y América*. Volume 3. Barcelona: Vincens Vives, 1957.

Vigil, Mariló. *La vida de las mujeres en los siglos XVI y XVII*. 2nd edition. Madrid: Siglo Veintiuno de España, 1994.

Vollendorf, Lisa. *The Lives of Women: A New History of Inquisitorial Spain.* Nashville: Vanderbilt University Press, 2005.

Williamsen, Amy. "Sexual Inversion: Carnaval and *La mujer varonil* in *La fénix de Salamanca* and *La tercera de sí misma.*" In *The Perception of Women in Spanish Theater of the Golden Age,* edited by. Anita K. Stoll and Dawn L. Smith. Lewisburg, Pa.; London: Bucknell University Press; Associated University Press, 1991.

Zuazo, Koldo. "The Basque Country and the Basque Language: An Overview of the External History of the Basque language." In *Towards a History of the Basque Language,* edited by José I. Hualde, Joseba Lakarra and R.L. Trask. Amsterdam: John Benjamins Publishing Company, 1995.

Zubiaur, José Ramón. "Euskara y castellano en el País Vasco en la época de Iñigo de Loyola." In *El pueblo vasco en el Renacimiento (1491–1521),* edited by José Luis Orella. Bilbao: Ediciones Mensajero, 1990.

Zucker, Kenneth *et al.* "Gender-Dysphoric Children and Adolescents: A Comparative Analysis of Demographic Characteristics and Behavioral Problems." *Clinical Child Psychology and Psychiatry* 7 (2002): 398–411.

Index